China & Pakistan

Pakistan and
adjoining areas

China & Pakistan

Diplomacy of an Entente Cordiale

Anwar Hussain Syed

The University of Massachusetts Press   Amherst

Oxford University Press   London, Karachi, Delhi

Published in Great Britain by
Oxford University Press

A Foreign Policy Research Institute Book

To my wife, Shameem, and our
children Sarah, Sameer, and Amir,
without whose frequent interventions
this book might have appeared sooner
but life would not be so worth living

Contents

A Note on Sources

For the most part, this study of Sino-Pakistan relations is based on printed materials. I have used Chinese newspapers and radio reports and commentaries as reproduced in the *Survey of China Mainland Press and the Peking Review*. Since the Chinese media are government controlled, their output may safely be considered representative of the official Chinese position. I have made frequent reference to three Pakistani newspapers—the *Pakistan Times* (Lahore), the *Morning News* (Karachi), and *Dawn* (Karachi)—in addition to a variety of other materials, including the works of Ayub Khan and Bhutto and, occasionally, the National Assembly *Debates*. The first two of these newspapers have, since almost the beginning of Ayub Khan's rule, been controlled by an official agency called the Press Trust of Pakistan. During much of the period under review, *Dawn* has been progovernment. Their reports and pronouncements may then also be deemed to have been fairly representative of the Pakistani official position on issues under comment.

I have discussed Sino-Pakistan relations with Pakistani diplomats, from time to time, over the last decade. More recently—in the summer and fall of 1973—I have interviewed a number of key Pakistani officials. A long interview with Prime Minister Bhutto on November 4 was devoted almost exclusively to this subject. I have also talked with Manzur Qadir, Pakistan's foreign minister from 1958 to 1962, and S. M. Zafar, who was law minister and one of Ayub Khan's close associates from 1965 to 1969. In addition, I have had in-depth interviews with the following diplomats in the Foreign Office (only their relevant posts are mentioned alongside their names): Agha Shahi, foreign secretary, formerly ambassador to China; Gen. N. M. Raza, foreign secretary (administration), formerly ambassador to Iran and twice ambassador to China; Sultan Mohammad Khan, ambassador to Japan, formerly foreign secretary and, earlier, ambassador to China; Sardar Shah Nawaz, "Officer on Special Duty," formerly ambassador in Iran; Akram Zaki, director-general, formerly minister in Washington, D.C.; Ahmad Kamal, director, China Section; Riaz Mohammad Khan, section officer, China Section, formerly third secretary in the Pakistan embassy in Peking and one of three Pakistani diplomats who are reasonably fluent in reading and speaking the Chinese language.

Prime Minister Bhutto and the officials named above were frank and forthcoming in their conversations with me, and for this I am most grateful. Only in a small number of cases did they decline to answer questions. I have the prime minister's permission to refer to my interview with him, and I do so where, in my judgment, it is necessary. But for reasons of prudence, which researchers in similar situations will readily understand, I do not name my other interviewees in the text while discussing matters that may be sensitive.

Acknowledgments

I have discussed the issues in this book with many friends and colleagues over the last several years, and I am indebted to them for giving me the benefit of their comment. Ferenc Vali, Franklin Houn, Howard Wiarda, Edward Feit, and Henry Korson, colleagues at the University of Massachusetts, read parts of the manuscript. Howard Wriggins and other members of the "National Seminar on Pakistan and Bangla Desh" at Southern Asian Institute, Columbia University, commented on an earlier draft of chapter 7.

William R. Kintner and Robert C. Herber at the Foreign Policy Research Institute in Philadelphia had occasion to read the entire manuscript; I am grateful to them for their interest and kindness. I should like to recall that my association with this Institute goes back to its beginning, to my younger days in the mid-1950s when I was a graduate student at the University of Pennsylvania and one of those who contributed to the first volume published under the Institute's auspices (*American-Asian Tensions,* [New York: Praeger, 1956]).

Friends in Pakistan—my brother, Ikram Hussain (a physician, poet, humanist, and one of the most astute students of Pakistani politics I know); Tariq Siddiqui (the proverbial gentleman and scholar and also a distinguished public servant); Muneer Ahmad, Hamid Kizilbash, Khalid Mahmood, and Iftikhar Ahmad, all at the newly established South Asian Institute in the University of the Panjab; Anwar Aziz (lawyer, businessman, and politician); Ismet Sahib, a founding member of the Pakistan People's Party; Waheed-uz-Zaman, Professor of History at the University of Islamabad—challenged some of my interpretations and, thus, contributed to the improvement of my mind.

Blame for the deficiencies the book may have is not to be addressed to any of these gentlemen. That I alone shall bear.

Grants from the University of Massachusetts Research Council and the Foreign Policy Research Institute enabled me to visit Pakistan and meet numerous other expenses connected with the preparation of this study. I am grateful for their generous assistance.

I should like to express my deep appreciation of the hospitality I received at the Pakistan Administrative Staff College in Lahore during a recent visit. I am grateful to Principal Hasan Habib, a great friend to Pakistani scholarship, and to his colleagues for their infinite courtesy and kindness. Words will not suffice to convey my appreciation of the wonderful hospitality and intellectual interaction provided by my old friend, Waheed-uz-Zaman, and his wife, Bushra, during my several visits to their fair town, Islamabad, in the fall of 1973.

I am grateful to Mrs. Leone Stein, Director of the University of Massachusetts Press, for her interest in this study and her encouragement while I revised an earlier draft.

I should like to take this opportunity of thanking Mrs. Virginia Goodrich, who has typed my manuscripts over the years, with competence and good humor.

Chapters 4, 5, and 7 below are substantially revised versions of material published in the Fall 1966, Fall 1967, and Winter 1973 issues of *Orbis,* and I am grateful to the editors for permitting me to draw on that material in preparing this volume.

One

Introduction

The study of international relations and the recent theorizing about them have been dominated by a concern with the behavior of great powers. While the distinction between the "elephants" and the "squirrels" of international politics is significant, it must be recognized that the great majority of actors in the international system today are the small and middle powers of the non-Western world. They have often been viewed as the stakes of great-power diplomacy, which indeed they were and are. But they do more than merely react to the cross pressures of great powers. In their own neighborhoods they are the "environment-determining actors." They act in pursuit of their own goals and thus create conditions and problems to which the great powers must in turn respond. Our explanations of international politics will remain insufficient if we regard the superpowers' "dominant system" as coterminous with the international system. The following study of Sino-Pakistan relations has been undertaken on the premise, among others, that the behavior of small nations merits more scholarly attention than it has traditionally received. The focus is therefore turned on Pakistan.

Scholarly writing on Pakistani foreign policy is by no means voluminous.[1] A few short surveys have been published in Pakistan and India, the latter being the more noteworthy for their abuse of Pakistan. Some of the dozen or so general works on Pakistan's government and politics, published in Britain and the United States, have a chapter each on her foreign relations.[2] The only full-scale work is that of S. M. Burke, a former Pakistani diplomat.[3] Pakistan's disputes and conflict with India, and her alliance with the United States, have received more attention. Sino-Pakistan relations are briefly discussed in the surveys referred to above and in somewhat greater detail in books on the international politics of South Asia. Especially noteworthy among the latter are: William J. Barnds, *India, Pakistan, and the Great Powers* (New York: Praeger, 1972); Bhabani Sen Gupta, *The Fulcrum of Asia* (New York: Pegasus, 1970); and Wayne Wilcox, *India, Pakistan, and the Rise of China* (New York: Walker, 1964). But the focus, even in these works, is not on Sino-Pakistan relations. Barnds turns it on the United States, Gupta on India, and Wilcox on Indo-Pakistan relations in an essay which not only is brief but covers only the initial stage of Sino-Indian conflict and Sino-Pakistan friendship. Khalid B. Sayeed's piece on "Pakistan and China: The Scope and Limits of Convergent Policies" in A. M. Halpern, ed., *Policies towards China: Views from Six Continents* (New York: McGraw-Hill, 1965), is useful especially for a preliminary discussion of Pakistani groups with a significant China interest, pro or con.[4]

Pakistan's foreign policy has gone through three distinct phases. Between 1947 and 1953 she seemed to act a nonaligned role. Her diplomats introduced the new nation to the outside world and sought to answer Indian attacks on the necessity and legitimacy of her birth. The Kashmir dispute with India, which developed into an Indo-Pakistan war within months of the subcontinent's partition in August 1947, occupied Pakistani policy makers almost to the neglect of other concerns. Her foreign minister, Sir Muhammad Zafrullah Khan, a distinguished public servant during British rule whose legal talents far surpassed his political skills, spent much of his time in New York, arguing Pakistan's case at the United Nations. Beyond that, Pakistan attempted to cultivate the Muslim nations of the Middle East in the expectation that her emergence as the largest Muslim state in the world would be received with considerable enthusiasm. But the Arab world, the original homeland of Islam and the base of its grand empire in an earlier era, did not take the bond of religion quite so seriously. Suspicion grew, especially in Egypt, that Pakistan coveted a dominant role in the region.

Psychologically, Pakistan's nonalignment was unreal. Her senior diplomats at the time had recently served the British in the army, the Indian Civil Service, or the Indian Political Service. Her politicians shared the professional men's strongly pro-Western outlook and orientation. They were all overawed by the allegedly high intellectual capacities and political wisdom of the British, and they looked to Britain for guidance in formulating their own foreign policy. But they soon discovered not only that Britain would not support them against India but that she was not the great power she once was. They turned to the United States, whose camp follower Britain herself had become.

The Pakistan-United States alliance made in 1954 remained operative for over a decade and yielded several billion dollars worth of economic and military assistance to Pakistan. It broke down because, instead of joining India to oppose China, Pakistan made friends with China and fought India, whom the United States wished to employ as an agency for containing China. Of this more will be said later.

Since the early 1960s, Pakistan has pursued an "independent" foreign policy, developing relations with other nations on a "bilateral" basis. Her relations with the great majority of states in Europe, Latin America, Asia, and Africa involve only a moderate degree of interaction, mostly commercial, with little, and only occasional, political content. Cultural exchanges and declarations of essentially nonexisting affinities on ceremonial occasions are made to relieve the boredom of routinized intercourse and partly to cover up inaction. The idea of bilateralism is significant with reference to Pakistan's relations with the great powers. In sum, it means that Pakistan and each of the great powers may have cooperative relations on the basis of such mutuality of interests as may happen to exist between them, without regard to either side's relations with third parties. Thus, during the 1960s, Pakistan was able to develop relations of limited cooperation with the Soviet Union, despite the latter's pro-Indian and anti-Chinese orientations.

Interpretations of Pakistan's relations with India, the United States, and the Soviet Union will be provided in the next chapter. Here a few observations with regard to her relations with some other countries may be helpful. Relations with Britain are predominantly economic and cultural. Tranquil for the most part, they are disturbed when Britain sides with India in the latter's conflicts with Pakistan or when the discrimination against the large Pakistani immigrant population in Britain goes beyond routinized patterns and levels. In early 1972 Pakistan left the Commonwealth because of Britain's hostile posture during the East Pakistan crisis and the war with India the previous year, her early recognition of Bangladesh as a separate state, and her lobbying, especially in Africa, for Bangladesh's recognition by other states.⁵ Many Pakistanis still attend British universities so that the old intellectual link persists. In France, de Gaulle's political style—his insistence on France's right to pursue an independent foreign policy, his desire to expel American influence from Europe, his initiatives toward the Soviet Union and China, his mass-based authoritarianism and his low regard for parliamentary institutions—commended itself to Pakistani leaders. Disregarding American policy on the subject, France has, from time to time since 1965, sold combat aircraft to Pakistan.

Pakistan's relations with Iran and Turkey have all along been cordial and cooperative. This is not in any great measure due to their membership in the Central Treaty Organization (CENTO), for that alliance has always been feeble. Despite the Regional Cooperation for Development (RCD), which the three countries established in 1964, the scale of their economic interaction has remained modest. Pakistan's trade with Iran and Turkey is an insignificant proportion of her total trade.⁶ Their relationship is essentially political. Iran and Turkey have invariably supported Pakistan in her conflicts with India. Recently the Shah of Iran, while in the process of acquiring two to three billion dollars' worth of sophisticated high-performance American weapons, repeatedly declared that his nation had a vital interest in Pakistan's territorial integrity and that Iran would come to Pakistan's assistance in the event of aggression against her.

Iranian interest in Pakistani security might transcend the shah's personal predilections. Iran herself does not live in an entirely congenial neighborhood. She is, and has been for many centuries, the only predominantly Shia nation in the world of Islam. This used to be an important, though not the only, reason for her historic tension with the Arabs. More recently three of her neighbors—the Soviet

Union, Iraq, and Afghanistan—have been unfriendly to her in varying measure. Diplomatic relations with the People's Republic of China were established as recently as 1971. On the other hand, Pakistan has not only befriended Iran unreservedly but honored her as a major source of inspiration in the development of Pakistani culture, particularly the literary and other creative arts. Afghanistan, a traditional rival of Iran, is hostile to Pakistan as well. A Baluchi separatist movement, looking to the creation of a greater Baluchistan that would include large areas of Iran and Pakistan, worries both governments. Perhaps paramount in Iran's consideration, however, is the likelihood that if Pakistan were dismembered again her territories would fall to India and Afghanistan. That in such an event parts of Pakistani Baluchistan might go to Iran is not a redeeming consideration. She cannot welcome the prospect of India, potentially a great power, pressing on her as an immediate neighbor. For similar reasons she does not wish to see Afghanistan enlarge at Pakistan's expense. It is then not without good reason that she has been urging peaceableness to both India and Afghanistan in relation to Pakistan.[7]

Pakistan's allegiance to Islam, aided by the romance of distance, gives her a fraternal feeling toward the Arabs that they are not inclined to reciprocate in full measure. They are happy to receive Pakistan's consistent and vigorous support of their causes. But they seem to feel that there is no need to reward Pakistan for doing something she does from the inner compulsions of her Islamic personality. Arab governments have supported Pakistan's Kashmir stand in the United Nations, where nothing of consequence happened. The conservative royal houses of Saudi Arabia and Jordan and the emirates of the Persian Gulf have had cordial relations with Pakistan. On the other hand, Egypt, Iraq, and Syria have often been closer to India.

Pakistan's relations with Indonesia, also a predominantly Muslim country, were cooperative beyond routine levels between 1962 and 1965. The two nations shared a developing pro-Chinese disposition during this period. Moreover, Sukarno's challenges to Western imperialism and neocolonialism, his intense nationalism, his oratorical skills and dramatic political style, appealed to Pakistani leaders, especially Bhutto.[8] Indonesia supported Pakistan unequivocally and, according to some reports, loaned her some naval craft during her war with India in 1965.

Pakistan's relations with Afghanistan have never been good. Since the departure of the British from the subcontinent in 1947, the Afghans have wanted to relocate the border that had separated them from British India since 1893 (the Durand Line). They have been sponsoring the notion of a separate state for the Pashto-speaking citizens of Pakistan to be called Pukhtoonistan. More recently, they have referred to Afghanistan as the "fatherland" of the Pathans and demanded a new state consisting of Afghanistan, Baluchistan, and other Pakistani areas stretching right up to the outskirts of Rawalpindi. Needless to say, Pakistan altogether rejects these ideas.

The two countries have had numerous border clashes over the years but no major outbreak of fighting. Afghanistan being land-locked, much of her commerce with the outside world is carried by the Pakistani rail and road transport systems. Pakistani gestures of goodwill and invocations of historic religious and cultural ties between the two countries make no significant or enduring impact on Afghan policy makers. From time to time, they heat up the Pukhtoonistan issue to suit the requirements of their domestic and foreign politics. Prince Daoud, who overthrew King Zahir Shah and seized power in July 1973, demands the cession of "Pukhtoonistan" to Afghanistan, threatening to use force if Pakistan does not negotiate a settlement. During a recent extensive tour of the Pashto-speaking tribal areas in the Northwest Frontier Province, Prime Minister Bhutto answered Prince Daoud by saying that Pakistan was quite capable of defending her frontiers.[9]

In this connection, it should be noted that Pathans along the Pakistan-Afghanistan border have friends and relatives on the other side. They have never paid much attention to the border and travel across it freely. This state of affairs facilitates Afghan diplomacy. Afghanistan does not have the capability of invading, or even seriously harassing, Pakistan; but with Soviet and Indian assistance she could pose difficult problems for Pakistan's national cohesion, which is tenuous in parts of Baluchistan and the Northwest Frontier regions.

Of the noncommunist nations in Asia (one might even say the world), since 1962 China's relations with Pakistan have been the most cordial and cooperative. This fact alone is of enough significance to justify a careful study of Sino-Pakistan relations, but there are other good reasons as well.

China's relations with Pakistan have generated stresses and strains in the latter's relations with the superpowers. The American decision to terminate military assistance to Pakistan in 1965, and the Soviet decision to assist India in dismembering her in 1971, cannot be fully understood without reference to these powers' anxiety over China's growing influence in Pakistan. Sino-Pakistan relations are thus entangled in a much larger web of relationships among Pakistan, India, China, the United States, and the Soviet Union. This complex interaction is therefore a recurring theme in this volume, involving considerable reference to South Asian politics and the goals and strategies of the great powers with respect to this region.

Why were China and Pakistan drawn together? Writing in 1967, Zulfikar Ali Bhutto, now the prime minister of Pakistan, observed that India's hostility toward these two countries had given them a "fundamental common interest," so that it was in Pakistan's national interest to seek China's friendship and in China's national interest to support Pakistan.[10] Security considerations and the compulsions of power politics have always been a vital factor in the development of Sino-Pakistan relations. But the relationship has now matured to a point where India's role as the common enemy is no longer essential to its sustenance. I will argue later that it will not only survive but, indeed, warrant a normalization of relations between China and Pakistan on the one hand and India on the other. Normalization should not, however, be confused with "friendship."

Both China and Pakistan are sensitive to the dictates of political realism: They act from considerations of vital national interests; both pursue power (military and related capabilities) as the most reliable means of countering hostile pressure in a world in which rivalries of nations persist and where the restraining role of international law and morality is still fragile. Given their goals and the relevant objective conditions, both would appear to accept functionality as a criterion of choice making. In this context, their motivations and their responses to external stimuli, especially threat perceptions, are similar to those of other nations. Yet, in terms of nuances and style, which add up to make a substantive difference, Sino-Pakistan relations do not quite fit the usual mold of relations between a great power and a small nation.

Other nations, most notably the United States, have assisted Pakistan's economic development and military capability on a much larger scale than has China. Yet the Pakistani sense of indebtedness to the Chinese is incomparably greater. This results partly from the two nations' identity of interests with regard to India, which had largely been absent from the Pakistani-American relationship. But another factor is also relevant. Despite their status as a great power, the Chinese are a developing, and a relatively poor, people. Their material assistance and their willingness to champion Pakistani causes against India in defiance of the superpowers have been seen as acts of sacrifice, self-denial, and courage; in sum, as evidence of real friendship. Many Pakistanis, including some officials in the Foreign Office, believe that the Chinese concept of friendship is similar to their own but different from that of the West, which in their view tends to be more expediential and somewhat commercial.

Pakistani Islam has not been a barrier to the development of friendly relations between the two countries. The view that socialism is repugnant to the Islamic value system has often been overstated. It is true that justification for capitalism, and a hierarchical social order based on economic differentiation, can be found in the holy books of Islam and the works of some of the great Muslim jurists. But the same books will also support the proposition that equality of access to the means of material well-being is more congenial to the Islamic ethos. The works of Iqbal, the "poet-philosopher" of Pakistan, the "progressive" writers, and Ghulam Ahmad Parvez have done much to popularize the latter thesis. Many Pakistanis are willing to believe that faith in God and the prophethood of Muhammad plus socialism add up to true Islam. It was on a platform of "Islamic socialism" that Bhutto's Pakistan People's party (PPP) won its spectacular victories in Punjab and Sind in the 1970 general elections. Some of China's socioeconomic values—social discipline, dedication and hard work, simplicity, outlawry of frivolousness, a puritanical approach to sexual morality, the state's commitment to provide the basic amenities of life to all citizens, selflessness and asceticism of her leaders and their publicized willingness to work with their hands alongside the ordinary worker—are regarded by many Pakistanis as truly Islamic values practiced by the Prophet and the four pious caliphs after him.

Pakistanis see China as a nonexploitative power. They feel she is not imperialistic; has no satellites in her camp; does not attempt to dominate Pakistan or extract concessions from her in return for her support; does not propagandize her ideology; and scrupulously refrains from interfering in Pakistan's domestic affairs. Pakistani diplomats share these perceptions of China and add that, as a rule, the Chinese do not even volunteer advice. When Pakistani officials seek counsel, the Chinese are careful not to be indelicate. They provide their analysis of the situation under discussion and then submit that it is up to the Pakistanis to make the decision.[11] This pattern of Chinese behavior is seen as a refreshing contrast to that of the Western great powers.

Pro-Chinese sentiment in Pakistan is truly amazing. On their return from visits to China, even right-wing dignitaries, who do not want any kind of socialism, Marxian or Islamic, praise Chinese virtues, referred to earlier, which they have no desire or intention of practicing in Pakistan. Pakistanis are inclined to believe that if Chinese support during their wars with India did not produce desired results, the blame must go to their own government, which agreed to a hasty cease-fire in 1965 and bungled the East Pakistan situation and then the war with India in 1971. Many people recognize also that in 1971 the Chinese were constrained by the overwhelmingly superior military power of the Soviet Union, which had allied itself with India. It is significant that this awareness of Chinese inferiority vis-à-vis the Soviet Union does not lower China in Pakistani esteem.[12]

The Chinese also have some "demonstration" impact on Pakistani opinion. It is argued that they too, like the Pakistanis, were once backward, corrupt, and disorganized, with a low social cohesion. If they were able to transform themselves, Pakistanis could perhaps do the same. Not all groups react to the Chinese experience the same way. The landless and the small peasants, artisans, tradesmen, urban workers, low-paid public servants, schoolteachers, unemployed and underemployed intellectuals, are more likely to favor Chinese ideas for establishing an egalitarian social order, provided they can be assured that their faith in God and the Prophet need not be given up. The propertied classes—landlords, big businessmen and industrialists, high-ranking civil and military bureaucrats, affluent professional men—applaud Chinese steadfastness in supporting Pakistan against India, but the great majority of them do not want any radical change in the social and economic status quo in Pakistan. They do not want to go the Chinese way. They controlled the government of Pakistan from 1947 to 1971. It is not therefore surprising that Pakistan's China policy has been cautious and that the rhetoric of friendship in Sino-Pakistan relations has been more advanced than their substantive content. But, as we will see later, rhetoric generates a momentum of its own that may carry the policy forward beyond its authors' original design.

Few Pakistani politicians or officials would now publicly admit that they were ever opposed to the development of friendly relations with China. Yet there can be no doubt that, during the early 1960s, influential men within the government were divided over this issue. Z. A. Bhutto pressed for a more forthcoming policy toward the Soviet Union and China. He was supported by S. K. Dehlavi and Nazir Ahmad, who were foreign secretary and defense secretary respectively. Subsequently, other leading officials in the Foreign Office—Aziz Ahmad, Mumtaz Alvie, Agha Shahi—argued for a new China policy. The more notable among the skeptics were M. Shoaib, finance minister; G. Ahmad, deputy chairman of the Planning Commission; A. B. Awan, director of the Central Intelligence Bureau; some high-ranking military officers; and the Nawab of Kalabagh, the great feudal lord who was not only governor of West Pakistan but Ayub Khan's close personal friend and advisor. Manzur Qadir, foreign minister between 1958 and 1962, and Ayub

Khan himself were cautious but willing to expand contact with the Chinese on an experimental basis. Some Pakistani diplomats observe that the president himself, as a result of a brainstorm, had been the one to initiate the idea of a border agreement with China.

It would be an exaggeration to attribute these individuals' policy positions to their ideological preferences or personal back-grounds. In those days, none of them, not even Bhutto, professed socialism. They were all good believers in private enterprise, the notion of a "mixed economy" being as far left as any of them would go. They were all Western-educated and/or westernized men.[13] More likely, their policy differences arose from their different per-ceptions of Pakistan's international environment, her security problem, and her economic development needs. Their roles in gov-ernment were also influential. Shoaib and G. Ahmad had to find ways and means of funding the Second Five-Year Plan, and much of the money came from the United States. They also had to con-tend with the Harvard economists who occupied key advisory posi-tions in the Planning Commission. It was Awan's and Kalabagh's job to suppress dissidents and radicals. The army had developed a measure of proficiency in the use of American weapons and wanted to be sure that supplies would keep coming. We will never know what policy recommendations Bhutto would have made had he been finance minister at the time.

The ideas of measure and balance are central to political realism. They refer not only to the balance of coercive capabilities between contending powers but also to the equation of ends and means in policy decisions. The Chinese have been good and loyal friends, but they are not omnipotent. Pakistan's confrontation with India represented a goal far out of proportion to her own means of sus-taining it. When, in 1971, her domestic dissension turned into a civil war and India became an ally of the Soviet Union, the balance between Pakistan's ends and means (including such as the Chi-nese might contribute) became badly deranged. The tragic failure of her policy—her defeat and dismemberment at Indian hands—resulted more from a precipitous enlargement of her security prob-lem than from any inherent defect in her China policy.

Until 1971 Pakistan had sought a cordial but not an exclusive relationship with China. At the same time, she wanted an actively cooperative relationship with the United States and, at least, a moderately cooperative relationship with the Soviet Union. The "new" Pakistan, under Prime Minister Bhutto, wishes to pursue essentially the same policy. It will be seen below that while this pattern of relations, analogous to walking on a tightrope, may survive a carefully controlled, moderate-to-low level of Indo-Pakistan tension, it is too delicate to bear the strains of serious Indo-Pakistan conflict. Nor will it hold if the "new" Pakistan does not resolve her problems of domestic reconciliation and cohesion. An internally turbulent Pakistan will inevitably invite foreign intervention.

In terms of a "macro" perspective, which is the one adopted in this study, some observers see Pakistan belonging to a Southern Asian subsystem that includes the nations of South and Southeast Asia.[14] If agreement on goals and cooperation in their fulfillment were irrelevant to the concept of a system and mere interaction, regardless of intensity or kind, were sufficient, the designation of southern Asia as a subsystem, and Pakistan's membership in it, would be technically correct. But such an exercise will not open any new windows on the behavior of member states. It is true that India provides the stimulus to much of Pakistan's international behavior. But in responding to the Indian stimuli, Pakistan interacts much more with the powers outside southern Asia than with those within it.

Pakistan's affiliations with international systems, other than the global system, may best be seen in a temporal context. Between 1954 and 1962 she belonged to a fairly tight bipolar system and two of its appendages, namely, CENTO and SEATO. But after a period of progressive loosening up the system itself became dysfunctional and largely inoperative. Since 1962, the international subsystem in which Pakistan has been the most active includes India, China, the Soviet Union, and the United States. There are indications that a new, and somewhat larger, subsystem relevant to Pakistan may emerge: this would include Pakistan, India, Afghanistan, Iran, China, the Soviet Union, and the United States. Iraq, Saudi Arabia, and the emirates of the Persian Gulf are also likely to interact with this subsystem. Within it two loose coalitions may develop: Pakistan, Iran, Saudi Arabia, some of the Persian Gulf emirates, and China on one side; India, Afghanistan, Iraq, and the Soviet Union on the other. The United States may act as the balancer of the system, albeit with a benevolent disposition toward the former coalition, which is also the weaker. This subsystem need not detain us, for it is still in an embryonic stage of development.

Two

The Context of Pakistan's China Policy

Pakistan's relations with China have developed largely in response to her security needs. They have been influenced by her relations with India, from whom the main threat to her security has been perceived as emanating; the United States, her main supplier of weapons until 1965; and the Soviet Union, which has, for the most part, sided with India in the protracted Indo-Pakistan conflict. A discussion of some of the more basic problems in Indo-Pakistan relations and a brief reference to the general character of Pakistan's relations with the United States and the Soviet Union follow, to provide the setting in which Sino-Pakistan relations have proceeded.

Pakistan and India: A Case of Antagonistic Perceptions

History and geography play a part in designating a nation's friends and enemies. In Pakistan's case, India has filled the enemy's role during the last quarter century. Not all of Pakistan's other neighbors have been entirely friendly. During the same period Afghanistan has pressed irredentist claims on Pakistani territory in the Northwest Frontier Province. But Pakistanis are likely to view this thrust of Afghan diplomacy as partly Indian inspired and, therefore, yet another expression of Indian hostility. India and Pakistan have had numerous specific disputes, some of which, notably the one regarding Kashmir, have led to a high level of tension, even military conflict, between them. But there can be no doubt that a basic reason underlying their hostility is to be found in their censorious perceptions of each other rooted in their historical experience. These

perceptions provide each side with a frame of reference for interpreting the other's behavior. The interpretations so derived often
confirm and sustain the perceptions. This cycle has generated a
deep mutual distrust in the two countries and, in Pakistan's case,
an acute sense of Indian threat to national survival. These perceptions merit study.

That for most practical purposes India is a Hindu polity, intolerant
of the Muslim community's cultural and political identity, is the core
element in the Pakistani perception of India. In the Pakistani interpretation, the Hindu hates the Muslim partly because for some hundreds of years, before the advent of the British, India's rulers were
Muslim. There is thus a large element of vindictiveness, a desire to
get even; but there is another disturbing reason for the Hindu attitude. The forefathers of a great majority of Indian Muslims were
once Hindu, and low-caste Hindu at that. By embracing Islam they
walked away from the Hindu social system and the constraints and
disabilities implicit in their previously inferior social station. Upper-
caste Hindus—traditionally dominant in politics, business, and the
profession—have reacted with the anger of a master whose slaves
have fled. The Hindu sees the establishment of Pakistan as a second act of fleeing, more infuriating than the first, for now a large part
of this "body of converts" has established itself as a sovereign state
and thus placed itself beyond the reach of Hindu domination.[1] The
more optimistic Pakistanis believe that even if India does not want
to annihilate Pakistan formally she does want to make Pakistan into
a satellite and thus destroy her capacity to be a free agent in her
domestic and foreign policy choice making. In Pakistani eyes India
is arrogant, aggressive, expansionist, illiberal, hypocritical, deceitful, and, above all, Pakistan's enemy.

In some ways, the current Pakistani distrust of India is an extension of the preindependence Muslim distrust of the Congress party
and its leadership. M. A. Jinnah, the founder of Pakistan, saw Gandhi as a "Hindu revivalist." He regarded the Congress as a Hindu
organization, determined to destroy Muslim culture; authoritarian,
indeed fascist, in its programs and methods; reactionary in spirit
and, under the guiding influence of Gandhi, dedicated to the establishment of Hindu raj in India.[2] Nehru, the more modern of the Con-

gress leaders, is thought to have had his own share of deviousness.
He ignored facts that happened to be inconvenient: he dismissed
India's communal problem by denying that it existed. In any case,
his professions of secularism, socialism, and modernism made no
significant impact on the Congress outlook, which remained Hindu
and retrogressive. They served only a propagandistic purpose
abroad, especially in the West, where they projected the Congress
as a modernizing agent. Congress rule in India's Hindu-majority
provinces during the years 1937-39 is thought to have been notable
for its atrocities against the Muslims. When Congress ministries
resigned toward the end of 1939, Jinnah asked the Muslims to cele-
brate December 22 as a Thanksgiving Day for their deliverance
from the Congress, which had "interfered with their religious and
social life, and trampled upon their economic and political rights."[3]
After independence there were numerous Indian assertions that
Pakistan would soon collapse and return to India. The Congress
resolution of June 14, 1947, accepting India's partition, proclaimed
that "the mountains and the seas" had made India's unity and pre-
dicted that once passions had subsided "the false doctrine of two
nations will be discredited and discarded by all." Gandhi, Nehru,
Patel, Kirplani, Pant, Lohia, Tandon, and other Congress leaders
mmade similar declarations. There were also a number of actions
calculated, as Field Marshal Auchinleck observed in a report to the
British prime minister on September 28, 1947, to "prevent the
establishment of the Dominion of Pakistan on a firm basis." For a
time the Nehru government would not release Pakistan's share of
the former government of India's cash balances. Nor did it give
Pakistan her share of the military stores, railroad carriages and
equipment, official records, and other assets. On several occasions it shut off canal waters flowing from India into Pakistan,
threatening to convert Pakistani fields into wastelands. It invaded
and conquered Junagadh, which had opted to join Pakistan, and
broke its pledges to hold a plebiscite in Kashmir. From time to time,
especially until the mid-1950s, it massed troops, including armor,
on the border to overawe Pakistan.[4]

In addition, India has tried to prevent Pakistan from assembling a
military capability sufficient to resist her. She visited unending con-

demnation on American military aid to Pakistan between 1954 and 1965. She has tried, with some success, to dissuade other major armament-producing nations from selling weapons to Pakistan.[5] Pakistanis feel that for many years India formented a secdessionist movement in East Pakistan and another, through the agency of Afghanistan, in the Northwest Frontier Province. The two nations have had many disputes, innumerable border clashes, and three wars, the last of which, in December 1971, dismembered Pakistan and made East Pakistan into a separate state called Bangladesh.

Pakistani observers see India as an expansionist power entertaining notions of imperial grandeur. They note that India holds Sikkim and Bhutan as protectorates and has endeavored, albeit without success, to impose a similar status on Nepal. She hoped to maintain the old British-Indian sphere of influence in Tibet, but in this she was thwarted by the vigorous exertions of Mao's China. They recall the statements of Nehru and other Indian leaders that a "leadership" role in Asia awaited India and that, in time, India would be the fourth great power in the world. They are disturbed by the projections and prescriptions of Indian theorists of "manifest destiny," such as K.M. Panikkar, who thought the political future of Afghanistan, Burma, Ceylon, Thailand, Indochina, Malaya, and Indonesia was "indissolubly bound up" with India and urged that the ancient Indian empire be re-created even if on a somewhat different basis.[6]

Pakistani opinion makers—newspaper editorialists, political leaders—are not inclined to concede Indian claims to higher moral virtue. The influential *Dawn* perceived Nehru as a "slippery customer," a covenant breaker, the "greatest living believer" in the efficacy of "deceit and force," a "wily Brahmin . . . with Chanakya [the ancient Indian theorist of power politics] lurking in his soul and Machiavelli swaying his intellect." Other commentators have seen India as a bully and an aggressor who has only contempt for the UN charter, a colonial power seeking to incorporate the nations of South and Southeast Asia into an Indian empire larger and grander than the ancient Mauriyan empire, a threat to the security of all her smaller neighbors.[7] They complain that Indian foreign propaganda agencies — whose fabrications, they feel, would put Goebbels to shame—project Pakistan as a friend of the Western imperialists with the objective of disrupting her friendship with Afro-Asian countries.[8]

The perceptions of political leaders have been similar. In the course of a foreign-policy debate in the National Assembly, Prime Minister Firoz Khan Noon, former Prime Minister Chaudhuri Mohammad Ali, and a former chief minister of Punjab, Mumtaz Daultana, described India as a brown imperialist-colonialist country bent upon subjugating Pakistan, a bully toward her smaller neighbors, a coward before equal or superior force, from whose "Brahmin-Bania" oligarchic rulers no justice could be expected.[9] Ayub Khan thought of India as an expansionist Hindu polity, whose leaders entertained a "deep," "implacable," "pathological" hatred of the Muslim and wanted to absorb Pakistan or turn her into a satellite. Bhutto saw India as a deceptive aggressor state whose leaders talked of peace while secretly preparing for aggressive war. He recalled that soon after assuring American audiences that "peace is a passion with us" Nehru had ordered the invasion of Goa. "Pakistan should be prepared for a similar manifestation of the Indian passion for peace," he told the National Assembly. Both Ayub Khan and Bhutto asserted that India wanted to build an empire extending from the Hindu Kush Mountains to the Mekong River.[10]

Pakistanis find confirmation of their perceptions of India in the writings of some Indian social critics and analysts. In this connection, the work of Nirad C. Chaudhuri, a Bengali Hindu widely known in Pakistan, is especially worthy of notice. Pakistanis will nod approval when they hear him say that, in his "unvarnished Indianness," the Hindu has no notion of balance or self-control; that the Hindu society is uncreative, unregenerated, ethnocentric, niggardly, and grasping; that even its gods are venal so that "the Hindu pantheon is as corrupt as the Indian administration"; that the Indian value system and temperament are incapable of sustaining democratic institutions; and that since independence the Indian people have been ruled by "an oligarchical one-party dictatorship which respects political freedom and personal liberty even less than the regime which it has replaced."[11]

Chaudhuri's Pakistani readers will also endorse his analysis of the Hindu's attitude toward the Muslim. The Hindu, he says, is a racist "by whose side the Nazi was a more parvenu." But Hindu hatred of the Muslim goes far beyond the somewhat generalized hatred of the outsider. This is a deep-seated, far-reaching, "maniacal" hatred, beginning with the arrival of Muslim rule in India and swelling with the passage of centuries. The Hindu nationalist, Chaudhuri says, made connections with India's ancient Sanskritic foundations; he even sought a synthesis of his tradition with that of Europe; but he saw no place for Islam or the Muslims in the system he wished to develop. "The new Indian culture of the nineteenth century built a perimeter of its own and put specifically Muslim influences and aspirations beyond the pale. In relation to it the Muslims stood outside as an external proletariat, and if the Muslims wanted to come into its world, they could come only after giving up all their Islamic values and traditions." Chaudhuri believes the Hindu must have someone to hate. He hated the British also; but after their departure from India "his undying hatred has again fastened itself on the Muslims."[13]

Rajni Kothari, one of India's better-known political scientists, also views India as a Hindu polity to whose nationhood—past, present, and future—hundreds of years of Muslim presence have no constructive relevance. Hinduism, he says, is "the solid bedrock and unifying framework" of modern Indian society. Kothari often uses the words *Indian* and *Hindu* synonymously. He observes that the Indian renaissance, following the establishment of British rule, arose partly from a revival of Hindu culture and its traditions and enabled the Hindu mind to regain the self-confidence it had lost during the period of Muslim rule. During that period there had been some interaction: Muslims adopted certain aspects of the Hindu caste system; Hindus adopted certain Muslim social usages, conventions, and artistic forms. "But with all this, the two religious and social systems remained separate and mutually exclusive." Muslim rule, Kothari goes on to say, demoralized the "people" (that is, Hindus) and their leaders. It was not until the advent of the British that the "Indian people eventually came out of the debilitating influence of Muslim power."[14]

Inasmuch as Pakistani leaders construe Indian hostility toward their state as an expression of the Hindu's hatred of the Muslim, the status of the Muslim minority in India remains relevant to the durability of their perceptions. They will argue that, while some enlightenment may have occurred since independence, the Hindu's hatred of the Muslim is still substantial, so that Indian claims of liberalism and her professions of peace and goodwill toward Pakistan cannot be taken at face value. In frequent communal riots the "wrath of fanatical Hindus has been visited upon the Muslims in the shape of violence, rapine, and slaughter."[15] Some Pakistani spokesmen have charged that India treats her Muslim citizens as "hostages" in her conflict with Pakistan. Ayub Khan wrote that Indian Muslims were kept as "serfs".[16]

Once again, Indian sources may be cited to support these interpretations. After independence Nehru often condemned Hindu communalism and warned that, like an "incubus," it would stifle nonconformists and destroy democracy. He noted that Urdu did not have its rightful place in India and that Indian Muslims felt their culture and tradition were being taken away from them.[17] More recently, his daughter, Prime Minister Indira Gandhi, told Parliament of the ferocious riots in the Indian state of Maharashtra. Home Minister Chavan spoke of "the merciless and brutal attacks on Muslims, who had borne the brunt of the violence." He reported that all the houses burned down during the riots had belonged to the Muslim community.[18] Mrs. Gandhi conceded that the government had "slept through" the mounting communal menace. It was consistent with this tradition that many of the state chief ministers whom she had invited to a meeting to discuss the communal situation did not come because of "more pressing" work.[19] In one of its comments on the riots, the *Hindustan Times* of May 30, 1970, spoke of the "dark and evil" forces that were spreading communal hatred and separateness. They were rewriting history to represent a "certain community" as a symbol of past tyranny. It noted also that between 1954 and 1968 communal riots had increased from 83 to 344 a year. During a tour of the riot-torn regions of Maharashtra, a newspaper reporter found that Muslims in the ruling Congress party and the provincial government were reluctant to speak their minds even in private conversations. They worked "under the shadow of their Hindu colleagues" and acted as their "satellites among the Muslims."[20].

An eminent Indian journalist, Pran Chopra, regards Indian secularism as a "half-alive ideal." The constitution is indeed secular. But that has not secularized Indian politics or made the Indian society secular-minded. Government officials at various levels show "shocking" indifference to the "destruction wrought by religious fanaticism."[21] B. G. Verghese has written in the same vein. The Indian Muslims, he says, feel they are a second-class minority. They live in the isolation of a "social-cultural ghetto." There is "an element of positive discrimination against the Muslims which is a disgrace and which must be fought and eliminated at every level." Urdu suffers neglect because it is regarded as a "Muslim language" and as "some kind of an insidious enemy of Hindi." He notes that it was not until a Communist government came to power in Kerala that an old Madras government ban on the construction and repair of mosques and madrasahs was lifted.[15] M. R. Dua has cited the amazing case of the government of Rajasthan once joining hands with the local Arya Samaj in a drive to convert the Muslim Meos of Alwar to Hinduism.[23] Krishna Iyer, a former judge of the Kerala High Court, has recently written of a large variety of routinized breaches of secularism at both official and nonofficial levels. India, he says, is a "curious hybrid, secular in speech but sacerdotal in its soul."[24]

Indian perceptions of Pakistan are somewhat more varied and complex. Not all Indian commentators are equally severe in their denunciation of Pakistan. Some of them have discussed Pakistani problems and concerns, including those involved in her relations with India, with considerable objectivity.[25] Nevertheless, there is a dominant image of Pakistan—a party line, if you will—that political leaders, public relations men, journalists, and a variety of other writers project. This dominant Indian view is presented below.

Generally speaking, Indian opinion makers do not fault the Pakistani people. They blame the Pakistani and/or Muslim leadership. The people on both sides of the border are said to be "brothers" in whose veins the same blood flows. They are simple folk, "pious, poor and ignorant." If in Pakistan they have turned against India, or the Hindus, it is because their reactionary leaders have misled them. Nehru professed to be emotionally attached to the Pakistani people and unable to think of them as "aliens."[26] Before independence, he insisted that there was no Muslim culture, personality, or identity different from that of the Hindus and therefore no Muslim rights that needed to be safeguarded. A few middle-class Muslims might have been influenced by the Persian language and tradition, but "the Muslim peasantry and industrial workers are hardly distinguishable from the Hindu."[27]

Indian commentators are virtually unanimous in the view that the partitioning of India and the establishment of Pakistan represented a great tragedy, "the vivisection of the living body of our dear motherland," an "unmitigated evil." Nehru maintained that the idea of a separate Muslim nationhood—and, therefore, the idea of Pakistan—was absurd, fantastic, mischievous, and "hardly worth considering."[28] Some Indian writers have asserted that nobody, not even the Muslims, wanted Pakistan. According to Sri Prakasa—a Congress leader and India's first high commissioner in Pakistan—Jinnah was shocked when Pakistan materialized and "did not know what to do with it"! He realized that Pakistan would hurt Muslim interests everywhere. But he was too proud to admit that his two-nation theory and his campaign for Pakistan had all been a "blunder."[29] Another writer asserts that the Muslim masses, who "have no concern with politics," have suffered from India's partition and would welcome its annulment "with a full heart."[30]

Then how did Pakistan come into being? According to a heavily advertised Indian theory, the British imperialists at home and their reactionary bureaucrats in India calculated that if they could not prevent independence they should weaken India so that she would not have the leading role in Asia she might otherwise play. Jinnah, who hated Gandhi and the Congress almost as much as did the British (and of this, more later), became their instrument and, at their urging, launched the movement for Pakistan.[31]

Let me now turn to Indian estimates of the men who may be regarded as Pakistan's founding fathers. Nehru speaks of Sir Syed Ahmad Khan as an "ardent" reformer and educationist who believed that Hindus, Muslims, and the other communities living in India all belonged to the same nation. But Nehru adds that in the context of the Indian political struggle, which was then beginning, Sir Syed was a reactionary. He wished to make the Indian Muslims "worthy and useful subjects of the British crown" and tried to keep them away from politics and the Congress. But his influence was limited to the Muslim upper classes; "he did not touch the urban or the rural masses." The Aga Khan, says Nehru, was an instrument of the British. At their instigation, he helped organize the Muslim League to divert the younger generation of Muslims from the rising current of nationalist politics and to keep them loyal to the British. Iqbal was a fine poet, but he was affiliated with the "old feudal order." He had considerable influence with the young people among the middle class at a time when the "Muslim mind was searching for some anchor to hold on to," but he too made no impact on the Muslim masses. Iqbal was among the early advocates of Pakistan, "and yet he appears to have realized its inherent danger and absurdity."[32] Other Indian commentators have echoed Nehru's disapproval of these early leaders of Muslim separatism. The characterization of the Aga Khan as a British agent is common. C. P. Ramaswami Aiyer wrote that Iqbal had "succumbed to hastily acquired prejudices," favored a "theocratically governed Muslim state," produced "dogmatic literature," and lacked a true understanding of Islam![33]

The intensity of Indian feeling toward Pakistan is best conveyed by the following characterizations of M. A. Jinnah, the founder of Pakistan. After his inconclusive talks with the Muslim leader in 1944, Gandhi declared that Jinnah's mind was "enslaved" so that he could not act as a free man; the British were using him as a "cloak for denying freedom to India."[34] Nehru wrote that, while "head and shoulders" above his colleagues in the Muslim League, Jinnah had become a willing "prisoner to their reactionary ideologies." Notwithstanding his modern exterior, he belonged to an older generation, "hardly aware of modern political thought or developments." He believed neither in India's unity nor even in democracy. He was evasive, never telling Nehru or the other Congress leaders what his, or his party's, goals or grievances were. He did not want a settlement. He left the Congress when he did because "he could not adapt himself to [its] new and more advanced ideology, and even more because he disliked the crowds of ill-dressed people, speaking Hindustani, who fled the Congress."[35] Subhas Chandra Bose also characterized Jinnah as a leader of the reactionary elements among Muslins.[36]

Virtually every Indian writer on national politics has something to say about Jinnah. It would be not only space consuming but repetitious to refer to a large number of them; a few representative types should suffice. There seems to be general agreement that Jinnah was able, upright, fearless, incorruptible, and a man of great determination. But the catalog of adverse descriptions is infinitely longer. Sri Prakasa projects Jinnah as a "rabid" communal leader, who thought he alone was right in whatever he said or did; he was dogmatic and intolerant of those who disagreed with him. Prakasa goes on to say that Jinnah was "an Englishman to all intents and purposes," fond of "pomp and show," and so vain he thought "the earth was not good enough for him to tread on." Yet he was petty in that he made frantic appeals to Prakasa, and through him to Nehru, for the safeguarding of his houses in Bombay and Delhi. His colleagues did not respect him and privately spoke ill of him.[37]

J. N. Sahni, once editor of the *Hindustan Times* and subsequently an Indian representative at the United Nations, describes Jinnah as superficial, pompous, arrogant, rude; a born actor; a career-seeking opportunist; a "pampered child" of the British bureaucracy; a small man.[38] B. L. Sharma, for many years a senior official in the Indian Ministry of Information, portrays Jinnah as an opportunistic, intensely ambitious, double-dealing fanatic, of whose thought processes "contradiction" was an outstanding characteristic. He announced principles and then worked to subvert them. He took back with one hand what he seemed to give with the other. No understanding or principle was sacred to him. "Blind to the past, irresponsive to tradition, cold to humanity, he preached the pernicious doctrine of religious hatred year after year.... No invasion of India in the past two thousand years had wrought such havoc and inflicted so much agony and suffering on its people, Hindu and Muslim alike, as had Jinnah from within."[39] After independence, he worked in many ways, overt and covert, to bring about India's dismemberment. In Pakistan he assumed dictatorial powers and permitted no freedom other than that of maligning India. This "structure of Jinnah's thought and actions," says Sharma, continues to guide Pakistani policy toward India.[40]

V. B. Kulkarni says Jinnah had no affection for the common man. There was no warmth in his heart, no laughter in his life, no interest beyond his work. He was uncooperative and stubborn, a master of evasion. Obsessed with hate of the Congress, he lacked the "mental serenity" necessary for true greatness. His "sudden" rise to a position of importance in Indian politics turned his head, and "delusions" overcame his mind![41] B. N. Pandey, a product of the Banaras Hindu University, asserts that Jinnah was unscrupulous in exploiting the masses and used Nazi propaganda techniques to consolidate his control over them. He had a personal reason for demanding Pakistan: "he could not reasonably aspire to the Prime Ministership of an Indian union. Was he then to be second man in a union cabinet headed by Nehru or Gandhi, or to be the chief minister of a Muslim-majority province?"[42]

Many Indian writers say also that once—until about the end of the 1920s—Jinnah was a fine man, a "true and great nationalist." Then something happened that turned him into a communalist meriting the characterizations noted above. The more popular explanation attributes this great change in Jinnah to his anger and frustration at the rise of Gandhi and Nehru to commanding positions in the national movement, which is said to have had the effect of relegating Jinnah to a minor role. Nehru himself maintained that Jinnah had become the leader of a Muslim separatist movement, "not because he really believed in Islam or Pakistan, but because it was a policy which would win him easy attention and secular power." It would also give him a "chance to lash back at Gandhi and those Congress leaders who had snubbed him."[43] Other Indian commentators accept and advance Nehru's interpretation. They allege that a "wounded sense of egoism" and a hatred of Gandhi born of thwarted ambition put Jinnah on the "warpath" and led him to demand Pakistan.[44]

Not all Indian interpretations of Jinnah are quite so harsh. Kanji

Dwarkadas, S. K. Majumdar, and Sasadhar Sinha have argued that it was Gandhi's ethos and ideology—his opposition to Western science and technology (including such things as Western medicine, railways, telegraph) and his espousal of slowness, simplicity, poverty, a return to nature and rural life—that repelled Jinnah. Jinnah opposed the Gandhi-dominated Congress, not the Hindu community of India. He wanted to save, if not all of India, the Muslim-majority areas of India from the hegemony of Congress. In this interpretation, Jinnah was a reasonable, moderate, sophisticated man. Twenty-five years of Gandhian leadership had made Congress politics increasingly metaphysical and oriented it toward Hindu revivalism. Gandhi did not understand politics and, under his influence, Congress never offered the Muslims a constitutionally guaranteed system of sharing power on an equitable basis. Jinnah left Congress because it had become illiberal.[45] It was the Hindu character of the Indian national movement and a Hindu desire to dominate the Muslims that encouraged Muslim separatism. A. K. Majumdar notes that Hindus had begun agitating against Urdu, calling it a Muslim language, as early as 1869. Tagore, he says, wrote poems about Rajput, Sikh, and Maratha heroes, but "except for the solitary poem on the Tajmahal where he had to bring in Shahjahan, no figure of Muslim India stirred his imagination to bring out a verse."[46]

Indian projections of postindependence Pakistan and her leaders have been just as derogatory. Nehru alleged that Pakistani leaders were driven by the old communal hatred of India. The adjectives he used to apply to the Muslim League before independence he now applied to the successive governments in Pakistan: they were reactionary, medieval, feudalistic, theocratic despotisms possessed of an irrational hatred of India. He described the Ayub regime as a "naked military dictatorship" without parallel in the "wide world today." Reacting to a firing incident at the Fazilka border in 1958, he characterized Pakistani "behavior" as barbarous gansterism.[47] Sardar Patel said of Prime Minister Liaquat Ali Khan's government that it broke its agreements, engaged in "dishonest and mischievous" distortions a la Dr. Goebbels, opposed India as a matter of habit, and fomented trouble in her territory.[48]

B. L. Sharma asserts that Jinnah's "irrationality" continues to sway Pakistani policy toward India. "Pakistani leaders howl with dismay if a problem is not settled, but howl with greater dismay if it is." They are deceitful: they talk of peace while preparing for war. In fact, they are war loving. They have no respect for law, equity, and justice. They recognize no obligations, "not even those arising from their own actions and agreements."[49] Sahni describes Ghulam Mohammad and Iskander Mirza as intriguers. He and Kulkarni project Ayub Khan as a "ruthless opportunist," an "artful performer," and a practitioner of political cynicism; Bhutto as a "fire-eating," hypocritical fanatic.[50]

Knowing perfectly well that India hates war and violence, Pakistani leaders continue to talk of an Indian threat to their national security and integrity! According to Indian spokesmen, this so-called Indian threat is an invention of Pakistan's rulers, calculated to divert attention from their oppression and exploitation of the Pakistani people. Moreover, Pakistani nationhood is fragile, built as it was on the "false" two-nation doctrine. The argument goes on to say that Pakistan suffers from a deep inferiority complex, a split personality, an acute identity crisis, and numerous other internal "contradictions," including a severe problem of regionalism. The ruling elite in Pakistan have determined that their projection of India as an enemy is a tactic of survival both for themselves and for the country. If Pakistan did not hate India, she would fall apart.[51]

Many Indian commentators assert also that Pakistan is an aggressive state dedicated to India's ruin, that she is expansionist with an insatiable territorial appetite, that she wants to "grab" not only Kashmir but the Indian Punjab, that she has invaded India several times, and that she has been promoting subversion in India ever since independence.[52] Sardar Patel often referred to Pakistan's "machinations" in Indian princely states designed to disrupt India's unification. He accused Indian Muslims of being loyal to Pakistan.[53] In similar vein, Sardar K. M. Panikkar has alleged that Pakistan hoped to disrupt and dismember India with the assistance of Indian Muslims and then become the dominant power in the subcontinent. These hopes have not materialized, and the consequent frustration has aggravated Pakistani hostility toward India.[54] Indian commentators assert also that for the last ten years Pakistan has been conspiring with China against India. She is an enemy that will not be pacified except by a show of superior force. India must be so powerful that just the thought of attacking her "should cause convulsions in the councils of Rawalpindi."[55]

In Indian eyes Pakistan is illegitimate. Ideologically, she represents a great heresy; functionally, a great tragedy. Foreign instigation guided the political process that brought her into being and the men who managed this process. She has continued to be in league with foreigners hostile to the neighborhood in which she lives. She is an enfant terrible. Her domestic political order has been a medieval, feudalistic despotism; her leaders aggressive fanatics; her policies pernicious and mischievous.

It is amazing how nearly identical Indo-Pakistan mutual perceptions are. Each side regards the other as reactionary, medieval, revivalist in spirit; irrational, even pathological, in its hatred of the other; "fascist" in the choice of its methods; deceitful, aggressive, expansionist, war loving; subversive of the other's good order and determined to bring about its ruin.

Just as Indian materials can be cited to confirm Pakistani perceptions of India, Pakistani sources can be cited to support some of India's perceptions of Pakistan. Pakistanis do not, as a rule, share Indian images of Jinnah, nor do they subscribe to the Indian view that Pakistan should never have come into being. But many Indian characterizations of the postindependence Pakistani political order will appear in Pakistani political writing also. Every successive government in Pakistand and its friends and allies have questioned the legitimacy, integrity, and sometimes even the patriotism of its predecessors and, in many cases, called them despotic, retrogressive, and feudalistic. The writings of Ayub Khan and Bhutto[56] and the columns of newspapers, such as the *Pakistan Times,* whose policy it is to support the government of the day, may be consulted as cases in point. Indian interpretations of Pakistan's policy toward India are not endorsed by Pakistani commentators, but even here an occasional exception may be found.[57]

Indian and Pakistani perceptions of each other can also be seen as stereotypes, that is, exaggerated characterizations that enable each side to justify its unfriendly behavior toward the other. They are based, in varying measure, on experience, received opinion, anecdotal descriptions, jokes, rumor, and gossip.[58] It is sometime said that the ruling circles—politicians in power, bureaucrats, dominant economic interests, and other power centers—in India and Pakistan perpetuate, if not also fabricate, unfavorable perceptions of the other side in order to maintain their own positions of profit and power. The drive for self-preservation is not peculiar to Indian and Pakistani elite: in all political systems, personal interest does often bear on the elite's policy choices and the rhetoric prepared and offered to justify them. It would be more accurate to say that there is a circular, and mutually reinforcing, interaction between the perceptions or stereotypes "already in the public domain," the media (books, magazines, newspapers, radio, television), and the ruling elite. The latter two further disseminate the current perceptions and enhance their credibility. It should be noted also that these perceptions not only legitimize but often circumscribe the elite's policy choices. Their limiting role should not be overlooked in discussing Indo-Pakistan relations. In each country, public opinion imposes a veto on contemplated change in established policy or posture toward the other. It was the Indian public's hostility toward Pakistan that induced the Nehru government to go back on its agreement to cede the Berubari enclave to East Pakistan.[59] Currently, the Pakistani public is more hostile toward India than the Bhutto government is.

Perceptions change quite readily when the change is from favorable to unfavorable, for, as Walter Lippmann once wrote, men are often willing to believe the worst about the foreigner,[60] especially the one with whom conflicts of interest have developed. Indian estimates of the Chinese changed abruptly when their border dispute and clashes became public knowledge. The change of American images of the Chinese in the nineteenth century is even more instructive. When they were needed as cheap labor in California, the Chinese were praised as "the most worthy of our newly adopted citizens" and characterized as thrifty, sober, inoffensive, law-abiding, able, and adaptable. It soon transpired that they were no longer needed as coolies, but instead of disappearing from the scene, they began competing with white Americans for job and business opportunities. They were now described as clannish, criminal, debased, deceitful, filthy, loathsome, servile, and vicious. They were said to smuggle opium and patronize prostitution and gambling.[61] The change from unfavorable to favorable is much more slow and difficult. Uncomplimentary characterizations of certain nations (Turk as cruel, Italian as quick tempered) and minority groups within the country (Jew as sly and grasping, Negro as superstitious and lazy) are not as widely shared among educated Americans today as they were, let us say, in the 1930s.[62] But they have not totally disappeared.

It is impossible to explain the rise and maintenance of unfavorable perceptions or stereotypes without regard to a nation's sense of threat, competitiveness, or conflicts of interest vis-a-vis the relevant "categories" (nations or groups to whom the stereotypes relate). American characterizations of Russia were much more unfavorable in 1948, when the Cold War had set in, than they had been in 1942, when the two nations were allies.[63] Since the Indo-Pakistan confrontation has been a going concern ever since the two nations became independent, there has been no reason or opportunity for their perceptions of each other to change for the better.

Generally speaking, international relations are inter-governmental relations. In most cases only an infinitesimally small proportion of a country's population knows, on a personal basis, the people of another country. Consequently, a population's perceptions of another nation are responsive to its own government's policy changes corresponding to changes in the levels of conflict or cooperation between the two countries. But Indo-Pakistan relations are, to an unusual degree, people-to-people relations with the result that their mutual perceptions are not as amenable to governmental manipulation as they might otherwise have been.

Once a young assistant, disturbed by the pervasiveness of international intrigue in North Africa, suggested to Lord Cromer, the British high commissioner in Egypt in the 1880s, that the powers might become cooperative if only they could come together and understand each other. To this Cromer replied: "My dear boy! The more they understand each other, the more they will despise each other.'' As we have seen above, Indian and Pakistani perceptions of each other are not without some substantive basis. It follows that even if hostile government propaganda were to cease the perceptions would not change until the relevent objective reality changed also. From the Pakistani standpoint, the most pertinent ''fact'' about India is that she is anti-Muslim. In the more generally advertised Indian perspective, the relevant ''facts'' about Pakistan are that she is ''theocratic'' and undemocratic.

The winds of change are blowing in both countries. Both are moving in the direction of modernity. Pakistan once again has a popular democratic regime. Since East Pakistan's separation from the west, the number of Hindus living in Pakistan is extremely small, so that any concessions a Pakistani constitution makes to the majority's Islamic sentiment need not be an irritant to India. The Indians, after all, are not agitated about the official rejection of secularism in Britain, where the queen is the Defender of the Faith, and Parliament, legally the supreme ecclesiastical authority, includes the Princes of the Church. But the success of secularism in India is vital to the improvement of Indo-Pakistan relations. Pakistani fear and distrust of India will not disappear until she can see that the Indian society treats her Muslims fairly, respects their cultural identity, and cherishes, instead of resenting, the Muslim contribution to her own heritage.[64] Secularism has indeed made gains in India. But as we saw earlier, India is still far from being a secular-minded society. Some Indian analysts are quite pessimistic about the prospect of a Hindu-Muslim reconciliation in India and, partly for that reason, the prospect of an Indo-Pakistan rapprochement. Krishan Bhatia feels Nehru's efforts to bring the two communities together have had no effect. Judging from the communal riots since independence, Hindu-Muslim relations appear to be more abrasive now than before.

There are psychological reasons that make the process of reconciliation nearly an impossibility. Hinduism has just emerged from centuries of political domination and helplessness. For the first time it is in a position to lay down the law to those outside the faith, and consequently there is a tendency to act arrogantly. . . . For a reli-

gion that does not advocate conversion from other faiths, Hinduism has a strangely acquisitive instinct and capacity to absorb other sects. It has assimilated Buddhism and Jainism. Christianity in India is increasingly acquiring Hindu characteristics. Islam, on the other hand, is fiercely individualistic and proud and has refused to become part of an amorphous culture. To Hinduism, Islam is a challenge; to Islam, Hinduism today seems a renewed threat.[65]

And again:

The very existence of Pakistan also represented a kind of defeat. Just as the Hindus were about to secure a position of dominance after centuries of subservience, the creation of Pakistan had restricted the area of their paramountcy. Thus, even those who were rational enough to rule out a future reunification of the two countries tended to regard Pakistan as an affront. Friendship and neighborly amiability were considered out of the question.[66]

With Indo-Pakistan hostility rooted deep in historical experience, and given the slow pace of social change and modernization in both countries, it is not surprising that relations have remained tense ever since independence. Pakistan's threat perception concerning India has been vivid, her security problem severe, and her sense of need for reassurance from other quarters great.

Pakistan and the United States

By the early 1950s the American policy of containing Soviet and Chinese influence was fairly well established. The United States adopted Pakistan as an ally in the process of building anticommunist coalitions in Asia and the Middle East. Pakistan welcomed this relationship, for it offered a way of strengthening her military capability, and thus her bargaining position, vis-à-vis India, whom, of all her neighbors, she feared the most. This divergence of threat perceptions and goals finally led to a breakdown of the alliance. The high points in the course of its development and dissipation may first be indicated.

In November 1953 news began appearing that Washington was

considering a military aid agreement with Pakistan.[67] On February 5, 1954 Pakistan formally requested aid and, three days later, President Eisenhower announced his adminstration's decision to extend it. On April 2 Pakistan and Turkey signed a treaty of friendship and cooperation, a prelude to their membership in the Baghdad Pact the following year. On May 19 Pakistan and the United States signed a mutual security agreement in Karachi. On September 7 they joined a number of other nations at Manila to establish SEATO. On March 5, 1959 they signed another bilateral mutual defense agreement. On October 20, 1962 the Indo-Chinese border conflict broke out. Ten days later Prime Minister Nehru made an urgent request for American military assistance which was promptly honored. The ensuing American program of military aid to India alarmed Pakistani leaders and began loosening the United States-Pakistan alliance.[68] Washington stopped military supplies to Islamabad when an Indo-Pakistan war broke out in September 1965. In July 1967 the American military mission in Pakistan was formally closed. On her part, Pakistan asked the United States to close her intelligence base in Peshawar on the expiry of a 10-year lease signed on July 18, 1959. The base was handed over to Pakistan on January 7, 1970. The alliance had clearly come to an end.

Both Pakistan and the United States reaped some advantages and some disappointments from their alliance. Between 1954 and 1965 Pakistan received, on a grant basis, more than 1 billion dollars worth of weapons, military training, and advice. By fiscal year 1970 the United States had obligated a total of $3,713.8 million in economic assistance—grants, loans, and agricultural commodities—to Pakistan and, by comparison, $8,246.7 million to India, a "non-aligned" nation.[69] But the fact or magnitude of aid to India should not be taken to mean that a "non-aligned" Pakistan would necessarily have received the aid she did.

In turn the United States had, until a little after President Ayub Khan's visit with President Kennedy in the summer of 1961, the satisfaction of having Pakistan's firm and consistent support in the Cold War. Pakistan opposed China's admission to the United Nations, withstood Moscow's intimidation and ignored its offers of expanded trade and economic assistance, and went out of her way to denounce Soviet "colonialism" in Eastern Europe. She supported American positions even to the detriment of her own foreign policy interests, as when Suhrawardy endorsed Dulles's proposal for a Suez Canal Users' Association. The United States established a strong political presence in Pakistan. American advisors guided the ordering of priorities in Pakistan's development plans (which some of these advisors later chose to condemn as having been exploitative of East Pakistan). There was hardly a university, government department, or military establishment where American advisors did not function. Policies were made and implemented, careers of individuals often advanced or thwarted, on the advice of these men. The United States AID organization in Karachi resembled a parallel government. The United States maintained an extensive communications base in Peshawar from where aerial and electronic monitoring and espionage activities against the Soviet Union and China were conducted.

Pakistan received a measure of American support in her disputes with India. While the United States had initially argued that India was within her legal rights in Kashmir, she later adopted a pro-Pakistan position, supporting the Kashmiri people's right to determine their own future through a free and fair plebescite under United Nations auspices. In January 1957 she asserted that an Indian-sponsored "Constituent Assembly" in Kashmir had no right to decide the state's affiliation. The following month an Anglo-American resolution in the Security Council sought to bring about the demilitarization of Kashmir with a view to preparing the ground for a plebescite. (The Soviet Union vetoed this move.) On numerous. other occasions, Washington asserted that earlier United Nations resolutions calling for a plebescite continued to be valid and therefore binding on India.

American support of Pakistan did not derive either from an ideological commitment to the Kashmiri people's right of self-determination or from a compulsion to be on the side of equity and justice (assuming they were readily apparent) in an international dispute. I would suggest that it was mainly an act of reciprocity in response to Pakistani support in the Cold War. But a radical shift in the alignment of forces occurred, and the whole complexion of the Cold War changed, when Sino-Soviet and Sino-Indian conflicts developed. Consequently, American interest in a Kashmir plebescite declined. Washington now favored a division of Kashmir that would leave Srinagar and the areas providing access to Ladakh with India. Under Anglo-American prodding, India and Pakistan were persuaded to renew their search for a settlement, but six rounds of talks, beginning December 1962, failed to produce agreement.[70] The United States continued to hope the dispute would go away. But she concluded that a resolution, if at all possible, could only come through bilateral negotiations, and that outside powers could do little to bring it about. The Indian position coincided.

Notwithstanding Pakistani perceptions and expectations, the United States did not have the opportunity to play an imperial role in the subcontinent and decree a settlement of Indo-Pakistan disputes. She regarded the Kashmir dispute as a nuisance in that it absorbed Indian and Pakistani energies which would be best spent elsewhere, but she feared that an attempt to pressure India would push her deeper into the Soviet embrace. The same result might be produced if Pakistan were enabled, with American military assistance, to seize Kashmir. American amunition supplies to Pakistan were therefore kept at a level where she could not deploy her American equipment for more than three to four weeks. That level of capability did not endanger the status quo preferred by India. Washington limited itself to "moral suasion," arguing that both India and Pakistan would, in the long run, gain by burying the hatchet. Not unexpectedly, each government took the position that it did not need American tutoring to discern its vital interests. Moreover, if only the other side were to see the light of reason, the dispute would be settled quite expeditiously.

The United States was more successful in helping with the resolution of another Indo-Pakistan dispute touching Pakistan's vital interests. The World Bank sponsored and assisted Indo-Pakistan negotiations over the distribution of river waters forming the Indus system. These tortuous and often delicate talks, lasting several years, finally produced a settlement reasonably satisfactory to both countries: President Ayub Khan, Prime Minister Nehru, and W. A. B. Iliff (World Bank vice president) signed the Indus Waters Treaty in Karachi on September 19, 1960. But for a substantial American financial commitment, and the patient diplomacy of the World Bank, the treaty would not have materialized. That the World Bank is an autonomous agency does not mean that American influence had no bearing on its endeavors.

The Pakistan-American alliance was not exactly popular in either country. President Eisenhower and Secretary Dulles, the Defense Department, and conservative, defense-oriented legislators, sensitive to the threat of communist expansionism, favored it. Many, though by no means all, liberals in Congress, the communication media, and the universities, who were more favorably disposed towards India and shared her perceptions of Pakistan, were opposed. But even to those who were sympathetic, Pakistan's intense concern with India seemed irrelevant to American goals and, therefore, distractive and worrisome. In Pakistan also the leftists were less than enthusiastic. In East Pakistan Maulana Bhashani led protest demonstrations against the alliance. The *Pakistan Times* of Lahore, then controlled by Main Iftikhar-ud-Din's Progressive Papers, Limited, denounced it in its editorials. The leftists objected that the alliance would suck Pakistan into the orbit of American imperialism and lead to the suppression of progressive forces at home. Pakistani politicians, the large majority of whom were conservative men of substance, defended the alliance when they were in power, threatened "agonizing reappraisals" occasionally, and denounced it when, ousted from power, they were thrown into the ranks of the opposition.

But no government of the day claimed to be wholly satisfied. Each in its turn complained that American support to Pakistan in her disputes with India had been insufficient, that massive American aid to India had given Washington an irresistible leverage which it did not apply because it did not wish to annoy India, that in fact it acted like a "neutralist" in the Indo-Pakistan confrontation, and that it still hoped to bring India into an anticommunist coalition, a vain hope resulting from a basic inability to understand the true nature and purposes of India's rulers. Opposition politicians lamented also that the alliance had compromised national independence and sovereignty without yielding any significant political advantage.

Pakistani and American pronouncements regarding their

alliance are best understood as an exercise in the diplomacy of contrived misunderstanding. Pakistani leaders—coming from successful professional careers, landed aristocracy, or big business—were not without an awareness of a communist threat, domestic and/or foreign, to their political and social order. But it is true also that they considered this threat to be remote rather than imminent. In their conversations with American officials they may have overstated their apprehension. At the same time, they made it clear that they were joining American alliances mainly to bolster their position in relation to India. Bogra did this at Bandung as early as April 1955 when the link with the United States was still in an initial formative stage, and leaders restated this position on many subsequent occasions. There can then be no doubt that Washington understood Pakistani goals perfectly well.

On the other hand, American officials made it equally clear that they did not wish to be a party to Pakistan's quarrels with India. They tried, without success, to limit Pakistan's military establishment to a size—five and a half divisions plus a proportionately small air force and navy—commensurate with the role they wanted to assign Pakistan in their global anticommunist strategy.[71] At Pakistan's persistent urging, they did promise to come to her aid in the event of Indian aggression. But they gave a similar assurance to India against Pakistan. It follows that each side understood that the other's reasons for being in the alliance were not the same as its own. Yet the alliance endured for more than a decade.

My own view is that each government's public posture revealed its inner calculations only partially. In the mid-1950s, when the alliance was made, Washington did not seriously expect either a Chinese thrust into South Asia or a Soviet invasion of Pakistan, Iran, or Turkey. Nor were Thailand or the Philippines in any apparent danger of external communist aggression. It follows that even if the United States had any intention at all of going to war against the Soviet Union or China in the defense of her Asian allies, a proposition not to be asserted without the greatest circumspection, she did not expect to have to wage such a war. To the extent that this calculation was made at all, it was most probably made in the context of contingency planning only. The relatively low level of Pakistan's sensitivity to the alleged threat of communist expansionism, and her much more vivid perception of an Indian threat, were therefore no serious impediments to her membership in the American alliance. For while the American rhetoric about the communist threat was much stronger, her considered assessment of the threat to treaty members was probably not much different from that of Pakistan.

America's Asian alliances were not military organizations expected to do battle with either the Soviet Union or China. Rather, they gave the United States the opportunity to maintain a military and/or political presence on the territory of these allies which would be advantageous if, contrary to expectation, she did have to go to war with one or both of the communist powers. Furthermore, they were intended to promote domestic stability and tranquility within the member countries. They created the impression of a western resolve to disprove the idea that communism was the "wave of the future," and bolstered the morale of conservative, or noncommunist, leaders in Asia, which needed some lifting after Mao's revolution in China and the Korean stalemate. The United States also wanted the allied governments to combat and suppress radicalism, subversion, or insurrections fomented by communists or "fellow-travelers." These American goals were not uncongenial to the ruling elite in Pakistan.

Ideally Dulles would have liked to induct both India and Pakistan into the American alliance system. He had to settle for Pakistan because India would not join. On second thought, Pakistan's Islam, its alleged aversion to communism, the "martial spirit" of West Pakistan, and the relatively good standing of the Pakistani army may have commended themselves to the American alliance-maker. Given India's periodic denunciations of American policies, and the distinctly pro-Soviet and pro-Chinese orientations of her "non-alignment," the idea of a Pakistani counterpoise to India may also have been viewed with favor.

The United States adopted a posture of near hostility toward Pakistan during the 1965 war on the subcontinent. In 1971 she did not take any effective steps to stop India from dismembering Pakistan. These matters will be discussed later. But it may be noted here that, within the limits of its terms of reference, the alliance would seem to have served American and Pakistani purposes reasonably well. Pakistan maintained conservative regimes at home, kept local communists in jail, promoted capitalism, and, for nearly a decade, kept contact with the Soviet Union and China to a minimum. On the other hand, the American connection enabled Pakistan to build a substantial military capability at relatively low cost to her own tax-payer. This capability was not large enough to coerce India, but it was sufficient to deter Indian military pressure, an attainment of no mean significance, considering that during the early 1950s India had seriously contemplated an invasion of Pakistan on two, and possibly three, occasions.[72] That Pakistan's protection from India was not a part of the original American design is immaterial. Pakistan was able to build a significant industrial base with U. S. economic assistance which, in the absence of this alliance, might not have been available to the same extent.

Some critics have argued that the alliance, instead of alleviating, aggravated Pakistan's security problem. It angered India so that Nehru repudiated the agreement to hold a plebescite in Kashmir, which he had made with Bogra in August 1953. It prevented Indo-Pakistan relations from settling into a "natural" mold, encouraged Pakistan to seek equality of status and power with India, and led to war between them. This argument implies that, in the absence of alternatives, Pakistan would have accepted a subordinate status in relation to India, which is what India desired.[73] But this is to ignore the Muslim state of mind that led to the establishment of Pakistan. It is quite possible, indeed likely, that Pakistanis would have considered a dependency relationship with India as the very negation of their separate national existence and resisted her even if their weapons were inferior. In the event of their being vanquished, the subcontinent might have been returned to a state of civil war the apprehension, and to some extent the reality, of which is often said to have persuaded Congress leaders to agree to India's division in 1947. Another response to the critic's argument can be made. William J. Barnds asserts that Nehru had no intention of giving up Kashmir, and that he had made it quite clear that any plebescite that might be held would be held under Indian auspices. India and Paki-

stan had fought a war in 1948 when the latter's alliance with the
United States was still half a decade away. On the other hand, Indo-
Pakistan relations were at their best between 1954 and 1962, when
Pakistan received American military aid. Instability and war
resulted when the United States began supplying weapons to India
also.[74]

The rationale of Pakistan's alliance with the United States began
to disappear when the Sino-Indian and Sino-Soviet conflicts came
to surface. American officials reacted to these developments with
quiet satisfaction. A deeper analysis of the split in the communist
world might have suggested a drive toward improving American
relations with China. However, the proverbial bureaucratic lag
made them seize the long-awaited opportunity to build India as a
counterpoise against China, a strategy already irrelevant to their
global aims but one to which their thinking had been attuned during
the 1950s. They began giving military aid to India. Pakistanis feared
that their ability to deter Indian military pressure would now be seriously weakened. They must look for additional sources of political
and military support. The Pakistan-American alliance, and American military aid.to Pakistan, might have gone on longer had the
Indo-Pakistan war of 1965 not happened and dramatized the divergence between Pakistani and American goals. The context and
assumptions of American policy in Asia would change again. But
that development was still some years away.

Pakistan and the Soviet Union

Soviet goals in South Asia have mainly been power-political rather
than ideological. In view of the troubles Moscow has had with internally cohesive communist regimes, established without the assistance of Soviet military power, such as those in Yugoslavia and
China, the prospect of communist revolutions in South Asia
might not be welcome in the Kremlin. The USSR has been more
interested in strengthening government-to-government than

party-to-party or people-to-people relationships. In the post-World War II period, as the United States built her political and economic presence in the areas south of China and the Soviet Union with the declared objective of containing these powers, Stalin's disdain for the national-bourgeois regimes in postcolonial Asia gave way to a more dynamic policy of influence-building. The South Asian sub-continent—by far the most populous and, next to Japan, politically and economically the most advanced region in noncommunist Asia—became the focus of Soviet interest. The USSR desired the "friendship" of both India and Pakistan. Confronted with the necessity of choice, she preferred India. Her choice-making became simpler when Pakistan made herself unavailable by joining an American anti-Soviet alliance and India gave her "non-align-ment" a pro-Moscow bias.

The pro-Soviet Indian posture, which began to solidify after Khrushchev and Bulganin declared in favor of the Indian position on Kashmir during a visit in December 1955, suited both govern-ments. The Indians were able to show that they were not without the support of a superpower. At the same time, they obtained massive economic assistance from the United States on the reasoning that, in the absence of such assistance, they would become excessively dependent on Moscow. They reserved the right to denounce Amer-ican Cold War policies, which they exercised quite frequently to Moscow's satisfaction. Since the Russians were not likely to be quite so tolerant of their detractors as were the Americans, the Indian government supported Soviet positions against the Ameri-can and remained silent when these positions were too obnoxious to support. Moscow was thus able to secure India's backing at a moderate cost: American assistance reduced the requests she might otherwise have addressed to the USSR; the political cost in terms of Pakistan's alienation could be discounted, for she was already in the American camp.

Yet Pakistan's physical location—her proximity to the Persian Gulf and the proximity of her northern areas to Soviet Pamirs and Chinese Sinkiang—was not without some strategic significance. Moscow knew also that Pakistanis were more interested in resist-ing India than in containing the Soviet Union or China. Their alliance with the United States might be an irritant but it did not pose a credible threat to Soviet security. While efforts might be made to disrupt it, there was no need to close the door on Pakistan. During the years of Khrushchev's supremacy in the Kremlin, the Soviet approach to Islamabad combined offers of mutually advantageous relations with hostile pressure and intimidation. Moscow provided India with weapons and supported her position on Kashmir, at the same time expressing an interest in expanding trade with Pakistan. The two countries signed their first trade agreement on June 7, 1956. In September 1958 Moscow opened a permanent show room in Karachi displaying a variety of Soviet machines, and in 1959 offered Pakistan technical assistance in the fields of irrigation, soil conservation, and water logging. Pakistan's exports to the Soviet Union and other communist countries rose from $5.1 million in 1955 to $35.8 million in 1960 (representing an increase from 1.3 to 8.4 percent of her total export trade). For the same years, imports increased from $0.6 million to $14.7 million (representing an increase from 0.2 to 2.3 percent of her total import trade).[75]

On the other hand, during 1958 and 1959, Soviet diplomatic notes and media repeatedly warned Pakistan of "dire consequences" should she participate in "imperialist war gambles" and permit American military bases on her territory. Moscow also took the position that the mutual defense pacts Pakistan, Iran, and Turkey planned to sign with the United States would be pacts of agression against the Soviet Union: they could not be defensive, for Moscow had no intention of attacking anyone.[76] But Pakistan would not be intimidated. *Dawn* hoped that "instead of riding the high horse, the Soviet rulers will try the methods of friendship for a change."[77] But these methods were still some time away. During a visit to Kabul in March 1960, Khrushchev roundly condemned Pakistan, comparing her "conduct" to that of her own former "colonial oppressors," and endorsed Afgananistan's irredentist claims in behalf of a "pukhtoonistan" in Pakistan's North West Frontier Province. A few days later, the new Soviet ambassador to Pakistan, Mikhail Stepanovitch Kapitsa, saw fit, minutes after presenting his credentials, to call for a plebescite to determine if Pakistani Pathans wished to remain in Pakistan, form an independent state, or join Afghanistan.

Once again the Pakistani press, more than the government, made a defiant response. The *Pakistan Times* characterised Khrushchev's "diatribe" as an "especially offensive" act of hostility.[78] *Dawn* called upon the government to send Kapitsa back home and close or curtail its own embassy in Moscow. It warned that Kapitsa's "masters" in the Kremlin had sent him to Pakistan "on a mission of mischief." Having failed "either to bribe or browbeat Pakistan into becoming a Soviet satellite . . . Mr. Khrushchev has now evidently decided to go all out to make himself as much of a nuisance to this country as he possibly can."[79] Khruschchev's statements in support of "Pukhtoonistan" had been "wild, untruthful, malicious, and brazenfaced." There seemed to be little prospect that a mutually beneficial relationship between Pakistan and the Soviet Union could be maintained.[80]

The diplomacy of pressure continued. On May 9, after it had become known that an American U-2 espionage mission over the USSR had originated from an airfield near Peshawar, Khrushchev threatened to rain rockets on Pakistan. Islamabad remained calm and ordered an "inquiry" into the incident. Pakistani newspapers, however, were more ready to do battle with Khrushchev. They dismissed his "bluster" as still another act of "cold war aggression," calculated to "drive a wedge" between Pakistan and the United States. Espionage, they wrote, was a routine function in international politics so that there was nothing unusual about the American U-2 missions over Russia. The Soviets themselves did plenty of spying in the United States and other countries, including Pakistan. Khrushchev's posture of "injured innocence" was therefore nothing more than a clever act of "showmanship." By contrast, there was something refreshing about the American admission that appropriate U. S. agencies had been collecting as much data as possible on Soviet offensive and defensive installations to safeguard the "Free World" against the possibility of a surprise Soviet attack. Khrushchev's threats against his small neighbors had shown him "not as a man of peace or even as a normal human being, but as a cruel bully."[81] A few days later, the *Pakistan Times* (May 30, 1960) likened him to Hitler, and *Dawn* May 19, 1960) wrote that he had sabbotaged the Paris Summit "deliberately, blatantly, and unashamedly." Recalling his threats to Pakistan, it went on to say:

Were the worst to befall, Pakistan will not be alone, and now is the time to make it clear that if a side had to be taken . . . then we should feel proud to be on the side of that which is right and just and honourable, and which, despite some of its irksome inconsistencies, upholds in the main those values of spirit and matter that make the life of man different from the life of animals, and therefore worth the living.[82]

It would be wrong to say that the U-2 incident had made no impact at all in Rawalpindi. Bhutto went to Moscow in the summer of 1960 and signed an agreement for Soviet assistance in Pakistan's oil and mineral exploration. The following year Moscow extended a credit of $32.4 million to develop Pakistan's oil industry. But neither Soviet threats nor technical assistance changed the Pakistani assessment that Soviet support encouraged Indian intransigence over Kashmir and aggravated her overall threat to Pakistani security. For instance, it enabled her to resist the Anglo-American suggestion, following her border conflict with China, that she make some concessions to Pakistan toward settling the Kashmir dispute. Ayub and Bhutto dismissed the alleged Chinese threat to the subcontinent as fanciful, asserting that India herself had precipitated the border conflict,[83] and that the real communist threat to the area would come, if at all, from the Soviet Union, not China.

Moscow, like Washington, was disturbed by Pakistan's "drift" toward China. But just as Pakistan had made her American alliance into a nonnegotiable policy in the 1950s, she placed her developing relationship with China beyond Soviet or American dictation during the 1960s. This is not to say that calculations of Soviet or American reaction had no bearing on the extent or depth of this relationship. Pakistan moved towards a policy of equidistance—or, if you will, a policy of balanced affections—with regard to China, the United States, and the Soviet Union. Moscow and Washington continued to caution Islamabad against the hazards of a close relationship with Peking. The Chinese, on their part, warned that "modern revisionists" and "American imperialists" were conspiring to help the "Indian reactionaries" against Pakistan. Nevertheless, Pakistanis persevered in pursuing a balanced relationship with the three great powers. Visits of dignitaries to China were matched by similar visits to the Soviet Union. Progovernment newspapers tried to give roughly equal coverage to news from the two communist nations.

A similar attitude developed in Moscow. Khrushchev's successors did not approve of the excessively pro-Indian bias of his South Asia policy. Thus, while in 1962 the USSR had vetoed an Irish resolution in the Security Council seeking merely to remind India and Pakistan of their obligations under the previous United Nations resolutions regarding Kashmir, in 1964 she called for a peaceful resolution of the dispute and, in so doing, recognized that a dispute did indeed exist. Kosygin described Ayub Khan's visit to Moscow in April 1965 as a "momentous event" in the development of Soviet-Pakistan relations. In their joint communiqué the two governments announced their "resolute" support for peoples seeking the right to determine their own future. Soviet leaders urged a peaceful settlement of the Rann of Kutch dispute when Shastri went to Moscow in May. They told him that they did not wish to get involved in India's quarrels with her neighbors, and that their ties with India were not directed against Pakistan, whose friendship they also desired. As the conflict in Kashmir escalated in August 1965, Pravda wrote:

Strengthening the ties between the USSR and Pakistan must be regarded as a part of a general policy aimed at ensuring peace in Asia and throughout the world. We would like Soviet-Pakistani relations, like our traditional friendship with India, to be a stabilizing factor . . . in Asia and to contribute to the normalization of relations between Pakistan and India.[84]

Moscow continued to send military supplies to India during her 1965 war with Pakistan. But it refrained from apportioning blame, adopted an apparent posture of neutrality, repeatedly offered its good offices, and finally mediated a formal end to the war at Tashkent. Kosygin went to Delhi toward the end of 1968 and again emphasized his view that there would be no stability in the subcontinent unless India and Pakistan developed a modus vivendi. Pakistani representations, in the post-Tashkent period, failed to halt the flow of Soviet weapons to India. But Moscow also provided Pakistan a small inventory of military vehicles (jeeps and trucks) and helicopters during 1966-67. In the wake of Pakistan's decision not to renew the American lease for the communications base near Peshawar, and partly to alleviate Pakistani anguish over the despatch of 100 SU-7 fighter-bombers to India, the USSR signed an arms agreement with Pakistan in July 1968.[85] At the same time, she assured India that she had no intention of upsetting the existing military balance in the subcontinent. In 1971 she would aid India in dismembering Pakistan. But of this more later.

The basic motivations of Moscow's South Asia policy are not difficult to discern. It had anchored its long-term influence-building operation in a growing relationship with India, a country several times as large, economically advanced, and militarily powerful as Pakistan. During the 1950s, while Pakistan improved her military position vis-à-vis India, the Soviets were content with a modest level of relationship with her. In the mid-1960s, after the emergence of an Indo-Soviet-American entente against China, the paring of American influence in South Asia came to have a lower priority at the Kremlin. The United States was now likely to lose influence in Pakistan; the USSR could only gain, for at this time she did not have much to lose. A moderate tilting of the balance of interest toward Pakistan would not impair her Indian connection. India was in secure possession of the larger part of Kashmir, and Pakistan, despite a decade of American military assistance, did not have the capability to take it away by force. Even a Pakistani-Chinese combination would not pose a serious threat to Indian security, given Soviet and American backing. The developing Sino-Pakistan relationship was to be discouraged because it opened the door to Chinese political influence in Pakistan, which might, in time, spill over into India and other neighboring countries to the detriment of pro-Soviet elements and forces there. A certain Soviet cultivating of Pakistan for the purpose of containing Chinese influence would serve the long-term interests of India also. It might then be argued that, even between 1965 and 1970, Soviet "neutralism" in the protracted Indo-Pakistan confrontation was more apparent than real. Soviet policy remained basically pro-Indian.

Needless to say, the USSR has been concerned with the safeguarding of her own vital interests, not those of Pakistan. She wanted "stability" in the subcontinent, and an end to Indo-Pakistan quarrels, so that Pakistan, instead of pursuing interests that conflicted with those of India, would join India in serving the common Indo-Soviet, and at this time also American, interest in containing China.[86] But in view of the Soviet Union's overwhelming military superiority over China, and considering that the Sino-Soviet and Sino-Indian rivalries are of a protracted nature, Pakistan's cooperation, while desirable, was not regarded as an urgent or crucial need in Moscow's calculations. There was then no compelling reason to pay her the price of Indian concessions towards a Kashmir settlement. The continuance of Indo-Pakistan tension might be regrettable, but it was not intolerable. Even an occasional war between them would not necessarily be an unmitigated evil. After destroying each other's weapons, both nations would be in the market for more weapons and credits to pay for them. This would not be bad for business: being one of the largest armament producers in the world, the USSR needed buyers for her surpluses.[87] Morever, armament sales would produce additional Soviet influence in both countries. At some future date, it might be substantial enough to induce Pakistan to redefine her national interests so as to be willing to support Soviet plans of regional cooperation in the area.

From time to time, Moscow has urged economic cooperation between India, Pakistan, and Afghanistan, on the one hand, and the Soviet Union, on the other. It would like to link its own vast system of overland transportation with the rail and road systems of Pakistan and India through Afghanistan, where it has built a network of roads. According to some Pakistani diplomatic sources, it would also like to establish a road link with the Pakistani port of Gwadar situated at the entrance to the Persian Gulf. This would be done by building a road through Baluchistan.[88]

Then there is the well-known Soviet proposal for an Asian security system, first unveiled by a Moscow commentator, V. V. Matveyov, in *Izvestia* of May 29, 1969. Attacking the argument that an Asian vacuum might develop following the withdrawal of British military presence east of Suez, he suggested that the nations of South and Southeast Asia—Afghanistan, Pakistan, India, Burma, Cambodia, Singapore, and others—were likely to organize a regional collective security system to resist foreign interference in their affairs. A week later Brezhnev endorsed the idea in a Moscow speech. No details were provided, but it was apparent that the proposed system would have the purpose of opposing the "aggressive forces" in Asia, that is, China. Soviet propaganda often warns the world that the "empire builders" in Peking, possessed of an insatiable expansionist appetite, are determined to bring all of South and Southeast Asia under their domination. Note also that Brezhnev's Moscow speech came three months after bloody border clashes between the Soviet Union and China had taken place.[89]

From Moscow's standpoint, the Indo-Soviet treaty of August 1971 might be regarded as a long step toward establishing a more inclusive anti-Chinese coalition.[90] In July 1971 it had become known that a Chinese-American detente was coming about. With some assistance from Islamabad, Henry Kissinger made a secret trip to Peking to arrange, among other things, the first visit ever of an American President to China. Washington was now forging a new and presumably friendly relationship with Peking. The earlier American collaboration with India and the USSR in opposing China had clearly ended. Moscow and New Delhi responded to this turn of events, extremely worrisome to both, by concluding that their own anti-China colaition must now be firmed up and formalized. Furthermore, as India prepared for another war with Pakistan, in which the latter might possibly have the support of China, she wanted to have a clearcut assurance of Soviet aid. On August 10, 1971 the two governments signed a treaty of "friendship" including provision for mutual defense assistance.

Moscow has not had any strong sense of commitment, one way or the other, with regard to Pakistan's territorial integrity or continued survival. As soon as Yahya Khan's military crackdown in East Pakistan developed into a civil war, in which India soon intervened on the side of the rebels, the Soviets, it seems, concluded that the "old" Pakistan, in which both parts of the country had been ruled by a strong central government, would no longer be maintained. Moreover, India had determined that, regardless of what others might say, the old Pakistan must not be permitted to remain. Moscow then chose to side with the parties most likely to win in the end. As early as April 3, 1971, Podgorny sent a tough note to Yahya Khan, which asserted that the Awami League had been supported by an overwhelming majority of the East Pakistani electorate in the preceding election, and asked him to stop the "bloodshed and repression." Moscow supported India's call for a "political settlement" of the Pakistani crisis, by which the Indian government meant Pakistan's voluntary agreement to East Pakistani secession or, at the most, a loose confederal connection between East and West Pakistan. But it is apparent also that, as part of the understanding leading to the Indo-Soviet treaty, the Kremlin had conceded India the option of military coercion in case Pakistan did not voluntarily agree to her own formal or virtual dismemberment.

During the months following the treaty, some minor concessions to Pakistani sentiment were made. In referring to East Pakistan, Moscow did not use the terms, "East Bengal" or "Bangladesh." On occasion, Soviet media urged a solution satisfactory to the "entire people of Pakistan" and one that would preserve her national integrity. But far more important is the fact that during the same period (August-November 1971) eight shiploads of Soviet weapons arrived in India.[91] In late October "consultations" under article 9 of the treaty, to remove the "threat" to Indian security, were held when Firyubin, Soviet deputy foreign minister, and Air Marhsal Kutakov visited Delhi. Soviet arms supplies continued during the war in December. At the United Nations, the Soviet ambassador accused Pakistan of "unprovoked aggression" against India and used his vetoes to block ceasefire resolutions while India completed her military victory in East Pakistan.

Pakistan's relations with the United States have been advantageous and, for the most part, cordial. Her relations with the Soviet Union have been difficult, from time to time tense, and, at their best, cooperative in a selective businesslike fashion. But neither the

United States nor the Soviet Union has viewed Pakistani security vis-à-vis India as a vital interest of her own. China too could not prevent Pakistan's dismemberment in 1971. I have argued later in this volume that Pakistan's survival depends largely on the national cohesion and integration she is able to build in the years to come. This will be a function mainly of her domestic politics. But to the extent foreign relations have a bearing on her national vigor and viability, the rationale for a cordial relationship with China will continue to exist in the foreseeable future. For of all the great powers, China alone has a lively sense of stake in Pakistan's continued existence as an independent state in Southern Asia.

Three

The First Beginnings

The first decade of Sino-Pakistan relations saw increasing contact between the governmental, professional, and intellectual elites on both sides; but it remained barren of significant political, or economic, content. Pakistani leaders met their Chinese counterparts, warmed up to them, but then shrank back, despite the awareness that, left to themselves, the two nations had no serious conflicts of interest to divide them. Given the state of international relations in Pakistan's neighborhood, Sino-Pakistan friendship seemed to have little relevance to Pakistani goals and aspirations. The United States, Pakistan's main supplier of modern weapons, seized of an evangelical anticommunist zeal, had made opposition to Russia and China into an article of "Free World" dogma. India, Pakistan's principal foe, and China were proclaiming brotherhood. Large-scale American military and economic assistance had just begun to arrive in 1955, and it would be some years before it could make a major impact on Pakistani capabilities. The maintenance of the American connection was thus an imperative to which successive Pakistani leaders submitted, even if with varying degrees of enthusiasm. Their differences in terms of personality traits, structure of domestic political support, attitudes toward communism, and the like might explain the peripheral detail of the general tone but not the crux of Pakistan's China policy during this period. Yet a relationship was begun during the 1950s that would expand substantially once the relevant international context changed as it did toward the end of the decade.

China, SEATO, and Pakistan

Even while Pakistanis struggled with the awesome problems of their own national survival during the years immediately following independence, they watched with some concern the civil war in neighboring China. They welcomed the end of that war and the emergence of a central government, even if communist, whose writ traveled throughout China. Some thought also that the new posture of China, a great Asian people rising from under long and ruthless foreign domination, augured well for Asia. They advised the government of Pakistan to establish diplomatic relations with the new Chinese government without waiting for other states to do so. China, they pointed out, was not only a neighbor, she contained a large Muslim population.[1] On January 4, 1950, Pakistan recognized the People's Republic of China, expressing the hope that the two countries would develop cordial and mutually advantageous relations.

At this time Pakistan did not share the American view that China ought to be kept out of the United Nations because her love of peace and regard for the obligations of the charter were insufficient. In September, 1950, she supported the Indian resolution seeking to replace the delegation of Nationalist China with that of the People's Republic of China. The government of Pakistan argued, in essence, that the credentials of the Nationalist Chinese delegate were bogus because his government no longer ruled China. Those who did actually rule China and who could, therefore, commit her capacities for war and peace should speak for her at the United Nations. China being a founder member of the organization, the quality or measure of her dedication to peace was irrelevant to the issue of her presence at the United Nations, just as it was irrelevant to the presence of other governments, such as the Soviet Union, whose commitment to peace, even in American eyes, was no firmer.

Pakistan, later, changed her mind about the urgency of seating China's representatives at the United Nations. From 1953 onward she voted with the United States to postpone consideration of the issue. Needless to say, this change resulted from the exigencies of her increasing dependence on the United States and not necessarily from a different view of the merits of the case. Not until 1961 would Pakistan again support China's admission. China regarded Pakistan's departure from her original position as an unfriendly move, but, on the whole, she does not seem to have cared much. Too, Pakistan did not go out of her way to oppose China. While she found North Korea an aggressor, she would not brand China as an aggressor in Korea.

As might be expected, the Chinese denounced America's anti-communist alliances. But their disapproval of Pakistan's participation in them was the more remarkable for its moderation. Chinese objections were not only political but legalistic. For instance, they argued that SEATO was not a proper regional organization within the meaning of articles 51 to 54 of the UN charter or in consonance with the Declaration of Bandung. Writing in *Kuang Ming Jih Pao,* Chen Ti-chiang, a council member of the Political Science and Law Association of China, pointed out that SEATO included only three Asian countries. Other Southeast Asian nations had not only declined to join it but opposed it. The United States, who "instigated and controls this outfit," lay more than ten thousand kilometers away. The alleged communist aggression being "of course non-existent," SEATO had in fact been formed to mount agression against China and other Asian peoples. The inclusion of Cambodia, Laos, and South Vietnam within its area of concern was merely an old-fashioned American attempt to create a sphere of influence. It sought to impose upon these countries the foreigner's will in disregard of their own.[2] Another commentator, Liang Chun-fu, reasoned that, in exchange for promises of "so-called aid" to the Asian members of CENTO and SEATO, the United States had acquired control over their foreign and domestic policies and military bases on their territories. These developments were incompatible with the principles of the UN charter and the Bandung Declaration which urged respect for the equality, sovereignty, and territorial integrity of all nations.[3] In the *People's Daily,* Tu Po wrote that far from seeking a pacific settlement of local disputes, as the UN charter enjoined, SEATO was given to creating and aggravating disputes. It came into being soon after the Geneva agreements on peace in Indochina were made, and it was determined to wreck those agreements. In establishing SEATO, "the United States was certainly not aiming at self-defense but at undermining peace in Indochina and maintaining tension in the Far East."[4]

The Chinese represented SEATO not only as an "illegal" organization but also as a tool of American "aggression" and imperialism. According to Chiang Yuan-chun, a *People's Daily* commentator, Washington planned "to link up SEATO with NATO and the 'Northern Tier Defense' system in the Middle East as well as its projected Northeast Asia bloc. It wants to form a military encirclement around the Soviet Union, China and the other people's democracies."[5] Worse still, the United States wanted to sow discord among Asians and to prevent them from cooperating with one another in mutually beneficial ways; undermine the spirit of Bandung; turn Asia into her sphere of influence, seize its strategic raw materials, and make its nations into satellites. "U.S. propaganda machines of all descriptions have long admitted openly that the U.S. interest lies really in the rich resources of strategic raw materials in this region such as tin, petroleum, rubber and iron ore."[6] The United States meant to "expand its armed intervention" against China, subvert the Geneva agreements, and "rekindle the flames of war" in Asia. Dulles intended to use as "cannon fodder" the troops of SEATO's Asian members, whom he would organize as "strategically placed reserves" to be coordinated with the "mobile striking power" of American naval and air forces.[7] SEATO's professed concern with communist subversion was seen merely as a pretext for suppressing national liberation movements and for intensifying American espionage operations in Asian countries. Commenting on a SEATO military leaders' conference at Baguio in April, 1955, Feng Chih-tan, a writer in the *People's Daily,* declared that American "subversive" and "interventionist" activities against the Chinese people were known to all. Now, he said, similar activities would be undertaken in Indonesia, Nepal, Afghanistan, and other Afro-Asian countries "distasteful" to the United States. Relying on a dispatch from London's *Daily Telegraph,* Feng accused Washington of having engineered the assassination of Adnan Maliky, assistant chief of staff of the Syrian army. He quoted a United Press report of

August 7, 1954, to the effect that the United States was engaged in
the biggest peacetime espionage operation in world history. He
went on to say:

*Washington has sent its agents, spies, assassins and saboteurs to
every corner of the world for subversion and sabotage.... It is no
secret that the so-called U.S. experts and technical personnel sent
to various countries under the point four program are engaged in
extensive espionage. These unscrupulous activities have become
a serious menace to social order in many Asian-African countries.
They are one of the basic causes for tension in the Asian-African
region, particularly in the Far East.*[8]

Peking maintained that U.S. economic aid to the Asian members
of SEATO, a small fraction of her military aid to them, served merely
to cloak her real "predatory" aims of colonial expansionism in Asia.
Since the creation of SEATO, the United States had been building
her military presence in Pakistan, Thailand, and the Philippines,
establishing military bases on their soil, interfering in their domestic affairs, and "fastening them to the American war chariot."[9]
These measures were designed to undermine Asian unity and
cooperation in maintaining peace and to bring all of Southeast Asia
under American control.

In these denunciations of SEATO and American goals, criticism
of the governments of Pakistan, Thailand, and the Philippines was,
of course, implicit. It is noteworthy, however, that Peking carefully
refrained from branding them as its foes. Not wicked, they were
only foolish: They had unwittingly permitted themselves to be drag-
ged into arrangements to whose sinister purposes they could not,
and should not, subscribe. Again and again the Chinese suggested
that the Asian peoples, including those whose governments had
seen fit to join SEATO, valued Afro-Asian solidarity. They had dis-
cerned, and they opposed, the ulterior motives behind American
expressions of interest in their security and welfare.[10]

On occasion Peking criticized Pakistan's ties with the United
States more openly and directly. For instance, in 1954, a *People's
Daily* commentator charged that Pakistan's pacts with Turkey and
the United States would menace peace in the Middle East and in

Southeast Asia. They would turn Pakistan into an American "war base" and jeopardize her security and sovereignty. He disputed the official Pakistani view that the pacts would strengthen the Muslim world, quoting Cairo radio and press to the effect that they were a catastrophe for Islam and that they would, like a sword, sever the ties between Pakistan and the Arab world.[11] He also quoted Vice-President Nixon and Sen. William F. Knowland as saying that Pakistan promised to become a key link in the "military crescent" encircling China and the Soviet Union. It was therefore not unreasonable that Pakistan's neighbors, notably India, were alarmed by these alliances. He recalled Nehru's statement that the progress made toward the solution of Indo-Pakistan differences over Kashmir had been "choked" by the supply of American military assistance to Pakistan, which was an intervention in the affairs of the subcontinent. "This explains why a wave of widespread protest has swept through Asia and the Middle and Near East against U.S. machinations in Pakistan."[12] Notice that even now the main thrust of China's criticism is directed at the United States and not at Pakistan.

More often, however, Peking chose the indirect form of rebuke: it contended that the people of Pakistan were opposed to their government's role in advancing America's imperialist goals in Asia. The New China News Agency gave regular and extensive coverage to statements of Pakistani notables, mostly left of center, criticizing Pakistan's alliances with the United States.[13] The main points of Pakistani criticism, as reported by NCNA, were that acceptance of American military aid and the concomitant obligations would make the country into an American satellite and isolate her from Afro-Asians. Chinese commentators attributed Pakistan's political instability during the mid-1950s to the pursuit of unpopular foreign and domestic policies by her government. They interpreted the Muslim League's great defeat in the East Pakistan elections of March 1954, as evidence that Pakistanis regarded their government's alliance with the United States as a threat to their independence and sovereignty.[14] "The elections in East Pakistan came at the time when the United States was intensifying its efforts to turn Pakistan into a military base." Commenting on Pakistani cabinet crises in 1956, Chiang Yuan-chun noted that the Muslim League's influence had declined because its policy of following the United States had brought about Pakistan's isolation in Asia, lowered her international prestige, and worsened her economic position. The people of Pakistan, on the other hand, wanted their government "to adopt a policy of peace and neutrality and take democratic steps in its domestic policy."[15] They did not favor American plans of creating tensions in Asia. There were urgings in the United States to increase aid to Pakistan with a view to bringing the situation there under control, but these efforts would prove futile, said Mr. Chiang, for "the Pakistani people will decide what they want."

That foreign bases exist on one's soil is liable to hurt the sensitivities of a newly independent people. In order to suggest that Pakistan's ties with the West had already compromised her sovereignty, the Chinese repeatedly charged that the United States had acquired the right to build, and had built, a whole string of military and air bases all the way from Rawalpindi to Gilgit.[16]

Why were the Chinese quite so gentle in their response to Pakistan's association with the American enterprise of opposing China? There is, first, the Indian explanation, which holds that right from the beginning the Chinese had perceived possibilites of exploiting Indo-Pakistan hostility to their own advantage.[17] They may have concluded that in receiving American arms Pakistan was concerned with strengthening her defenses against Indian, not Chinese, aggression. This explanation is probably correct, but it is not adequate, for the Chinese were equally moderate in their criticism of the other two Asian members of SEATO, Thailand and the Philippines. It might be recalled that in 1952 they had launched their policy of peaceful coexistence with the independent states of Asia. In the following years they permitted a certain amount of relaxation in their foreign and domestic policies. At home they spoke of letting "a hundred flowers bloom" and "all schools of thought contend." At Bandung, and also later, Chou En-lai projected an image of reasonableness and moderation in his contacts with Asian leaders. With considerable success he tried to convince them that his government desired peace, not aggrandizement, and that it did not seek to subvert their political systems. The Chinese repeatedly invoked the spirit of Bandung, which meant, among other things, that ideological differences were no bar to Afro-Asian solidarity.

The Chinese maintained also that in contemporary international relations all serious "contradictions" resulted from the conduct of Western imperialist powers. Relations of Asians with one another were not infested with "mutually antagonistic" contradictions. And any contradictions that might seem to exist in their relations were really of a nonantagonistic nature and could be resolved by peaceful negotiations. In other words, no fundamental conflicts of interest existed among Afro-Asians. All they needed to do to preserve this basic harmony was to keep the Western imperialist at a safe distance. Furthermore, one must distinguish the principal contradiction from the nonprincipal and the principal aspect (or component) of a given contradiction from its nonprincipal aspects. Having done this, one must concentrate on surmounting the principal contradiction or the principal aspect of a given contradiction, as the case may be—the expectation, of course, being that after the principal contradiction has been subdued the resolution of subordinate contradictions will follow. Accordingly, China reserved her more emphatic denunciation for the United States, the leader of the coalition directed against her, and adopted a tolerant attitude toward its smaller Asian members. Any acknowledgment that these Asian powers were apprehensive of her intentions would weaken her criticism of the United States as an imperialist meddler in Asia. This approach was of a piece with her attitude toward America's European allies and, later, toward the allies of the Soviet Union. Britain, for instance, was admittedly a hostile imperialist power, but in the Western anticommunist coalition she represented merely a "nonprincipal" contradiction. Therefore, Peking exercised remarkable caution in commenting on the future of Hong Kong. It even expected that Britain, believing that China did not threaten her interests, would exert a restraining influence upon American policies toward China. Its approach toward Outer Mongolia, whose rulers are just as "revisionist" as any and follow the Moscow line, has been likewise marked by considerable moderation and restraint.[18]

Bogra and Chou En-lai: Toward a Better Understanding

Personal contact between Prime Minister Mohammad Ali Bogra of Pakistan and Premier Chou En-lai of China at Bandung went a long way toward improving the tone of Sino-Pakistan relations. It is clear that Bogra went to Bandung with an open mind and a modicum, at least, of good will toward China. Pakistan, it will be remembered, was one of the Colombo Powers—the others being Indonesia, India, Burma, and Ceylon—that had sponsored the Bandung Conference. She believed, as did the other sponsors, that China must be brought out of her isolation, which, they thought, was largely responsible for her "warlike attitude." They wanted "to lay a firmer foundation for China's peaceful relations with the rest of the world, not only with the West but equally with themselves and other areas of Southeast Asia peripheral to China."[19] They also wanted to bring about China's diplomatic independence from the Soviet Union. These objectives, they thought, would be served by enabling the Chinese leaders to meet with other Afro-Asian leaders. Each side could then get a more realistic view of the other's posture and policies. Kahin believes that this happened.

Certainly many delegations left the Conference with their image of China looking less grim and forbidding than before. Chou En-lai's conduct at Bandung had done much to convince previously skeptical delegates that . . . peaceful coexistence with Communist China might be possible after all. Even such strong supporters of American policy as Mohammad Ali Bogra, Prince Wan and General Romulo had become persuaded that at least for the near future China sincerely wanted peace.[20]

At Bandung, Bogra and Chou had at least two private meetings during which SEATO was "explained" to the Chinese premier.[21] Addressing the political committee of the conference, Chou declared that he and the Pakistani prime minister had reached an understanding on matters of "collective peace and cooperation." He had received the assurance that Pakistan would not support any aggressive action that the United States might launch against

China under the SEATO treaty and that she neither opposed China nor apprehended aggression from her.[22]

What did Bogra tell Chou En-lai? It may be assumed that he stressed Pakistan's fear of India, her state of virtual defenselessness at the time, and the necessity therefore of strengthening her relative military position even if this must be done through American assistance. Chou's understanding of Pakistani concern regarding India may have been enhanced by the patronizing and overbearing attitudes of Nehru and Krishna Menon, which antagonized several delegations at Bandung, notably the Indonesian and the Ceylonese.[23] But in any case, the connection between Pakistan's fear of India and her alliances with the United States was not a mysterious affair. Consider, for instance, Carlos P. Romulo's answer to Nehru's criticism of SEATO:

Why have my country and other countries joined this regional grouping? Let us answer frankly. . . . If I ask my good friends from India and Pakistan why almost half their national budgets are going into military preparations, both would say this is being done not because the governments or peoples of each nation are spoiling for a fight, because both are peaceful, but because there is a situation in Kashmir which might be even more difficult to settle fairly if only one side were armed.[24]

The Pakistani delegation at Bandung lent the Chinese significant support on a crucial issue. The representatives of Cambodia, Thailand, and the Philippines had expressed concern about direct and indirect Chinese aggression against their countries. Later in the debate the question of communist colonialism arose. Bogra of Pakistan, Abdoh of Iran, Jamali of Iraq, Zorlu of Turkey, and Kotewala of Ceylon, among others, argued that one could not reasonably condemn Western colonialism in Asia and Africa without at the same time condemning Soviet colonialism in eastern Europe. Bogra, however, emphasized that in this context China must be distinguished from the Soviet Union.

China is by no means an imperialist nation and she has no satellites. Therefore when the Prime Minister of Ceylon raised this issue with which some of us are in complete agreement he was directing his criticism against the Soviet form of imperialism by which many countries have been made satellites.... The distinguished delegate of China should not misunderstand the purpose which makes the Prime Minister of Ceylon raise this issue. We have the friendliest relations with China; China is certainly not imperialistic; she has not brought any other country under her heel. Therefore it is not directed against ... a fellow delegate who, we appreciate very much, has shown a great deal of conciliation.[25]

On his part, the Chinese leader tried to blunt the edge of Nehru's denunciation of SEATO by saying that he did not expect aggression from Pakistan or SEATO's other Asian members. He had private meetings with Prince Wan of Thailand whom he invited to visit China, especially Yunnan, to see for himself that no Thai-speaking Chinese were being trained there for the purpose of infiltrating his country. He paid a visit to General Romulo of the Philippines and invited him also to visit China. He offered to sign nationality treaties eliminating dual nationality of Chinese residents in Thailand and the Philippines. At Bandung Chou En-lai presented himself as a model of conciliation. He observed that while, being a communist, he believed that his system was a good one, he realized that there were other systems in Asia and Africa. These differences should "not prevent us from seeking common ground and being united." No one was being asked to give up his views. Since the Chinese were opposed to external intervention in their own affairs, how could they want "to interfere in the internal affairs of others?" He upheld the freedom of religious belief and called attention to the presence of a Muslim imam (religious leader) in his delegation at Bandung! This should have gone well with Bogra and the leaders of other Muslim countries at the conference. Emphasizing Chinese tolerance, he went on to say that his people respected the right of Americans to maintain their own way of life and political and economic systems. Repeatedly he declared that his government did not want war with the United States. Even the liberation of Taiwan could proceed without the use of force.[26]

After the Bogra-Chou talks at Bandung,[27] cultural contacts between Pakistan and China expanded rapidly. During 1955-56 hardly a month passed without a delegation of Pakistani and Chinese dignitaries visiting the other side. They included politicians, parliamentarians, lawyers, industrialists, writers, artists, public officials, and even mullahs. Among the more important Chinese visitors to Pakistan were Mme. Li Teh-chuan, vice-president of the All China Democratic Women's Federation; Sheikh Nur Mohammad Ta Pu-sheng, an officer of the China Islamic Association; Mme. Soong Ching-ling, vice-chairman of the Standing Committee of the National People's Congress; and Vice-Premier Marshal Ho lung. Notable among the Pakistani visitors were: Maulana Ehtashamul Haq; Dr. Bashir Ahmad, vice-chancellor of the University of the Punjab; Begum Shahnawaz, a legislator and women's leader; Raja Ghazanfar Ali, a veteran politician and diplomatist; Sheikh Mujibur Rehman, then minister of commerce in the government of East Pakistan; Mirza Aboul Hasan Isphahani, an industrialist and diplomat; Mahmud Ali, politician of the National Awami party in East Pakistan; and Said Hasan, vice-chairman of the National Planning Commission.

These exchanges produced no spectacular political results, but they did, at least on the Pakistani side, improve the general tone of Sino-Pakistan relations. It is difficult to assess the impact, if any, that Pakistani visitors may have made on Chinese opinion outside the officialdom. The Chinese visitors left a favorable impression with Pakistani audiences and thus built a reservoir of popular goodwill which later became a determining factor in Pakistan's China policy.

On their return from China, Pakistani dignitaries spoke of the Chinese Muslims' religious freedom, referred to China's rapid strides in the fields of technological and economic development, and praised the sense of mission, devotion, and selflessness of her leaders.[28] Raja Ghazanfar Ali, for instance, lauded the "tremendous voluntary effort embracing every development project in the country." Dams, reservoirs, and irrigation projects had been accomplished in a matter of months. He was vastly impressed by the rapport between China's top leaders and ordinary workers. He reported that once, when a dam was being constructed, Premier Chou En-lai worked on the project eight hours a day for several days. Talking about religious freedom, he observed that twelve out of Peking's eighty mosques had been built during the regime of Mao. Libraries contained large and good collections of books on Islam.[29] Returning from a similar visit, Mahmud Ali told an audience in Dacca that "if democracy means rule by discussion, real democracy exists in China." He added that Islam was freer in China than elsewhere "because Muslims have no worries to disturb their minds." They enjoyed religious freedom, and their social customs were respected.[30]

The Chinese, on their part, emphasized certain political themes: both nations had formerly suffered colonial exploitation; being Asian, both were devoted to peace and Afro-Asian solidarity; differences of ideological affiliation should not be permitted to stand in the way of their friendship and cooperation. President Liu Shao-chi told Sheikh Mujibur Rehman: "Although we speak different languages and have different political systems, these are no impediment to the establishment of friendly and cooperative relations between our two countries."[31] Speaking from Radio Pakistan on January 29, 1956, Mme. Soong Ching-ling reiterated the same theme, to wit, that different social and political systems could coexist peacefully and cooperate with each other in many ways. Mankind had lived in different systems all along. Both Pakistan and China had contributed to the success of the Bandung Conference, which meant that they were opposed to colonialism and war. Both were peace loving, and the "growing friendship and goodwill" between them would advance the cause of peace in Asia and the world.[32]

Suhrawardy: A Return to Skepticism

At Bandung Chou En-lai had invited Mohammad Ali Bogra to visit China. Before he could do so, he had to give way to Chaudhuri Mohammad Ali as prime minister. The latter twice planned, but then postponed, a visit to China, causing speculation that he had acted under American advice. H. S. Suhrawardy, who became prime minister in September, 1956, did finally visit China for twelve days the following month. He and his hosts exchanged pleasantries and gifts: he gave the Peking Zoo a baby elephant to amuse Chinese children. He joined the Chinese leaders in declaring that friendly contacts and a "commerce of goodwill" between the two countries dated back more than two thousand years. They recalled the visits of the famous Chinese travelers, Fa Hsien and Huang San, to parts of the subcontinent that now compose Pakistan. Apart from anti-colonialism and Afro-Asian solidarity, Chou En-lai and other senior communist officials emphasized the following themes: there were no conflicts of interest between Pakistan and China; both were developing countries, facing similar problems, with much to learn from each other's experience; both were devoted to the principles of peace adopted at Bandung; cooperation between them could be strengthened despite their different social systems and their different views on "certain international questions."[33]

Suhrawardy had an exceedingly cordial welcome wherever he went in China, and the Chinese press and radio gave him favorable and extensive coverage. Some Chinese commentators went so far as to claim that he intended to pursue an "independent" foreign policy. The *People's Daily* referred to the steadily growing cultural and commercial contacts between the two countries ever since the "frank and sincere" Chou-Bogra talks at Bandung. It praised Pakistan government's efforts to improve relations with socialist countries. It welcomed the withdrawal of Suhrawardy's initial support for the American proposal to establish a Suez Canal User's Association, for this revised position was more representative of the Pakistani people's desire "for peace and friendship among nations and their opposition to colonialism."[34]

During the first few days of his visit, Suhrawardy would seem to have directed his eloquence, of which he had plenty, at the innocuous. He professed to have come in the spirit of Fa Hsien and Huang San, "to see, to understand and to learn." He praised the splendors of China's past, the continuity of her civilization, the beauty and gracefulness of her cities, the healthfulness of her children, the discipline and industry of her people, the wisdom and devotion of her leaders and their tolerance toward religious minorities, and the rapid rate of her technological and economic development. Replying to Chou En-lai's banquet speech, he remarked:

> Throughout recorded history, China has stood as a symbol of much that is the finest and the best in human achievement. Its contribution to the sciences and to the arts, to philosophy and literature has enriched human civilization. One particularly impressive fact . . . is the continuity of the Chinese civilization, the enduring quality of its spirit and essence, which has withstood and absorbed and made its own, the many and varied influences which have shaped China's long history.[35]

On political matters he remained sober. He conveyed the "highest regard" and the "warm feelings of friendship" of the Pakistanis for the Chinese people. He wished *all countries* would live in "amity and friendship, whatever their aims and methods of achieving them," and cooperate with one another "to further the welfare of the *human race.*" Peace was essential to progress, for without it no plans of social and economic development could succeed.[36]

After a few days of conversation with his hosts, Suhrawardy warmed up a bit. At a Pakistan embassy reception he professed to be convinced of the Chinese desire for peace. "I see this country wants friendship with every other country. It wants to go out to assure every country that it means well. If China seeks the friendship of the world, it is the duty of the world to seek the friendship of China."[37] On October 24, 1956, before going out on a tour of the country, he expressed the hope that his discussions in Peking had removed any "misunderstandings" that might have existed between the two governments. Their objectives—socioeconomic development of their peoples and international peace and cooperation—being similar, they need have no conflicts. "Our ways may not be the same," he said, "but they are not far apart; our methods may be different but they have much in common. There is no reason therefore why we cannot cooperate with each other in the achievement of our common aims."[38]

But this is as far as he would go. In their joint statement the two prime ministers claimed that their "frank and informal" discussions had further strengthened their friendly relations. They pledged to carry forward the spirit of Bandung and do "all in their power'' to relax international tensions and promote peace. They agreed to seek solutions of their *respective* problems on the basis of peace and justice. They recognized the need for increasing cultural and commercial contact between the two countries.

Barely two months later Chou En-lai was in Pakistan returning the visit. At a colorful tribal ceremony in the Northwest Frontier area, the nawab of Hoti placed a Pathan turban on Chou's head while the assembled Yusafzai elders and notables applauded. Thus the Pathans accepted him as a "sworn brother." The nawab assured him that they would stand by him "through all ordeals." Evidently pleased, Chou observed that while he had become a brother of the Pakistanis he hoped that they in turn would become the friends and brothers of the Chinese people.[39]

The declarations made and the assurances exchanged during Chou's visit were substantially the same as those professed during Suhrawardy's visit to China two months earlier. The two propositions Chinese officials had repeatedly urged on their Pakistani audiences—there were no conflicts of interest between the two countries; ideological differences should not prevent them from strengthening their friendship—now found their way into the final joint statement of the two prime ministers.[40] This time Chou En-lai was much more vehement in his attack on the "colonialists." They had left a legacy of disputes in Asia and Africa which they were exploiting to serve their own "ulterior" ends. In the past they had prevented Pakistan and China from coming together, but this they would no longer be able to do.[41]

Now, as at Bandung, Chou En-lai presented himself and his colleagues as men of moderation and humility who sought peace passionately because it was indispensable to the success of their development plans at home. At a civic reception at Karachi he observed:

True, in their task of national reconstruction, the people of China have attained some achievements, but these achievements are meagre. . . . My country is still very backward economically as well as culturally. . . . Through our own personal experiences, we, the Chinese people, have realized that it is an immense task to build a backward country into a modern one. Essential in this connection are not only the concerted efforts of the people all over the country but also a peaceful international environment. Any war may interrupt our work in peaceful construction.[42]

Kashmir was not mentioned publicly when Suhrawardy was in Peking. Now in Karachi reporters questioned Chou En-lai on the subject. He maintained that like other disputes among Afro-Asians the Kashmir dispute could be settled amicably. Not much more than "sincerity" on both sides was needed, and, of course, the "colonialists," who had originally caused the dispute to arise, must not be allowed to meddle with it. Beyond this he would not go, for he and his government were still studying the matter. Pending completion of this study, he would follow the Chinese "principle" that "one has no say on a question until he has studied it."[43]

As Chou told reporters, Kashmir had figured in his talks with Suhrawardy at Peking and Karachi and in his talks with Nehru just before coming to Pakistan. His reluctance to adopt a clearly pro-Pakistani position on the issue and his insistence that the dispute had resulted from the colonialists' (and not Indian) machinations caused some disappointment in Pakistani circles. Suhrawardy endorsed the idea of peace among nations with the qualification that it must be just. At a banquet for Chou he declared: "We shall always strive for peace and are prepared to extend our hand in cooperation to all friendly countries. We, however, think that peace without justice is an illusion. As long as grievous wrongs remain unredressed . . . and lust of power continues, the threat to world peace will persist. Mere lip-service to slogans, however appealing they may be, cannot remove the causes of friction."[44]

The exchange of visits between the two prime ministers did not lift Sino-Pakistan relations from the domain of cultural and professional contacts that by this time had become a fairly routine affair. In politics their agreements were still confined to platitudes such as the greatness of Bandung, the glory of international peace, the virtues of Afro-Asian solidarity, and the evils of colonialism. In a modest way the visits may have further improved the environment, in terms of public feeling, in which Sino-Pakistan relations would proceed. But the better understanding each claimed to have gained of the other's purposes and policies did not draw the two governments any closer.

In 1957 Pakistan's relations with China took a turn for the worse. But before we deal with this development, it would be appropriate to sum up Pakistani and Chinese attitudes toward each other's major political concerns. Regarding Kashmir, Pakistan received some limited satisfaction from China. Unlike the Soviet Union, China did not concede that Kashmir belonged to India. But beyond this she adopted a neutral position, favoring neither India nor Pakistan. It would appear also that she wished to see the dispute settled. The Chinese welcomed the 1953 Bogra-Nehru agreement to have talks on holding a Kashmir plebiscite. "All countries and peoples which stand for the settlement of international disputes through peaceful consultation," declared the *People's Daily,* "rejoice at this news."[45] It urged the normalization of Indo-Pakistan relations and maintained that, with genuine desire for peace on both sides, all disputes between them could be settled. The Indo-Pakistan communiqué was especially welcome because the projected talks would be held bilaterally to the exclusion of the United Nations which, during its five years of handling the matter, had only aggravated the Kashmir dispute. Moreover, the UN was a mere instrumentality of the United States, who wanted to convert Kashmir into a "colony and a military base." The *People's Daily* had something agreeable for both sides. It endorsed the right of the people of Jammu and Kashmir "alone to determine their own fate and future." It also defended Nehru's ouster and subsequent arrest of Sheikh Abdullah on the ground that he was "a tool of the American agents."

I have already referred to Chou En-lai's equivocal statements on Kashmir when he came to Pakistan in December 1956. During a visit to Ceylon in February, 1957, he joined the Ceylonese prime minister in urging India and Pakistan to resolve their Kashmir dispute by direct negotiations and not to take it to the United Nations. He opposed the idea of sending UN troops to Kashmir. It is clear that at this time the Chinese were not concerned with the specifics of any settlement that India and Pakistan might make. They wanted, first and foremost, to exclude Western influence from the affairs of the subcontinent. They would have welcomed a settlement, regardless of which side came out winning, as long as it was accomplished without Western participation. Any settlement would bolster their doctrinal position that Afro-Asians could resolve their disputes if the West, which had created the differences in the first place, would stop interfering in their affairs. A settlement might also have the effect of easing Pakistan's security concern, therefore loosening her links with the United States. This would be desirable, for the Chinese overtures for deescalating the Sino-American cold war had been rebuffed by Dulles. As might be expected, the Chinese were looking at Indo-Pakistan disputes from their own, not Pakistani, perspectives.

It may be argued that Pakistanis had no reason to expect a more sympathetic Chinese attitude toward their problems with India. It is nevertheless worth mentioning that they were irked by the Chinese tendency to blame the West, rather than India, for the impasse in Kashmir. Some Pakistanis had hoped that Chou En-lai would prevail upon his friend Nehru to be "reasonable." In view of China's neutralism and Russia's openly anti-Pakistan stand, *Dawn* observed that it was the communist world, not the West, that hoped to gain from the continuance of Indo-Pakistan conflict over Kashmir.[46] Speaking in the National Assembly in September, 1958, Prime Minister Noon lamented that the two "great Asian powers"— China and Russia—had done nothing to promote a peaceful solution of the Kashmir problem.[47] It was not until Sino-Indian border tension reached crisis proportions that China began to move toward the Pakistani side of the issue.

The Pakistani position on an issue of some importance to the Chinese—their presence at the United Nations—was no less ambivalent. Outside the UN, Pakistani newsmen, politicians, and even government officials declared in favor of admitting Communist China. At an Independence Day reception in 1955, for instance, the Pakistani ambassador in Peking told his guests, including Chou En-lai, that Pakistanis, both in and outside the government, wished to see China restored to her "legitimate position" in the United Nations.[48] In a press conference on June 18, 1955, Prime Minister Mohammad Ali Bogra urged high-level talks between China and the United States to remove tension over Taiwan. Among the measures he reportedly proposed for relieving tension were the seating of Communist China at the UN, Kuomintang evacuation of the Chinese offshore islands, and departure of the U.S. Seventh Fleet from the Taiwan straits. In a London interview in July 1956, Hamidul Huq Chaudhri, Pakistan's foreign minister at the time, declared: "we have always been of the view that in order to create a stabilizing influence in South and Southeast Asia, the admission of China into the UN is necessary."[49] He added that his government would support every effort that might be made to resolve Sino-American differences, for peace would not come to Asia until these differences were resolved.

But despite these declarations of sympathy, when the time came to act, the Pakistani delegate at the United Nations dutifully supported, year after year, the American move to postpone consideration of the question of China's admission. The more recent Pakistani analyses have tended to attribute this lag between words and deeds to the nation's domestic political weakness which, between 1953 and 1958, is said to have invited Western, especially American, pressure. Consider, for instance, the following statement of Z. A. Bhutto before the National Assembly of Pakistan in November 1962:

When the Central Government of the People's Republic of China was established we recognised their new regime and initially supported its admission to the United Nations. Thereafter, advantage was taken of our position.... What is tragic is the willingness easily to succumb to pressures. This inevitably happens when there is internal weakness. The very fact that the same allies could not prevail upon the present government to continue the previous policy ... is evidence of the independence of our present foreign policy.[50]

Bhutto's claim regarding the "present government's" vigor was overstated, but of this more later.

In 1957 Sino-Pakistan relations began to deteriorate. In the summer of that year, Prime Minister Suhrawardy visited the United States where he joined John Foster Dulles in denouncing communist colonialism. In addresses to the House of Representatives and the Senate, he declared that "peace is safe" in American hands. He praised America's moral integrity without which, he maintained, the world might have been shattered at a time when this country alone possessed atomic weapons. Pakistan was proud of being an American ally in the "great adventure" of "establishing in the world the rights of the individual and in opposing the measures that tend to trample that spirit."[51] In a subsequent interview he described the Chinese posture as one of aggressive expansionism that threatened peace and freedom in Asia.

Why did Suhrawardy go out of his way to condemn a government with whose leaders he had so recently exchanged assurances of goodwill and cordiality? Several considerations might have weighed with him. In a Security Council debate on Kashmir earlier in the year, Pakistan had received strong "moral support" from the Nationalist Chinese delegate.[52] This might have impelled Suhrawardy to reciprocate the Nationalist Chinese favor by saying something nasty about their foes. Then there were the usual considerations of Pakistan's dependence upon the United States for military and economic assistance, which had been heightened by the inner convulsions of Suhrawardy's own government. It will be recalled that he presided over a coalition in which his own party was the smaller, and therefore junior, partner. His foreign minister, Firoz Khan Noon, who later succeeded him as prime minister, came from the Republican party, which comprised the larger group in the coalition. Note also that both he and Noon were exceedingly pro-Western in their orientation.[53] It is not surprising that during a visit to the Middle East President Nasser of Egypt would not even meet him.

In October 1957, while Suhrawardy was still the prime minister, the Pakistani delegation at the United Nations adopted a rather curious course of action on the question of whether China's admission should even be considered. First it abstained from voting, but then on second, "and by no means wiser," thought, it changed its position and asked to be counted among the opponents of the resolution calling for a consideration of the issue.[54]

The Chinese were irritated by Suhrawardy's remarks. But, once again, they were surprisingly moderate in expressing their reaction. The *People's Daily* thought it "quite understandable" that he should want to say pleasant things about the Americans in order to get more aid. But he "overreached himself," it added, when he joined Mr. Dulles in "slandering" China.[55] Ironically, it is a measure of Washington's tendency at the time to take Pakistani docility for granted that, despite his unequivocal and thoroughgoing support of American policies in Asia and the Middle East, Suhrawardy received virtually no press coverage and only a modest amount of official attention during his visit to the United States. He was dismissed as a "camera bug" who was also "jovial."[56] According to the *New York Times,* "some specially posed footage" of Eisenhower and two helicopters for emergency use during floods were among the more openly avowed results of his talks in Washington.[57]

Ayub Khan Era: The Initial Phase

The downward trend of Sino-Pakistan relations, characteristic of Suhrawardy's tenure as prime minister, continued through the first two years or so of Ayub Khan's presidency. On coming to power, Ayub made certain observations that suggested the possibility of a shift of emphases in the nation's foreign policy. He criticized the preceding government for having needlessly strained Pakistan's relations with countries such as the UAR, USSR, and China. He would instead pursue a policy that Pakistan's interests and geography dictated. He also referred to the celebrated rule that nations have no eternal friends or enemies, only eternal interests. But these expressions of realism did not immediately produce a visible impact upon Pakistan's relations with China. Indeed, these relations worsened.

To begin with, the president and his ministers partook of the same pro-Western orientation that had characterized their predecessors. As defense minister in the government of Pakistan during 1953-54, and earlier as commander in chief of the army, Ayub Khan had taken a leading part in the negotiations that eventuated in Pakistan's alliance with the United States. As commander in chief he had presided over an organization that benefited substantially from American military assistance. He knew also that the mountains in the north and the northwest had never excluded invasions of the subcontinent. It is, therefore, likely that the president readily accepted the American estimate of international communism as a threat to peace and freedom, and of China (which was said to be still some way from "mellowing") as an even greater menace than the Soviet Union. At a press conference in May 1960, Manzur Qadir echoed this American view and observed that China's admission to the United Nations would not mitigate her expansionist urges.[58] Later in the same year, Bhutto told reporters at the United Nations that China had made extensive "incursions" into Kashmir and thus violated the UN resolutions concerning the stationing of troops in that area.[59]

Specifically, three issues strained Sino-Pakistan relations: the Chinese suppression of the revolt in Tibet; her interpretation of certain Pakistani actions and statements as implying support of a two-China policy; and Ayub Khan's proposal for a joint defense arrangement between India and Pakistan. Pakistan did not endorse the Chinese action in Tibet. "It goes without saying," wrote *Dawn*, "that in this country there is as much sympathy as anywhere in the Free World for the Dalai Lama and the Tibetan people whose traditional autonomy has been suppressed."[60] The events in Tibet, *Dawn* added, were just as reprehensible as the continued Indian aggression against the people of Kashmir. In October 1959, Pakistan voted in favor of placing the Tibetan question before the United Nations General Assembly.

The Chinese action would seem to have heightened Ayub's concern regarding a communist threat to the subcontinent. The Chinese were building military bases in Tibet. The Russians, for several years, had built airfields and strategic roads in Afghanistan. Ayub saw that if the communist powers chose to advance on the subcontinent they would have the facilities to do so. Accordingly, he made his well-known offer of a joint defense arrangement to India, which, however, Nehru at the time rejected, exclaiming, "defense against whom?" Interpreting the trend of Pakistani policy, the *Pakistan Times* wrote:

They [the government of Pakistan] *also realized that, so long as India and Pakistan remained at daggers drawn, preparations for effective defense of the sub-continent against possible aggression by the Communist giants in the north would remain extremely difficult. The Chinese onslaught against Tibetan freedom earlier this year lent strength to their belief in the necessity of an Indo-Pakistan rapprochement.... The soundness of their approach was readily appreciated by those whose vision could reach beyond the exigencies of the present differences between India and Pakistan, and who could see the mortal perils lurking for both in the aggression and expansionism inherent in the creed of the two formidable neighbors in the north.* [61]

Talking with a *Times of India* correspondent in October 1959, Manzur Qadir expressed disappointment at Nehru's rejection of Ayub's joint-defense proposal. He also observed that he did not understand why Nehru meekly took "slap after slap" from the Chinese, pretending at the same time that he had not been slapped at all. [62]

The Chinese have always reacted sharply to the suggestion that there might indeed be two Chinas. Pakistan was never enthusiastic about this possibility, but some Pakistani statements and moves could have been seen as bearing a two-China slant. For instance, in March 1957, a member of Pakistan's delegation to the United Nations, K. Sarwar Hasan, an influential commentator on foreign affairs and secretary of the Pakistan Institute of International Affairs, spoke of a recent Security Council debate on Kashmir. He praised the "moral" support Pakistan had received from the Nationalist Chinese delegate, Tziang Ting-fu, whom he described as a "great statesman." He thought it remarkable that "this China," even while lacking the advantage of location on the mainland, should have displayed a high regard for moral standards. At this point, an official of the Chinese embassy in Karachi, who had been listening to Mr. Hasan, left the meeting protesting that his people "resolutely opposed" any statement or attempt aimed at creating two Chinas. [63] In 1958 when tension was high in the Taiwan straits, the Pakistani ambassador in Peking declined, in a note of October 7, to concede that Taiwan was a part of China. He argued that the question of Chinese sovereignty over Taiwan and Penghu Islands was "unclear"—a position not unlike that of Chou En-lai when he refused to commit himself on the Kashmir issue on the ground that he was still studying the matter.

In 1959 a group of Nationalist Chinese Muslim pilgrims to Mecca stopped over at Karachi for a few days, met Pakistani religious leaders, made statements and speeches, and chatted with the Pakistani foreign minister. The Chinese protested and used the occasion to vent their frustration over the course of Pakistan's China policy during the two previous years. Their note, dated July 21, 1959, charged that a delegation, headed by a lieutenant general of the "Chiang Kai-shek clique" usurping the name of Chinese Muslim Haji Mission, had been permitted to come to Karachi, "slander" China, and damage Sino-Pakistan relations. Pakistani press had insulted China by covering the statements of this group. And the foreign minister, Manzur Qadir, had made a serious "provocation" against the Chinese people and government by receiving the so-called pilgrims. This was not an isolated incident. "In the past few months, the Pakistani government has been stepping up its following of the U.S. plot to create two Chinas and has made repeated utterances flagrantly interfering in China's internal affairs. Thus it undisguisedly shows its slight of China's sovereignty and territorial integrity."[64] The Chinese noted also that from April 7 to May 12, 1959, the Pakistani foreign minister and other high officials had repeatedly abused China for putting down the "rebellion of a handful of reactionaries" in Tibet, thus interfering in China's domestic affairs "and waging cold war in the footsteps of the United States."

An "observer" writing in the *People's Daily* went further. He charged that ever since the establishment of diplomatic relations between the two countries, the government of Pakistan had taken an unfriendly attitude toward China on many issues. In the 9th, 10th, 12th, and 13th sessions of the UN General Assembly, it had followed the United States in opposing discussion of the question of Chinese representation. During the preceding two years, Pakistani officials had openly denied Chinese sovereignty over Taiwan "by calling Taiwan a 'country' and by placing Taiwan and 'mainland China' on the same footing." The "observer" concluded that "since the Ayub Government came to power, the Pakistani stand of following the US 'two Chinas' scheme and showing hostility to the Chinese people has become worse."[65]

On their part, the Chinese too had "interfered" in Pakistan's domestic affairs. In February, 1959, Ayub Khan's government arrested two leftist leaders, Faiz Ahmad Faiz (a renowned poet) and Maulana Bhashani. In a cable to the president, a Chinese Committee for Afro-Asian Solidarity professed shock and indignation at the detention of these "distinguished peace partisans and leaders of Afro-Asian solidarity movement" and warned: "Their continuous arbitrary detention by your government will be condemned by people of Asia, Africa and the world who cherish peace and justice. We resolutely demand Bhashani and Faiz to be immediately released by your government."[66]

It is well known that after the Tibetan crisis Chinese policy hardened both at home and abroad. Her denunciation of SEATO (that "out-and-out aggressive bloc") became harsher. NCNA accused Pakistani newspapers of "turning black into white" in writing about the happenings in Tibet. Needless to say, Ayub's call for Indo-Pakistan cooperation in defending the subcontinent irritated the Chinese. They noted that he had only recently signed an "aggressive" military pact with the United States and had sent his foreign minister to a SEATO meeting in Washington "where a series of military and political plots against Asian countries were worked out."[67]

Looking back at the spectrum of Sino-Pakistan relations between 1950 and 1961, one will notice three distinct phases. There is the pre-Bandung period, 1950—54, when these relations followed a pattern of humdrum routine: a modest amount of trade and occasional exchange of visits exhausted the interest of Pakistan and China in each other. During the two years following Bandung, one could see a great deal of cultural exchange and talk, especially from the Chinese side, about peace, goodwill, cooperation, Afro-Asian solidarity, and colonialism. In this chorus, Pakistanis joined also, but with much less enthusiasm. Beginning with Suhrawardy's visit to Washington in the summer of 1957 until shortly after Ayub Khan's visit with Kennedy in the summer of 1961, Sino-Pakistan relations remained in low key.

Neither side was able to get the other's support for its political goals. Each settled for limited gains. China concentrated on cultivating Pakistan's public opinion and building a reserve of goodwill that might some day be helpful. Pakistan, limited by her con-

frontation with India and alliance with the United States, went spas-
modically from rhetoric of goodwill to that of her Cold War
obligations.

A further word should perhaps be said about the principals, on
the Pakistani side, who charted the course of relations with China.
It might be puzzling that the man to initiate the thaw in Sino-Pakistan relations should have been no other than Mohammad Ali
Bogra, who was outstanding for his pro-Western sympathies. He
was neither an astute politician nor an especially skillful negotiator,
but he was noted for personal warmth and forthrightness that
inspired credibility. These qualities enabled him to convince Chou
En-lai that Pakistan was no enemy of China. He was assisted at
Bandung by Gen. N. M. Raza, who had earlier served as Pakistan's
ambassador in Peking and is said to have had Chou's respect and
confidence. Furthermore, China's "peace offensive" was in full
swing at this time so that the American view that China meant to
subjugate Asia might have seemed exaggerated even to a man like
Bogra. Note also that American leverage on Pakistani policy was
not as powerful in early 1955 as it became a year or two later.

In Ayub Khan's case one or two considerations other than those
already mentioned may be important. He came to the presidency
believing that Pakistan's major difficulties, domestic and foreign,
had resulted from her political instability and governmental mis-
management. He expected that, once he had put the country back
on an "even keel," there might be a reasonable prospect of settling
Pakistan's disputes with India. Although Indian leaders had
greeted him with shouts of "dictator," some improvement in relations between the two countries did materialize within less than two
years. The Indus Waters dispute was resolved in 1960. Nehru personally came to Karachi to sign the treaty. Ayub took him to the hills
of Muree, had long walks with him, gave him flowers, talked about
the need for Indo-Pakistan cooperation and of dangers from northern neighbors. But each time he mentioned Kashmir, Nehru
became tense and taciturn. Ayub did not abandon hope, at least
not yet.

It should be remembered also that for eight years (1953-60) during the period under review Eisenhower occupied the White House
and John Foster Dulles, for the most part, made American foreign

policy. Dulles was a loyal supporter of America's allies.[68] Until his meetings with President Kennedy in mid-1961, where he apparently learned better, Ayub had hoped that stronger American interest might finally lead to a solution of the problem of Kashmir; hence his relative coolness toward China during the two years or so following his accession to the presidency. But major changes in Pakistan's international environment would soon develop and prompt her to seek China's friendship.

Four

Toward an Entente Cordiale

Sino-Pakistan relations got their first major intake of substantive content, above and beyond the rhetoric of goodwill, when the two nations made border and air-travel agreements in 1963. These agreements were significant, for they implied, especially on the part of Pakistan, a recognition of basic change in the salients of her international environment. It had been public knowledge since the summer of 1959 that Sino-Indian relations were moving away from Panchasheel and "brotherly" cooperation toward confrontation. On the other hand, the Kennedy administration in Washington, coming to office in the beginning of 1961, downgraded American alliances in Asia which some of its spokesmen derided as symptomatic of a disease named "pactitis." The president himself, a long-time advocate of generous American assistance to India to insure the success of her political and economic development models, wished to see her assume a leadership role in Asia and act as a counterpoise to China. In this context, a settlement of Indo-Pakistan disputes would be welcome. But Kennedy would not use American assistance as a lever to pressure India into making concessions to Pakistan. If a settlement on Pakistani terms could not be had, he would rather that Pakistan learn to live with the status quo in Kashmir or revise her terms so as to make them acceptable to India. Pakistan's cooperation with India in opposing China would be valuable, but it was not crucial.

The agreements were significant also in terms of their impact on American thinking with regard to the efficacy of the alliance with Pakistan. They dramatized Pakistan's unwillingness to redefine her basic foreign-policy goals to suit the changing requirements of

America's global strategy. This assertion of independence, shocking to Washington officials used to a Pakistani posture of acquiescence, initiated a process of reappraisal that, after the Indo-Pakistan war of 1965, led to a virtual termination of the alliance. Some nonofficial reactions were harshly critical. Writers in popular magazines designated Pakistan as the "friend of our enemies" and portrayed Ayub Khan as playing "footsie" with Chou En-lai.[1] Even sober commentators referred to Pakistan's new China policy as "flirtation" and deplored the agreements under reference as breaches in the "Free World" solidarity. Pakistan, they said, was getting closer to China only to spite India, blindly following the dictum that the enemy of one's enemy was one's friend.

Needless to say, these interpretations were exaggerative. Tension with India was indeed a major factor, but other influences were also at work: a desire for diversification of commercial connections and profit; an assessment that the Chinese threat to the subcontinent was, at worst, remote; domestic political stability permitting a greater degree of independence from Western aid givers, especially the United States, in shaping her foreign policy; the general thaw in the Cold War and the resulting view in Rawalpindi that the United States herself might eventually ease relations with China as she had done with the Soviet Union. Note also that the agreements did not come as a sudden or impulsive Pakistani response to the Sino-Indian conflict. They represented a deliberate choice.

The Border Agreement

Three years before the Sino-Indian border dispute erupted into armed conflict and the United States dispatched military aid to India, there began a process that culminated in the Sino-Pakistan border agreement of 1963. In September 1959, the government of Pakistan received a Chinese map showing parts of Hunza as Chinese territory. This mountainous area, abounding in glaciers, lay east of 75° longitude and north of 36.5° latitude. The Chinese line began at Mintaka Pass below the point where the Afghan-Pakistan-

Chinese boundaries met, came down to Shimshal Pass, and turned east toward Tibet.[2] Apparently, the Pakistan Foreign Office took it all rather calmly. Foreign Minister Manzur Qadir stated that his government would take no official notice of the map, for maps, by themselves, did not constitute violation of territory. The foreign secretary, Ikramullah, remarked facetiously that Pakistan might respond by publishing maps that showed Chinese territory as Pakistani.[3] But it seems that in fact the Chinese maps were engaging the government's serious concern. The Foreign Office, a spokesman told the press, was collecting "authentic, internationally acceptable material to have a clear line demarcated between Pakistan and China."[4] On October 23, 1959, President Ayub Khan announced that his government would soon propose border talks to China. Within a month a proposal to this effect went forth, but there the matter rested.[5]

China did not respond immediately to the Pakistani initiative. Throughout 1960, which was the year of the U-2 incident and heightened East-West tensions, Sino-Pakistan relations remained in low key. When Ayub Khan visited the United States in the summer of 1961, his pronouncements revealed the tentativeness of his thinking about China. He still talked of the danger from the north and urged Indo-Pakistan cooperation to meet it. To great applause he told a joint session of Congress that Pakistan was the only country in Asia upon which the United States could rely in time of crisis. At the same time, he explained his government's intention to normalize relations with the Chinese and to define the common border with them. In a "Meet the Press" interview in New York on July 16, 1961, he suggested that a formula for accommodating both China and Taiwan in the United Nations might be found.[6] In an interview with NBC's Welles Hangen he asserted: "The Chinese have their ideology, and we have our ideology. They have no faith in our ideology and we have none in their ideology. But we are neighbors and we would to like live as good neighbors. We have no cause to quarrel over our undemarcated border and all we have said is: let us define it and let us see what comes out of it."[7] The Chinese could not have welcomed Pakistan's continued advocacy of joint defense with India and her implied support for a two-China policy. It is hardly surprising that at this time they paid little attention to the proposal for border demarcation.

Pakistani foreign policy came under considerable stress and strain during 1961. Relations with Afghanistan reached the breaking point in May. Ayub failed to dissuade Kennedy from sending arms to India. In December India occupied Goa, convincing Pakistanis more than ever before that she was irredeemably disposed to aggression. The United States seemed unable to influence Indian policy toward either Goa or Kashmir. Pakistan now leaned a bit in China's direction and, in December, voted in favor of seating China at the United Nations. The Chinese were apparently impressed; on January 14, 1962, their ambassador in Pakistan characterized Indian press reports of Chinese claims on Pakistani territory as "pure fabrications." This did not allay Pakistani concern altogether. The Chinese maps were recalled, and it was noted that Chinese claims on parts of Hunza, Gilgit, and Baltistan might be asserted in the course of negotiations. But when would negotiations begin? In a mood of cautious optimism, the *Morning News* observed: "It is true that Pakistan requested China long ago to proceed with the actual demarcation of the border and China has not yet replied to it. It is not unlikely, however, that the trend of recent events may induce China to proceed with demarcation talks. Pakistan's recent vote for the admission of China into the United Nations may be an important factor in the process."[8]

In the middle of March 1962, more than two years after Pakistan had first proposed negotiations, Peking decided to discuss the border question. A Chinese note on the subject was regarded in Karachi as a step forward. S. K. Dehlavi, the new foreign secretary, described Pakistan's relations with China as "cordial with prospects of closer understanding in fields where such understanding is possible and desirable." Later he told newsmen at Rawalpindi that he was not aware of China having occupied any Indian territory.[9] On May 3, with a view to "ensuring tranquility on the border" and developing "good neighborly relations" between them, Pakistan and China announced that they had agreed to negotiate a provisional demarcation line between Sinkiang and "the contiguous area the defense of which is under the actual control of Pakistan."

The projected agreement would expire upon the settlement of the Kashmir dispute between Pakistan and India, at which time the sovereign authorities concerned would negotiate a permanent settlement.

The news of China's willingness to discuss the border, and unconfirmed reports that she had offered Pakistan a treaty of commerce and friendship and assistance in mineral exploitation and industrial development, evoked enthusiastic response in Pakistan. At the same time, commentators went out of their way to express the hope that the United States would not object to Sino-Pakistan economic cooperation. They were clearly loath to have to choose between the United States and China, as, similarly, Washington had never welcomed the prospect of having to choose between Pakistan and India. Since a number of newspapers—notably *Dawn,* the *Morning News,* and the *Pakistan Times*—maintained excellent liaison with Ayub Khan's government, it would be fair to assume that their interpretations were not far removed from thinking in the Foreign Office. These are noted here in some detail.

The developments under reference were, first of all, attributed to the peace-loving character of both governments: both wanted quiet borders and good relations with all their neighbors. Pakistan had reached border agreements with Burma and Iran and had settled most of her border disputes with India; China had concluded similar agreements with Burma and Nepal. Peking's troubles with India, according to these newspapers, arose from the latter's choice of a militant path and abandonment of the spirit of Panchasheel. "Nehru may have made sure of a couple of billion dollars in aid, but he has created dangerous tensions."[10] Congratulating leaders of both nations for their high statesmanship, *Dawn* singled out Foreign Secretary Dehlavi for special commendation, since he had "perhaps done the hardest work in this connection."[11] In an editorial entitled "The Glow in the North," it welcomed the emerging "entente cordiale" between Pakistan and China.

The new Chinese gesture will be received with deep appreciation all over the country. Pakistan will readily grasp the hand of friendship extended by its great neighbor. It will be against our grain not to do so. Indeed, men of goodwill all over, who sincerely long for a world free of tensions, would welcome this move which may well bring about the removal of misunderstandings in this region. But there are others also who would recoil at the very thought of good neighborly relations between China and Pakistan.... Strenuous attempts will also be made to sow fresh seeds of discord and create misunderstandings between Pakistan and the United States.... But for men of vision, a Sino-Pakistan pact of friendship and economic cooperation, or better still, of non-aggression, would be something to be happy about. It will vindicate the stand of this country that our alliances are only for purposes of defense against aggression ... that Pakistan's friendship with China is not incompatible with the feelings of fellowship we have for the American people. A Pakistan closely allied to the United States and having an equally close alliance with neighboring China will be ... an outstanding example of the triumph of reason over fear and short-sighted self-interest.[12]

Other commentors advanced essentially the same argument without waxing so eloquent. Dealing with the subject at a more mundane level, the *Morning News* noted that Ayub Khan's government, having defined the national interest in "broad" terms, did not view alliances with the West as a barrier to friendly relations with China and the Soviet Union. Earlier, the agreement with the Soviets for oil exploration in Pakistan had been "a refreshing departure from a policy of isolation and aloofness that previous regimes had imposed upon the country because of their internal weakness rather than any external compulsion." Economic cooperation with China need not hurt Pakistan's relation with the United States. Indeed, "if the experience of India is any guide, the Americans will be more responsive to our needs than they have hitherto been.[13]

In June 1962, Mohammad Ali Bogra became Pakistan's foreign minister and dispatched General Raza as ambassador to Peking. The general had served in that post in the early 1950s and reportedly established "a close personal relationship" with Chou En-lai.[14] Following Raza's arrival in Peking in mid-July, the two governments exchanged maps and discussed procedural matters. Actual negotiations began on October 13, a week before the Chinese attacked Indian positions along the Sino-Indian border. On December 26 China and Pakistan announced "complete agreement in principle" on aligning their common border. Evidently, the conflict with India had pushed the Chinese toward agreement. In the National Assembly, Zulfikar Ali Bhutto explained: "No state would want to have unresolved situations on two fronts. At any rate, we were the gainers. We saw no reason to delay the matter since we ourselves had initiated it."[15]

Once again Pakistani commentators emphasized that no sinister designs against any other country lurked behind the agreement, which had been motivated solely by the desire of the signatories to coexist peacefully. It had, they thought, proved that both governments were realistic and reasonable. Although "the salutary principle of settling disputes through negotiations," which Pakistan advocated, had unfortunately not commended itself to the government of India, it was hoped that wiser counsels, instead of "armed instigation from distant cold war capitals," would eventually prevail in New Delhi.[16] Bhutto called the agreement "a signal triumph for the procedure of peace," and Dehlavi hoped Pakistan's friends would welcome it because it safeguarded her legitimate interests and insured peace.

The actual border agreement was signed on March 2, 1963. It covered a 200-mile frontier beginning at the trijunction of Afghanistan, Pakistan, and Sinkiang and running in a general southeasterly direction up to the Karakoram Pass. China ceded to Pakistan 750 square miles of territory beyond the main watershed of the Karakoram range, comprising the Oprang Valley and the Darband-Darwaza pocket including its salt mines. Pakistan surrendered no part of the territory under her control. In drawing up the agreement the two sides relied on the customary boundary line, following the principle of the main watershed. Waters draining into the Indus system remained with or came to Pakistan, while waters draining into the Tarim system remained with China. The Shaksgam Mustagh drainage area of about 1,050 square miles, which at one point Pakistan had claimed, remained with China. But then, as one spokesman explained, even the British had not asserted claim over this area when they proposed the McDonald Line to China in 1899.[17] It is interesting to note that the boundary line emerging from the agreement "corresponds along much of its length—passes and all—with that claimed by the Indian government itself in its correspondence with Peking; the barren southern slopes of the Aghill mountains seem the only significant stretch of ground to be bargained away.[18]

The new territory brought Pakistan some modest economic advantages—grazing grounds and the Darband-Darwaza salt mines which would be useful to Pakistanis in adjacent areas, especially the Hunzans. Secure possession of the waters draining into the Indus system must also be reckoned as an advantage in view of Pakistani apprehensions about the future of streams flowing into West Pakistan from the Indian-occupied part of Kashmir. Pakistan's share future included six of the seven mountain passes in the area and three quarters of K-2, the world's second highest mountain. This region is not easily reached, and its strategic value is dubious. However, the agreement was significant politically. It mitigated the potential for conflict between the two countries. It placed China formally and firmly on record as maintaining that Kashmir did not, as yet, belong to India. As Pakistanis saw it, the agreement showed also that they, and the Chinese, were willing and able to resolve their international disputes by peaceful negotiation; if the Kashmir dispute had defied solution for a decade and a half, responsibility for that must be placed at Nehru's door.

Reaction to the agreement abroad was mixed. It was generally conceded, sometimes grudgingly, that Pakistan had come out of the negotiations well: She had taken areas she did not have before and had given up none from under her control. The United States had viewed the thaw in Sino-Pakistan relations with misgivings. When China and Pakistan agreed to hold talks in May 1962, officials in Washington regarded this development as a setback for American relations with both India and Pakistan.[19] Reacting to the actual agreement in March, 1963, the State Department noted that Pakistan's interests in the area had been met but expressed concern that it might endanger the Indo-Pakistan talks on Kashmir then in progress.[20]

India, as might have been expected, declared that the agreement was "illegal": China and Pakistan had no common border, for all of Kashmir, including the part on the Pakistani side of the cease-fire line, belonged to her. Indian officials also charged that Pakistan had "given away" thousands of square miles of "Indian" territory. But as a special correspondent of the *Times* (London) noted, the total area in dispute amounted to only about 3,400 square miles, out of which China had turned over 750 square miles to Pakistan. Pakistan merely gave up claims on maps, while China gave up actual territory, from which she withdrew her armed forces and administrative personnel.[21] Commenting on Pakistan's advantages from the agreement, the *Manchester Guardian* wrote:

It can of course be argued that the Chinese have been so generous for malicious reasons: to upset Indo-Pakistani relations, to woo the Pakistanis from their Western commitments, above all to prove to the Indians once more how much they are missing by not coming to terms. If so, it was up to the Pakistanis to make the most of these fortuitous diplomatic advantages, as they have done. Nothing in the agreement is inconsistent with Pakistan's alliances, and the two parties have safeguarded India's interest as far as they can by including a clause that provides for fresh negotiations if the Indo-Pakistan dispute over Kashmir is settled.[22]

A Matter of Timing

The agreement in principle on December 26, 1962, was announced hours before the Indo-Pakistan talks on Kashmir—inspired by the United States and Britain—were scheduled to begin. The border agreement itself was signed and announced on March 2, 1963, that is, ten days before the opening of the fourth round in the Indo-Pakistan talks. On both occasions, certain quarters, notably Indian and American, judged that these announcements had been badly timed and would dispose the government of India against settling the Kashmir problem. The *Times of India* wrote that the government of Pakistan had announced "this shady agreement" two hours after the Indian delegation had called upon President Ayub.[23] Swaran Singh, the chief Indian negotiator, declared that the announcement of Pakistan's agreement with India's enemy was "certainly not helpful in paving the way for a mutually satisfactory solution."[24] The *New York Times* viewed the announcement as a "deliberate provocation" and observed that the timing was intended to pressure India into making concessions on Kashmir. By using China "as a bogeyman," Pakistan hoped to induce the United States also to put pressure on India toward the same end.[25] Similar dissatisfaction was voiced in Washington and Delhi when Bhutto went to Peking in late February 1963, to sign the agreement. Dean Rusk called in the Pakistani ambassador to warn that the agreement with China would endanger Pakistan's negotiations with India.[26] Nehru told the Indian Parliament that the "announcement is deliberately timed to upset our talks." A few days later he charged that China was trying to "poison" Indo-Pakistan relations and had timed the agreement to prejudice the outcome of the talks.[27]

What was behind the timing of these announcements? Let us consider the one of December 26, 1962. The government of Pakistan asserted that the timing had been determined in Peking and that the announcement coming when it did was purely coincidental.[28] On December 27 President Ayub Khan told American Ambassador Walter McConaughy and the British high commissioner, Sir Morris James, that Ambassador Raza had had instructions to sign the agreement as soon as the Chinese met certain demands. A telegram that the Chinese had accepted these demands and that Raza had signed the agreement had arrived in code at 8:30 the previous evening. The government of Pakistan decided not to suppress the news because Peking would have announced it anyway. Moreover, as Dehlavi pointed out, the government wanted the Indians to know of the agreement before, rather than during, the talks.[29]

The Chinese would, of course, deny that they wanted to wreck the Indo-Pakistan discussions. They might refer to Chou En-lai's statement in the second week of December welcoming the forthcoming talks. At a Pakistan embassy dinner in Peking, Chou observed that his government had "always entertained the hope that Pakistan and India would settle their dispute over Kashmir through negotiations. We are glad to see that [they] have reached agreement on the holding of such negotiations."[30] He went on to express hope that the negotiations would achieve "positive results." A statement like this might be taken to mean only that the Chinese were being ingenious. But if the official Indian theory that the Kashmir dispute is merely a symptom, and not the cause, of the bad state of Indo-Pakistan relations is correct, the Chinese need not have feared a Kashmir settlement. In this connection, a growing section of official and unofficial opinion in Pakistan refused to consider relations with China as a bargaining point in the country's relations with India. A comment in the *Morning News* of December 6, 1962, is instructive: "the solution of Kashmir will not be a means to an end. Those who are obsessed with the defence of India against China should know that Pakistan has no human fodder to offer to the big guns that are being assembled in the underbelly of the Himalayas."

A more plausible explanation suggested that the Chinese wanted to show the world—especially the Afro-Asians, some of whom were trying to bring the Sino-Indian dispute back to the conference table—that their difficulties with India arose largely from the latter's intransigence. It is significant that they signed a boundary agreement with Outer Mongolia, an ally of the Soviet Union, on the same day that they signed the agreement in principle with Pakistan, an ally of the West. They had already settled their border disputes with Nepal and Burma. As the *Times* wrote, in neither case—Pakistan or Outer Mongolia—was there any urgency to sign and announce the agreement. The Chinese took the opportunity to emphasize that they could be reasonable with those who would be reasonable with them.[31] In the process they hoped to regain the sympathy of the nonaligned world. In this view, the Chinese had engineered "a strikingly successful operation that demonstrated formidable skill and power. These are qualities that must be recognized, and Moscow has at least as much reason to worry as the West has."[32]

As a correspondent of the *Daily Telegraph* reported from Karachi, China's sudden acceptance of Pakistan's conditions apparently took Rawalpindi by surprise.[33] Left to themselves, the

Pakistanis would probably have chosen a different time for announcing the agreement. However, they have had little reason to regret the timing chosen by Peking. Nehru, under considerable pressure from the United States and Britain, had agreed to discuss Kashmir with Pakistan in the wake of India's humiliating defeat in the brief border war with China. That he had done so reluctantly became obvious, raising serious doubts about his willingness to make the concessions that might break the Kashmir deadlock. Almost immediately after signing a joint communiqué with Ayub Khan, announcing their agreement to hold talks, Nehru stated publicly that it would be "very harmful" to alter the status quo in Kashmir.[34] Then, three days before the talks were to open, he accused Pakistan of adopting an "attitude of blackmail" and the West of exerting pressure tactics on India. He told an American newsman: "While we are prepared for greater contacts and greater trade between Kashmir and Pakistan and for adjustments of the present cease-fire line, which is not a very sensible one, we are persuaded that any major change would be the ruin of the Valley [of Kashmir]."[35]

Two days after the talks had begun, they were already being viewed in Delhi as superfluous. "With the Chinese now talking peace, there is less feeling in India that Kashmir concessions are necessary," the Associated Press reported.[36] When two rounds of talks had been held without yielding any progress, the *New York Times* commented: "The crux of the problem lies in the failure of India to manifest any readiness to make important concessions."[37] Western pressure on India, it should be noted, had taken the form only of an appeal to her enlightened self-interest. It had not made Anglo-American military assistance contingent upon a settlement with Pakistan. At a Calcutta news conference, U.S. Ambassador Galbraith assured the Indians that his government had never intended to link its arms aid to them with a Kashmir settlement: "We do not do business with our friends that way!"[38] While urging a settlement of Indo-Pakistan differences in a letter to Prime Minister Nehru, President Kennedy professed to understand India's difficulties concerning the Kashmir problem and left the impression that its resolution would not be a prerequisite to long-term American military assistance to India.[39] There were even some reports to the effect that the United States would prefer India's retention of the Valley of Kashmir because she needed it for defending Ladakh.[40]

India's professions of shock at the Sino-Pakistan agreement in principle were difficult to take at face value; for as the *Manchester Guardian* pointed out, Nehru had agreed to talks with Pakistan "in the full knowledge that Pakistan was negotiating with China and success was at least a possible outcome."[41] At any rate, the announcement under reference would seem not to have affected the talks, which went through six rounds. The subject of territorial adjustments was broached during the third round, but the two governments were so far apart that progress was virtually ruled out.

The question of timing arose again when Bhutto went to Peking to sign the actual border agreement on March 1, 1963. On this occasion, it was evidently an act of choice on both sides. After three rounds of talks with India, the government of Pakistan had apparently concluded that its handling of the border agreement with China would have little relevance to India's disposition with regard to Kashmir. After Bhutto had signed the agreement, Nehru declared that he would withhold the concessions he had earlier intended to offer Pakistan.[42] But in his dealings with Pakistan Nehru rarely had difficulty in finding reasons for changing his mind. Commenting on the theory that the Sino-Pakistan border agreement would jeopardize the Kashmir talks, a British observer wrote:

Perhaps it will. But the Pakistanis may be excused for thinking that a bird in the hand is worth two in the bush. They have got very little from talks with India over the past decade or so, and the results of the present round are entirely speculative. There is still no evidence that India is ready to concede their minimum demand. Certainly the agreement with China may be used by India as a justification if the negotiations fail. But the Indian Government has never been at a loss for such justifications in the past.[43]

The Air-Travel Agreement

The Sino-Pakistan border agreement was followed by a trade agreement, which is not discussed here because of its routine

nature, and an air-travel agreement. The latter evoked considerable interest and comment in international circles, since it was
the first of its kind that China had made with a noncommunist country. The idea of commercial air service between Pakistan and China
was not altogether new. As early as 1956 Saifuddin Azizi, the governor of Sinkiang, had broached it with visiting Pakistani editors.
Kashgar, he explained, could not be much more than one jet hour
from Rawalpindi. Air service to Peking via Sinkiang would remove
the necessity of going through India and Hong Kong. PIA (Pakistan
International Airlines) examined the suggestion at the time but did
not follow it up for security reasons.

Toward the end of 1962, however, PIA was looking for new business. It had a thriving service to London but lost money on its Lon-
don-New York run, even though making only two round trips a
week during the peak season and one a week otherwise.[44] It wanted
to extend travel to Tokyo, but the British prevented this by refusing
to grant landing rights in Hong Kong. It was under these circumstances that Nur Khan, PIA's managing director, went to Peking in
May 1963, to discuss the possibilities of landing rights in China. The
following month he announced a preliminary agreement providing
for direct commercial air service between the two countries. "Rout-
ing our service via Canton and Shanghai will enable our airline to
extend its European service to the Far East and will provide the fast-
est service from this part of the world to Tokyo.[45] The final agreement was signed in August 1963. Nur Khan made it clear that the
agreement contained no unusual provisions or restrictions. The
Chinese had granted PIA all normal traffic rights without any conditions regarding the nationality of passengers carried into or transi-
ting the country. He observed also that the airline expected to profit
from the Chinese route. The growing number of trade fairs in the
Far East and of Europeans visiting China would make this
possible.[46]

The air agreement put additional strain on Pakistan's relations
with the United States, which had already suffered in some measure from the Sino-Pakistan border accord. Officials in Washington thought Pakistan was "playing with fire in inviting a militant
communist nation to the doorstep in this part of Asia." They were

concerned that this breach in China's containment might become the impetus for a route system reaching eventually into Africa and Latan America.[47] As a gesture of disapproval, the United States "postponed" a four-million-dollar loan to Pakistan that she had earlier agreed to advance for modernizing Dacca airport so that it could receive jet aircraft.

Considering that American aid to Pakistan at this time averaged about 500 million dollars a year, postponement of a four-million-dollar loan served merely as an irritating pinprick. The government of Pakistan decided to start work on the airport with its own funds. Peking welcomed this turn of events. Now, wrote a commentator in the *Peking Review,* the project would cost less and Pakistan would not have to have American advisers. Pakistan had done well in making this decision. "When the choice had to be made between national pride and the American dole with all its accompanying insolence and insults, Pakistan preferred to uphold the honour of its people... Pakistan, by deciding to resist American pressure and build with its own resources, shows that self-reliance is a weapon that can help the new emerging nations safeguard their national independence."[48]

In the first week of September 1963, President Kennedy sent under secretary of State George Ball to Rawalpindi to inquire how far Pakistan intended to carry her "flirtation" with China. Although they assured Ball of continued fidelity to their alliances with the United States, Pakistani leaders put up a show of firmness and independence. They told him the American policy of arming India without securing a Kashmir settlement had left them no alternative to seeking friendly relations with China.[49] Soon after Balls's return, the United States decided not to make an issue of the Sino-Pakistan air agreement. Officials indicated that the Dacca Airport loan would be reinstated. With a touch of exaggeration, Phillips Talbot, assistant secretary of state for Near Eastern and South Asian affairs, declared: "We regard our relations with Pakistan as firmly based today, as they have been, on a joint understanding of the importance of maintaining the United States-Pakistan alliance against Communist subversion and aggression.[50] A few months later, PIA disclosed that the U.S. State Department had authorized the use of

Boeing jets for the new service and the stockpiling of spare parts worth about $500,000 within China.[51]

A protocol and related documents on technical and operational arrangements were signed by Pakistan and China on March 8, 1964. The first PIA jet touched down at Shanghai International Airport at 4:34 P.M. on April 29. The Chinese hailed the service as a "milestone in the history of friendly relations between the two countries." More than a thousand Chinese met the flight at the airport, which had been decorated with Pakistani and Chinese national flags and huge placards affirming Sino-Pakistani "friendship." At a reception for Nur Khan, Foreign Minister Chen Yi significantly observed: "We would like to point out that those who tried to isolate and blockade China have failed."[52]

It may incidentally be noted that in 1963 Pakistan concluded an air-travel agreement with the Soviet Union which for the first time gave a foreign airline the right not only to land on Soviet territory but to go on from there to other countries. The agreement provided for the establishment of four points beyond Moscow for PIA's Karachi-Kabul-Moscow service, which began to operate on April 1, 1964. PIA thus became the only International Air Transportation Authority (IATA) member serving both China and the Soviet Union.

Pakistan's air agreements, especially with China, were rated as something of a diplomatic triumph. It was pointed out that Western airlines, notably BOAC, had for years tried in vain to obtain landing rights in China. A commentator in the *New Republic* observed that Pakistan's China policy was calculated to serve her own national interests and not those of Peking. Ayub Khan was developing the "most active foreign policy in Asia," designed to restore control of Asian affairs to Asians. In the border agreement Pakistan had gained beyond her expectations. Her air agreement, under which she alone was operating the flights so far, was no more "sinister" than India's long-standing agreement with the Soviet Aeroflot.[53] Other observers suggested that noncommunist nations should welcome the Sino-Pakistan air agreement. Pakistan's success in securing landing rights in China was a precedent that others should want to follow. The Chinese, on their part, would be able to go to Europe, Africa, and other places without first having to go to

Moscow. If and when they operated their own flights under the agreement, the passage of their delegations through Dacca and Karachi would not necessarily threaten Pakistan's security. "Dealings with China," wrote the *Times*, "are difficult enough for almost every country at the moment not to concede such contacts as do seem possible and even beneficial in the long run."[54]

The Shadow of a Sino-Pakistan Alliance

Since 1962 Pakistani spokesmen have often insisted that "friendship" with China is a growing factor in their foreign policy. Pronouncements about China have been sympathetic and even laudatory. Zulfikar Ali Bhutto maintained that there could be no rational hope for strengthening the rule of law in international relations while a nation of 700 million people remained excluded from the United Nations. Nor could enduring peace be achieved in South and Southeast Asia without Chinese participation in the endeavor. China was among the more important forces seeking the salvation of Afro-Asians; Pakistan should collaborate with her in liquidating the "forces of colonialism and its ramparts still maintained by Portugal and India."[55] On July 17, 1963, Bhutto made a statement in the National Assembly that caused a stir in Pakistan and abroad, leading to speculation that China and Pakistan might already have made an alliance against India—a thesis Indian officials, press, and propaganda organs had been advancing for quite some time. Arguing that India, lacking the will—and a genuine reason—to fight China, might eventually direct her increasing military power at Pakistan, the foreign minister declared:

This much we know and can say that if, God forbid ... India were, in its frustration, to turn its guns against Pakistan, the international position being what it is, Pakistan would not be alone.... An attack by India on Pakistan would also involve the security and territorial integrity of the largest state in Asia. This new factor that has arisen is a very important one. I would not, at this stage, wish to elucidate it any further.... A defeated Pakistan or a subjugated Pakistan would not only mean annihilation for us but also cause a serious threat to other countries of Asia and particularly to the largest state of Asia. From that point of view and as a result of the other international factors that have recently come into operation, I think I can confidently say that everything is being done . . . to see that our national interests and territorial integrity are safeguarded and protected.[56]

Not all of Bhutto's listeners in the National Assembly were impressed. An Opposition leader, Mohammad Yusuf Khattak, observed that in the past Pakistanis had, "by sheer romantic imagination," attributed to others intentions that did not exist. He cautioned the foreign minister against reading "too much in the Chinese expression of friendship."[57]

Bhutto's assertion received little credence abroad. American officials, for instance, were annoyed that Pakistan should look to China for help against India but doubted that a Sino-Pakistan alliance had been, or would be, made. Such an alliance, they reasoned, would jeopardize Pakistan's ties with the West. It was one thing for Pakistan to improve diplomatic and commercial relations with China but quite another to seek her military support. Bhutto could not have meant what he said; he was merely expressing the "depth of Pakistan's dissatisfaction" with American plans for long-term military assistance to India.[58]

At a press conference, President Kennedy offered a similar interpretation. He conceded that American military supplies to India weakened Pakistan's position in the South Asian balance of power. Pakistan would protest at this policy, and her protests would be received with understanding. But all of this would be much different from a formal alliance with China, which "would change completely . . . the SEATO relationship and all the rest."[59] During his visit to Rawalpindi, George Ball had already taken the position that a close relationship between Pakistan and China would "nullify the sense of alliances" between Pakistan and the United States. He was assured that while Pakistan would maintain her relations with China in good order she had no intention of changing sides in the Cold War. According to Thomas Brady, an "extremely authoritative" Pakistani source told Ball: "we are still loyal members of the military alliances with the United States."[60]

At home Bhutto's speech provoked debate on essentially the same issue Washington had raised: To what extent was Pakistan's growing friendship with China compatible with her membership in SEATO? Many members of the National Assembly argued that the two did not go well together. But the desire for consistency led most Opposition speakers to question the wisdom of remaining in SEATO rather than that of close relations with China. Farid Ahmad, a veteran member, professed to be puzzled:

In view of the fact that we have an alliance of friendship, that we have succeeded in resolving all our disputes with China . . . what is the good and what is the sense in continuing the SEATO Pact any longer? . . . The only logic of our continuance as a member of that Pact would have been that there was a threat of communist attack from China. Today we are told, Sir, that we are on the best of terms with China and an attack on our territory will also involve them. In view of that fact, Sir, it would have well fitted the External Affairs Minister if he had taken his own logic to its conclusion. . . . But I must say, Sir, that . . . he has been asked to sponsor and argue a very bad case.[61]

The leader of the Opposition, Sardar Bahadur Khan, thought it was "ridiculous" that after making a border "deal" with China the government should want to stay on in SEATO on the ground that it was a defensive alliance that furthered Pakistan's interests. Another Opposition member observed that SEATO had been designed mainly to thwart the aggressive designs of communist countries such as China. "What justification can there be for you to remain in these Pacts when you have joined hands with China?" he asked.[62]

Most members who adopted this line of reasoning urged the government to withdraw from SEATO, although they recognized that breaking the pacts with the West would be a complicated and serious affair. One member, Syed Mohammad Habibul Haq, asked how Pakistan could abandon ties with the Anglo-Americans when she had received a "tremendous amount of aid" from them and was so deeply committed to them. He urged Ayub Khan to resign, "to surrender your powers to the people," who would then establish a coherent foreign policy![63] Zulfiqar Ali Bokhari, though usually a proponent of an "independent" foreign policy, was among the few speakers who urged caution in conducting relations with China. "Sir, this assurance from China, this flirtation with China, has been again on the rebound. It is not backed by or based on some solid ground ... or similarity of thought. And, Mr. Speaker, Sir, once again I feel that our energies, our whole attention, should not be directed towards China alone so far as the Eastern bloc is concerned."[64]

Bhutto repelled Opposition demands for terminating the alliance with the United States. He reasoned with critics that in the "cold ruthlessness of international politics" one could not expect to find a perfect alliance or a "state of relations which would be ideal from our point of view alone."[65] Repeatedly in the National Assembly, even when he threatened the West with "agonizing reappraisals," he ended by declaring that his government contemplated no "basic" or "radical" change in its foreign policy. A week after his controversial speech of July 17, 1963, he pleaded:

We wish to rehabilitate our relationship with the Western powers, to revive our happier past association with them. ... We value their friendship. They have assisted us in many ways. They have made a valuable contribution to our economic growth and to our military security. We are not unmindful of these facts. We are not ungrateful. All that we are doing is to ask the West to appreciate the fact that India's increased military strength can only be directed against Pakistan.[66]

In their public pronouncements Bhutto and his colleagues maintained that cordial relations with China were not incompatible with SEATO and other ties with the United States. SEATO being a defensive alliance, a member state need have no quarrel with China unless the latter should attack the former's territorial integrity or that of another member state. Commenting on reports in 1962 that China had offered, or intended to offer, Pakistan a nonaggression pact, Bhutto observed: "This offer cannot be regarded as inconsistent with our alliances with the West. Our alliances are for self-defense. A non-aggression pact further reinforces the defensive character of these alliances."[67]

Needless to say, Bhutto was arguing from premises regarding SEATO's purpose that its other members did not share. The United States, its chief architect and patron, viewed the SEATO alliance as an instrument for containing not only overt Chinese territorial expansion but also China's influence. But the rationalistic quibble over consistency was really irrelevant to the issues set in pragmatic terms. Pakistan's border, trade, and air-travel agreements and exchanges of pleasantries with China were consistent with her ties with the United States because the parties concerned did not seriously object. China had repeatedly declared that she did not regard Pakistan's membership in SEATO as an impediment to the improvement of Sino-Pakistan relations. American officials urged upon Pakistanis the wisdom of keeping the Chinese at a safe distance, and occasionally they made harmless gestures of disapproval, but they did not object strongly enough to confront Pakistan with the necessity of choice. It would seem that the United States did draw the line on the question of a Sino-Pakistan alliance or even a nonaggression pact. That no such pact was made should confirm this interpretation.

Chinese Objectives in South Asia: A Pakistani View

The pattern of Pakistan's relations with China that emerged during 1962-63 cannot be explained without some reference to her assessment of Chinese objectives in South Asia and to her new leaders' inclination toward independence, self-assertion, and realism in formulating their foreign policy. At one time Ayub Khan had warned Nehru of dangers from the "north" and had urged him to settle the Kashmir dispute and organize a joint defense arrangement with Pakistan. Surely the north in this context included China. But it is apparent that he did not see a "clear and present" Chinese danger to the subcontinent. The Chinese threat was remote and latent, arising from her potential as a great power, not from any inherent aggressiveness. One should be on guard against the dynamism of all great powers. India, too, was potentially a great power and therefore deserving of her neighbor's watchful concern. Arrangements for containing India's imperialist impulse were just as much in order as those for restraining the Chinese; indeed, more so, in view of her long record of highhandedness in Junagadh, Kashmir, and Goa and her generally domineering attitude toward Pakistan. Pakistanis' reactions to the Sino-Indian border clash revealed their conviction that for the foreseeable future it was India, not China, that posed the greater threat to the independence of smaller nations in South and Southeast Asia.

On October 20, 1962, Dawn's editor declared that "all this talk about the Chinese being the aggressors [was] tommyrot." India had provoked the conflict in the Northeast Frontier Agency at the instigation of her patrons in Washington, London, and Moscow. She had discarded the mask of neutralism and seemed to glory in the role of a "naked military aggressor." The United States, Britain, and the Soviet Union were competing with one another to win over and use Nehru's India. "Be it said, therefore, to the eternal shame of India's present leadership, that they should seem so willing to play the role of the White Man's stooge and act as agent provocateur against a fellow Asian nation."

I noted earlier Dehlavi's denial that the Chinese had seized any Indian territory. He now deplored that India had seen fit to pursue policies of aggression and expansionism in utter disregard of Gandhi's teachings.[68] Pakistan's ambassador in Japan, General Sheikh, told the Ashai Evening News that India had been the original aggressor in her conflict with China. As early as April 1962, said the ambassador, the Indian army had mounted an offensive in Tibet and established forty-seven advanced check posts. Some of these went deep into Chinese territory and outflanked Chinese posts.[69]

The government of Pakistan consistently held that China had no intention of invading India; India had no intention of fighting a war with the Chinese; the so-called Sino-Indian war was a mere border clash that the Indians themselves had provoked; the problem could and should be resolved by negotiations; eventually India would settle her dispute with China, but in the meanwhile she was seeking Western military assistance only to be able to dominate her small neighbors; and the Western powers, on their part, were willing to support her because they wanted to make her into a satellite. This position was taken by Ayub Khan, Bhutto, and members of the National Assembly from both the Treasury and the Opposition benches.

In a statement of November 5, 1962, Ayub Khan observed that the Sino-Indian conflict must be limited in nature because of the terrain over which it was being waged. It would have started sooner if the parties had meant it to be otherwise. October was no time for a long war in the Himalayas; the weather would soon bring military operations to a halt. In a broadcast to the nation on October 1, 1963, he addressed himself to the subject more fully:

That there is no possibility of a major war between India and China is believed even in the capitals of those countries which are rushing arms aid to India. Then, why are they doing so? The reasons are best known to them. But we can see that they wish to take advantage of the anti-Chinese feeling in India to align her to the West or at least to range her against China. In this they are sadly mistaken.... I am sure that India will, sooner or later, come to terms with China.... If these warlike preparations go on in India ... what is more natural than a war of conquest against the smaller nations. And we head the list.[70]

On November 26, 1962, speaking at an emergency session of the National Assembly, Bhutto characterized the Sino-Indian conflict as a "phony war." Nehru's government, he said, had whipped up war hysteria to obtain massive military aid from the West. The Western powers had been quick to oblige India, because they wanted to aggravate her conflict with China and to seduce her into their sphere of influence. He quoted from Nehru's book, *Glimpses of World History,* to the effect that the imperialists had exploited China. In trying to rectify the McMahon Line, the Chinese were now struggling to right the wrongs they had suffered at the hands of the colonial powers.[71] India, he thought, should return to the negotiating table, but he doubted that she would do this in the near future. Being a vain, deceitful, and imperialist power, she wanted to dominate the entire land mass from the Hindu Kush to the Mekong River. Since she was unable to fight the Chinese Colossus, she would turn her recently augmented military power "against the helpless peoples of South and Southeast Asia."[72] By contrast, the Chinese were a peace-loving people. They had offered to negotiate an amicable settlement and had unilaterally stopped the fighting. India had declined the Chinese invitation, thus repudiating "Nehru's sermons" on the virtues of settling international disputes peacefully. Many members of the National Assembly voiced sentiments and interpretations similar to those expressed by Ayub Khan and Bhutto.[73]

The objectives of China's India policy are controversial. Some writers believe the Chinese have never forgotten that once all of the Himalayan regions, along with Nepal, Bhutan, and parts of northern India, were included in their empire. They assert that the Chinese now want to regain their old frontiers.[74] Other observers tend to the view that Chinese aims are more modest. As early as November 22, 1962, a *New York Times* analysis quoted "specialists" as maintaining that the Chinese really wanted only the northern hump of Ladakh through which the Sinkiang-Tibet road passed and that they had already achieved this objective during their brief conflict with India. The Chinese then offered implicit recognition of the McMahon line in the northeast in exchange for Indian acceptance of their claim in Ladakh. The Chinese cease-fire should not be taken as a retreat effected under Soviet pressure; it meant merely that, having taken what they wanted, they were ready to stop fighting and withdraw from the areas they did not wish to keep.[75]

A few months later the United States and British governments were reported unable to accept the Indian estimate that a Chinese attack on that country should be expected in the near future. Arguing from its own premise in this regard, the government of India had requested about two billion dollars worth of military assistance. The two Western powers did not think India was capable of absorbing such a vast quantity of military aid. But beyond that, Dean Rusk and Duncan Sandys, who were in Delhi at the time, argued that China would need time to digest what she had acquired the previous year.[76] The fact that U.S. military aid to India, in terms of both quantity and the type of material provided,[77] remained modest and was halted altogether after the Indo-Paki-

stan war in the fall of 1965 would suggest that American assessment of the Chinese military threat to India had not been greatly different from that of Pakistan. Apparently, Washington too had
concluded that this threat was, for the most part, potential rather
than specific or imminent.

Territorial considerations were probably a minor part of the Chinese strategy with respect to India. By inflicting a humiliating defeat
on India, China sought to show that India was not much of a rival for
the leadership of Asia. Given the record of Indo-Pakistan relations,
Pakistanis would not be greatly upset if India's potential for becoming the dominant power in South and Southeast Asia were weakened. But if China were to vanquish India, would not Pakistan be
next in line? Once again, Pakistanis did not believe China would
ever come down to the Indian plains to fight a war.

A New Look in Pakistani Foreign Policy

By the end of 1962, when the agreement in principle regarding the
Sino-Pakistan border was announced, Ayub Khan's government
had been in power for four years. It had achieved considerable self-
confidence in both foreign and domestic affairs. Its policy makers
knew they needed American economic and military assistance. But
they knew also that the United States would not threaten to withdraw her assistance each time they talked with the Chinese. There
might well be limits beyond which cordiality with China could not be
carried without disrupting the alliances with the United States. But
within those limits there was room for maneuver. Men who filled
positions of power in the government, such as Bhutto and Dehlavi,
possessed the initiative and the ingenuity to explore this opportunity. They were prepared to make and assert their own judgments
about the state of international relations and Pakistan's interests. A
number of things became apparent to them. The Cold War was in a
state of thaw. The edge of the Soviet-American conflict had been
blunted. NATO was loosening, and deGaulle was bent upon
expelling American influence from Europe. China and India, which

only a few years before had proclaimed their brotherhood, were
engaged in a border conflict. The Soviet Union, once China's ally,
seemed to share the American interest in containing China.
Friends of yesterday were enemies of today. Who could say that the
enemies of today would not be friends tomorrow? Even Mohammad Ali Bogra, well known for his feelings of friendliness for the
United States, partook of this mood. In a speech to the National
Assembly on November 23, 1962, he said:

*I want to assure the House [that] we shall exploit and explore all
possibilities in the economic, commercial and other fields in the
best interest of Pakistan.... That should give a clear indication of
the positive independent line we are adopting—the criterion being
what is in the best interest of Pakistan, not what suits others....
There is no eternal friendship in international relations and there is
no eternal enmity. As situations change, enemies can become
friends and friends can become enemies. But the most important
and eternal fact is the question of national interest, national safety,
national integrity and national security, and that is of paramount
importance.*[78]

Pakistan knew that already there were many voices in the United
States urging openings to China such as cultural exchanges,
trade, and her admission to the United Nations. Could the two
countries remain isolated from each other forever? How long
before the United States herself might begin to normalize relations
with China? In a broadcast to his people on November 1, 1963,
President Ayub Khan gave his estimate of the winds of change.

*Last month, I spoke about the normalization of our relations with
our great neighbour, China. There had been criticism and disapproval of it in certain countries of the world. I am glad to learn that
in the same countries, there is now a move for the normalization of
their own relations with China. The New York Times has urged it.
The United States President has admitted that there will be no real
world disarmament unless China is a party to it. And I see in some
American newspapers that the State Department has approved
that the West Coast businessmen should develop trade relations
with China. Mr. Harry Truman ... has written an article that America*

should supply free wheat to China. Therefore, the foundation is being laid to normalize relations with China. We are doing just that. So, where is the cause for suspicion of our intentions?[79]

Was it in Pakistan's interest to forgo opportunities to establish mutually advantageous relations with a neighboring great power until the United States thought the time for such a course of action had arrived? And could one be sure that in making this determination the United States would take into account Pakistan's vital interest? Was it really dangerous to come close to the Chinese, as Americans had warned? Did Americans understand the Chinese and know how to deal with them without being seduced in the process, while others, especially Asians, did not? Needless to say, Ayub Khan and his colleagues answered these questions in the negative. If American officials had confronted them with the necessity of choice, they might *conceivably* have pulled back from their projected border, trade, and air-travel agreements with China. They were not so confronted, and they made the agreements. But there is no indication that the agreements represented anything like the "eternal friendship" of which signatories to international arrangements sometimes boast. It should be instructive to recall Ayub Khan's observation, at a Rawalpindi Bar Association meeting on July 16, 1963, that "lying in between three very powerful countries [the USSR, China, and India] we have to make sure that we attain a certain measure of security against the incursions of *any* of these three countries."[80]

Pakistan's fear of India and her resentment at American military aid to that country were doubtless important factors impelling her to seek China's goodwill. Expectation of profit must have been another consideration: the agreements under discussion promised larger exports, more business for PIA, and some new territory. But it should be noted that China was not the only country on the other side of the fence to receive Pakistani attention. During 1962-63 Pakistan exchanged dozens of delegations and made numerous commercial contracts and agreements with the Soviet Union and nations of eastern Europe. Sino-Pakistan agreements were essentially a product of this new look, this spirit of independence, in Pakistan's foreign policy.

Five

China and the Indo-Pakistan War of 1965

In August 1965, sporadic fighting broke out between India and Pakistan in Kashmir.[1] Then on the morning of September 6, 1965, the Indian army invaded West Pakistan, directing its attack at Lahore, the provincial capital, located about fifteen miles from the border and regarded by many, including its own two million citizens, as the "heart" of Pakistan. As is customary on such occasions, many foreign government leaders deplored the fighting and expressed the hope that it would shortly cease. Some took sides. Of Pakistan's allies, Iran and Turkey supported her vigorously, as did such others as Jordan, Syria, Saudi Arabia, and Indonesia. But of all of Pakistan's supporters, China spoke the loudest. She gave Pakistan unqualified moral support and, at the same time, threatened India with "grave consequences" for allegedly violating Chinese territory along the Sikkim border. Her policy created widespread apprehension of a general war in Asia. By linking the Sino-Indian and the Indo-Pakistan conflicts, the Chinese fostered a sense of urgency among the powers about terminating the Indo-Pakistan war.

Chinese diplomacy produced other significant results: it inhibited some of the great powers, especially the Soviet Union, from siding openly with India and from putting as much pressure upon Pakistan as they might otherwise have been inclined to do; it contributed, intentionally or inadvertently, to bringing about a cease-fire on terms acceptable to Pakistan; and it made a deep and long-lasting impression on Pakistani public opinion, giving it a distinctly pro-Chinese disposition.

The Chinese Ultimatum to India

The Chinese position toward the Indo-Pakistan conflict was unambiguous: Peking deemed India the aggressor and held her solely responsible for the conflict; it supported the Kashmiris' right to self-determination which, it maintained, the Indian government had "perfidiously" usurped; it accused the United Nations of acting, under Soviet-American direction, to the detriment of Pakistan on the Kashmir issue; it charged Soviet-American "collusion" in encouraging the Indian attack on Pakistan and, subsequently, in attempting to force Pakistan to acquiesce in India's possession of the part of Kashmir already under her control; and it asserted that India's attack on Pakistan and her "intrusions" into Chinese territory were all part of the same Indian design of aggressive expansionism.

On September 4, 1965, while the Indo-Pakistan fighting was still confined to Kashmir, the Chinese foreign minister, Marshal Chen Yi, stopped at Karachi on his way to Mali. At a news conference that evening, he condemned India's "provocative violations" of the cease-fire line in Kashmir, supported Pakistan's "just" action in repelling the Indian attacks, and maintained that India's rule in Kashmir had produced the current struggle of the freedom fighters there. The Kashmir problem, he said, ought to be solved according to the wishes of the Kashmiris and the commitments made to them in this regard by both India and Pakistan.[2] The following day, the *People's Daily* advised India "to stop its domineering and arbitrary practice of bullying its neighbor." It justified Pakistan's counter-attack on Indian positions in Kashmir.

In an official statement issued on September 7, the Chinese government denounced the Indian attack on Lahore as an act of "naked aggression," by which India had enlarged a local conflict into a general war. The Indian action, it added, "not only is a crude violation of all principles guiding international relations, but also constitutes a grave threat to peace in this part of Asia. The Chinese Government sternly condemns India for its criminal aggression, expresses firm support for Pakistan in its just struggle against aggression and solemnly warns the Indian Government that it must bear responsibility for all the consequences of its criminal and extended aggression."[3] Speaking at a North Korean reception two days later, Premier Chou En-lai repeated the substance of the above statement. He added that by not naming India as the aggressor and by professing to be neutral as between the contestants, the United States and the Soviet Union were, as usual, confounding the distinction between right and wrong, "aggression and antiaggression." The Indian "reactionaries" were "outright aggressors both in the local conflict in Kashmir and in the general conflict between India and Pakistan."[4] Vice-Premier Hsieh Fu-chih expressed similar sentiments at a rally in Lhasa on the same day.

On September 11 an editorial in the *People's Daily* held that India alone had provoked the conflict. Indian assertions that Pakistan had sent "infiltrators" across the cease-fire line and had "invaded" Indian-held Kashmir were "absurd." A genuine popular uprising had occurred on the Indian side as a reaction to Indian oppression. Prime Minister Shastri's claim that in attacking Lahore India was only taking "defensive measures" was a typical example of "gangster logic" which the Indians had learned "entirely from U.S. imperialism." The *People's Daily* declared: "In short, it was not Pakistan but India that first crossed the cease-fire line in Kashmir.... It was not Pakistan but India that first threw its air force into action and bombed peaceful cities of the other side. It was not Pakistan but India that first crossed the international border.... So, India is in every case the aggressor and Pakistan its victim."[5] Similar expressions of support for Pakistan and condemnations of India continued to issue from Peking until well after the cease-fire.

The Chinese warned that Pakistanis and Kashmiris should not expect justice from the United Nations, which had had a "bad reputation" in the matter of Kashmir. For eighteen years it had permitted India to act "lawlessly" without "lifting a finger" to restrain her. On this, as on other issues, it had shown itself to be "a tool of U.S. imperialism and its partners." An editorial in the *People's Daily* noted that on August 14, 1965, the Indians had crossed the cease-fire line and occupied the Kargil area, on August 25 the Tithwal area, and on August 28 the Uri-Poonch area, all on the Pakistani side. But on none of these occasions had the UN Security Council uttered a "single word of disapproval." It became active only when Pakistan hit back on September 1 and the Indian troops "found themselves in difficulties." When U Thant's report at the council session of September 4 referred to armed men, not in uniform, crossing the cease-fire line from the Pakistani side, he gave India a much-needed justification for her own breaches of the cease-fire line. Later, when India attacked Pakistan, the Security Council, instead of condemning India as an aggressor, spoke merely of the "extension of the fighting," thus blurring the distinction between the aggressor and the victim. "All this shows that the United Nations' partiality for India has a long history. . . . The United Nations, consistently reversing right and wrong and calling black white, has always served the interests of aggressors. . . . Today, [it] is again siding with the aggressor on the Kashmir issue and the Indo-Pakistan conflict and . . . has become a sanctuary for the Indian aggressor."[6]

Peking advanced the view that the United States and the Soviet Union were more favorably disposed toward India than toward Pakistan.[7] For many years the two had vied with each other in giving India money and arms. This great-power competition for their goodwill had emboldened the Indians into thinking that they could do whatever they desired; hence, their "domineering attitude" toward their neighbors. The two great powers, who treated the present Indian leadership as "their darling child," supported it in its war against Pakistan, which they had earlier instigated. Of late the United States had shown increasing irritation with Pakistan's independent foreign policy and had decided "to cut [her] down to size through the military aggression launched by the Indian reactionaries." Washington, "feigning impartiality," had suspended military aid to both India and Pakistan even while admitting that this would make Pakistan weaker still in relation to India.[8]

The Chinese placed a similar interpretation on Soviet efforts to resolve the Indo-Pakistan conflict. They pointed out that as far back as 1955 Khrushchev had declared Kashmir to be an integral part of India. Thus, the Soviet Union had also assisted India in "sabotaging" international agreements on Kashmir and annexing it. When the Indians, after first attacking Pakistan, met firm resistance and began to suffer reverses, Moscow came up with an offer of "good offices" to end the war. "What the Soviet leaders intend to do is, in the name of 'good offices,' to aid the Indian aggressors to force Pakistan to accept India's annexation of Kashmir as legitimate."[9]

Peking also charged that India had attacked Azad Kashmir and later West Pakistan with the prior knowledge and approval of the United States. Premier Chou En-lai, in his speech at the North Korean embassy, declared that the Indian government "could not have engaged in such a serious military adventure without the consent and support of the United States."[10] The Chinese were to find support for their thesis in a front-page report, splashed in banner headlines, in the September 13 issue of London's conservative paper, the *Daily Telegraph*. The reporter, Victor Anant, who had flown out of Delhi to dodge the Indian censors, suggested that the U.S. Central Intelligence Agency, having worked for a time at securing the overthrow of President Ayub's government, had come to believe that a coup was imminent and had so advised the Indian government. He also implied that the United States knew of, and possibly connived at, the impending Indian attack.[11]

The Chinese propositions noted above fully coincided with the corresponding Pakistani views and interpretations. Consider, for instance, the editorial comments in *Dawn* of September 17 and 19. After dragging its feet on the Kashmir issue for eighteen years, said *Dawn,* the Security Council was waking up to it only after Pakistan had begun to teach the Indians a "fitting lesson." But even so the council tended to "equate the aggressor with the aggressed." The question before it being one of "freedom against oppression, right against wrong," it must name India the aggressor if it wanted to restore peace in the subcontinent. The editorial of September 19 was even more explicit and emphatic. Commenting on U Thant's suggestion, contained in his five-point plan submitted to the Security Council on September 17, that Ayub and Shastri meet in a third country to discuss the current situation and the "problems underlying it," *Dawn* protested:

The phraseology chosen by the Secretary-General shows how much at pains he has been to evade the very mention of Kashmir.

... What Secretary-General U Thant is trying to do under pressure ... is to come to the aid of the Indian aggressor and not only bail him out of his difficulties but inflict from U.N. headquarters in New York a military defeat on Pakistan which the Western stooges in India themselves cannot do.... Let not the enemies of Pakistan and their friends and allies in Washington, New York and elsewhere suffer from the delusion that the Government of Pakistan can be browbeaten into accepting the cease-fire on terms which would amount to a virtual and unconditional surrender to the aggressor who is on the run.

Ever since the Sino-Indian conflict in 1962, the Chinese had periodically accused India of a variety of "provocative" acts, including transgressions of their territory. The pungency and frequency of these complaints rose sharply during the Indo-Pakistan war. Beginning with a note dated September 8, Peking addressed numerous protests to New Delhi, charging that Indian armed forces had repeatedly intruded into Chinese territory, built military structures on it, fired on Chinese personnel, kidnapped Chinese citizens, and stolen cattle. Each of these notes threatened "grave consequences," and one, that of September 16, went forth as an ultimatum. Yang Kung-su, a deputy director in the Chinese foreign office, summoned the Indian chargé d'affaires in Peking to his office at 1:00 A.M. on September 17 and handed him a note demanding that India dismantle within three days her "aggressive military works" built on the Chinese side of the Sino-Sikkim border, return the kidnapped men and sheep and yaks, and "pledge to refrain from any more harassing raids across the boundary."[12] Otherwise, responsibility for the consequences, once again "grave," would be entirely Indian.

Chinese communications to India during September and October of 1965 represented both Pakistan and China as victims of India's aggressive expansionism. Dispatched ostensibly to protest India's alleged violations of Chinese sovereignty, they also contained digressions on India's policies in Kashmir and her attack on Pakistan. Indeed, one inevitably received the impression that India's actions vis-à-vis Pakistan were as much responsible for occasioning the protest as any injuries that China might herself have sustained at Indian hands. This linkage of Sino-Indian and Indo-Pakistan conflicts was evident in almost every note that the Chinese government addressed to India during this period. The Chinese also found occasion to assert in these notes that, come what might, they would not be stopped from supporting Pakistan's fight against Indian aggression.

Take, for instance, the Chinese ultimatum of September 16. It consists of a little more than one thousand words, of which more than three hundred are devoted to an exposition of the Indo-Pakistan conflict. It accuses the Indian government of following the logic that the territories they have seized belong to them and those they would like to "grab," but have not yet taken, also belong to them. The Chinese government, it goes on to say, pursues a policy of "non-involvement" in the Kashmir dispute in maintaining that it should be settled by the Kashmiris themselves.

But non-involvement absolutely does not mean failure to distinguish between right and wrong; it absolutely does not mean that China can approve of depriving the Kashmiri people of their right of self-determination or that she can approve of Indian aggression against Pakistan. . . . So long as the Indian Government oppresses the Kashmiri people, China will not cease supporting Pakistan. . . . This stand of ours will never change, however many helpers you may have, such as the United States, the modern revisionists and the U.S.-controlled United Nations.[13]

The second ultimatum to India, dated September 19, contained a similar digression, as did the protest notes of September 8 and 26 and official statements on September 7 and 9. Peking kept up the pressure on Delhi. A note dated September 20, following within hours the second ultimatum, protested fresh Indian violations of Chinese territory. The day after the Indo-Pakistan cease-fire, a group of Indian demonstrators, shouting that China wanted to start a world war over a few sheep and yaks, tried to deliver 800 sheep at the Chinese embassy in Delhi by way of a settlement! This occasioned still another Chinese protest on September 26, stating that while the kidnapped men, sheep, and yaks must be returned— "every single one of them"—there were other matters also: India's "subversive activities" in Tibet, her occupation of more than 92,000 square kilometers of Chinese territory, and constant armed provocations and intrusions. All these "accounts" must be settled.

The government and the press in Pakistan did not acknowledge that the Chinese allegations against India had anything to do with the Indo-Pakistan conflict. In fact, they tried to disentangle the two situations. In an editorial on September 21, *Dawn* insisted that "the Chinese move has nothing whatever to do with Pakistan's defensive war with India." Yet there was recognition on both sides that China had indeed played a significant role. The Chinese protest to India on September 26 made the usual digression from its main subject to announce that "the whole world now sees that it was India which launched a war of aggression against Pakistan . . . *and it was China and other justice-upholding countries which by their firm anti-aggressive stand punctured your aggressive arrogance.'"*[14] In an editorial on September 27, *Dawn,* after advocating China's presence in the United Nations, observed: "China is the greatest power of this continent and no issue of war and peace can be decided without its participation in international deliberations . . . . *The role that this great country played recently during India's aggression against Pakistan helped immensely the cause of peace and justice in this part of the world [emphasis added]."*

The Chinese Impact

What precisely was China's role? The Indian government and the press charged "collusion" between Pakistan and China. The Chinese dismissed the Indian charges as a "fantastic tale," and Pakistani spokesmen described them as sheer propaganda designed to agitate certain sections of opinion in the United States. In a television interview with the American Broadcasting Corportion, Pakistan's ambassador in Washington declared that "there have been no promises, no agreements, no collusion of any kind between my Government and China.'"[15] American commentators—supplying their own analyses and quoting officials in Washington, the United

Nations, and important world capitals—tended to reject the "collusion" theory.[16] Some doubted that there could ever be any really deep collaboration between the Chinese and Pakistani governments as currently constituted. In this view the latter happened to be "the kind of conservative, strong-man regime that the Chinese Communists would overturn at the first opportunity. Cooperation between the two . . . can be given only warily and with mutual suspicion."[17]

Strictly speaking, the Indian charges of Sino-Pakistan collusion were incorrect. But it is true that cooperation between the two did not proceed without considerable reservation. Ayub Khan did not wish to throw away the long-term advantages of Pakistan's connection with the United States in the process of obtaining Chinese support during the war. The following information, not generally available at the time and conveyed to me by Prime Minister Bhutto and senior Pakistani diplomats in recent interviews, may be of some interest.

During a meeting in 1965, Chou En-lai, after hearing Ayub Kan's discourse on Kashmir, is said to have observed that a "just" settlement of the dispute would not materialize unless Pakistanis were willing to make "sacrifices." When Chen Yi stopped at Karachi on September 4, he was told that Pakistanis were now ready to make sacrifices! At the same time, Pakistani diplomats emphasize that the Chinese have never encouraged Pakistan to go to war with India. Nor have they endorsed the idea of such a war as a means of reactivating lagging world interest in the Kashmir dispute. Prime Minister Bhutto and his colleagues are inclined to interpret Chou En-lia's reference to the necessity of making sacrifices as a philosophical statement and not as a specific policy recommendation. They add that the Chinese had not been consulted *before* the government of Pakistan made the decision to send "freedom-fighters" to the Indian side of Kashmir. In fact, hardly any of Ayub Khan's ministers or other high officials—beyond Mr. Bhutto, General Akhtar Malik (who trained the "freedom-fighters" and apparently not so well), and a few other generals—knew of the plan. When, after a few days of the Indian invasion, the war entered a stalemate so that Pakistani ammunition stocks were being depleted without making a significant impact on the battlefield, President Ayub Khan "frantically" appealed to the Chinese to "do something." After the Chinese sent an ultimatum to India, the American and British ambassadors advised him that the Chinese action might lead to a general, and possibly nuclear, war. Unwilling to risk a break with the United States, and unnerved by the thought of a larger war, Ayub Khan now appealed to the Chinese to withdraw the ultimatum.

Ayub Khan's approaches to Peking were, at the time, known only to a few individuals in the two governments. Others responded to the developing situation on the basis of current interpretations of Chinese intentions. During the first week or so of the conflict, the Chinese threats to India were not taken seriously. The *Times* of London dismissed the Chinese note of September 8 as a "war of nerves" that might not even be related to the Indo-Pakistan war.[18] Victor Zorza of the *Manchester Guardian* saw it as a routine affair, no more menacing than dozens of previous Chinese notes to India or their threats of action in Vietnam.[19] The Indians were reported "rattled" but not unduly alarmed. Washington officials and analysts, familiar with the "strident" vocabulary of Chinese diplomacy, detected no imminent danger of Chinese military action against India. They believed that while the Chinese were watching the situation closely, they would not risk for Pakistan what they had been unwilling to risk for North Vietnam. Their support to Pakistan would continue to be largely political.[20] The Soviets, apparently, were more apprehensive, as indicated by the strong language of their statement of September 13: they invited the whole world to join them in condemning "certain powers" that sought to aggravate the Indo-Pakistan conflict by making "incendiary" statements. They warned also that if the Chinese intervened "many states might find themselves drawn into the conflict one by one."[21]

The Chinese ultimatum of September 16 commanded a somewhat higher degree of credibility than did the previous threats. But even so, the reaction was mixed. Indian officials, on the one hand, claimed that the Chinese were about to do something "sinister." C. S. Jha, Indian foreign secretary, declaring that a "fateful moment in history" had arrived, observed that the Chinese meant to humble

India.[22] In Washington and Moscow the Indian ambassadors sought public declarations of support in the event of a Chinese attack. Back home in Delhi, on the other hand, they viewed the ultimatum chiefly as a Chinese effort to encourage Pakistan. At the Indian Defense Ministry, observers found a calm and "complacent" disposition, "undoubtedly genuine," if not quite logical.[23] The Indians did not seem to expect any serious trouble on their border with China. In the West some observers were inclined to deemphasize the Chinese threat. *Newsweek* (September 20, 1965) quoted a "leading sinologist" as saying that "China will make a lot of noise in order to keep the Indians guessing but, so far as direct action is concerned, it will most likely remain uninvolved." Some officials in Washington viewed the ultimatum more as a "psychological gambit" to unnerve India and to embarrass the United States and the Soviet Union than as a military threat.[24]

Yet none of these observers and analysts, official and other, could say confidently that the Chinese were only bluffing. The Chinese had made a "cunning move," wrote the *Christian Science Monitor,* "calculated to reap the maximum dividends with the minimum effort." They had been astute also in choosing the location of their threatened action. Crossing the Sikkim border in a swift maneuver, they could cut off Assam from the rest of India in a matter of hours. They meant to show Sikkim, which had long wanted the status of a sovereign state, that India could not protect it.[25] The consensus seemed to be that while the Chinese did not comtemplate a major attack on India they could mount an action serious enough to trouble the Indians but not large enough to evoke U.S. military intervention. Even if they confined themselves to taking a few Indian posts, India would either have to fight on two fronts or suffer another great humiliation. Moreover, U.S. officials explained, with only a small effort the Chinese could pin down a substantial number of Indian troops, thus aiding Pakistan. This would put Pakistan in debt to the Chinese, giving them a new "leverage in the tangled affairs of the sub-continent."[26]

China's impact on the conflict issued precisely from the uncertainty surrounding her intentions. No one knew what, if anything, she was about to do. Some courses of action might be considered unlikely; none could be ruled out. This presented the United States and the Soviet Union with a painful dilemma. If China launched a major attack on India, the result might be a world war. If she made only small, pinprick advances and the two great powers did not go to India's aid, they would alienate Delhi. And if they did aid India, they would alienate Pakistan and push her closer toward China. The Indo-Pakistan war had been a nuisance; it now became an intolerable situation. It must be terminated. This heightened concern was apparent in the statements of high officials and the columns of influential journals. The British foreign secretary, Michael Stewart, described the Chinese ultimatum as a "serious, indeed, dangerous development." At the United Nations, Ambassador Goldberg warned that "new and serious developments" had enlarged the threat to peace. He urged India and Pakistan to realize the "overriding" reasons for accepting a cease-fire and avoid "truly disastrous consequences." A *New York Times* editorial called for a cease-fire, warning that "it is important most of all because Communist China is openly intervening with all its sinister influence—in the form of propaganda, ultimata and political threats today—but quite possibly with military force tomorrow. . . . Until a cease-fire is in effect, China will obviously be encouraged to continue her blackmailing tactics against India, with consequences that could be catastrophic not only in Asia but throughout the world."[27]

At the United Nations on September 22, 1965, India and Pakistan finally agreed to a cease-fire, which went into effect at 3:00 A.M. the following day. Commenting on the Chinese influence on the course of events, the *Nation* wrote:

The paradox of the cease-fire, in a sense, is the fact that China is perhaps the power responsible for it. Whatever China's intentions may have been—and we shall probably never know—it was the specter of direct Chinese intervention that got things moving. The Chinese demonstrated once again that they know how to put on, and take off, the pressure; the timing was excellent and the action got results. And it is a bit difficult to imagine that the cease-fire was not part of China's intentions from the outset; Chinese diplomacy does not often produce "accidental" results. In this instance, even

Pakistan may have been moved to accept the cease-fire in part because of its uncertainty over what the Chinese might do.[18]

The *Nation* was probably correct in suggesting that the government of Pakistan was also troubled. It could not have regarded with equanimity the prospect of a general war. Moreover, having China as a military ally in a real war, entailing the presence of Chinese troops on Kashmiri and Pakistani soil, represented a possible turn of events that Ayub Khan's government could not have welcomed, Indian propaganda notwithstanding.

Chinese Goals and Pakistani Responses

What did the Chinese hope to accomplish? Many Pakistanis thought that China only wanted to be helpful to them in their hour of need. Others, including some Indian observers, suggested that China actually wanted to bring about a cease-fire and that her ultimatums to India were intended to secure the best possible terms for Pakistan by putting pressure on all concerned, especially the great powers in the Security Council.[29] The *Times* (London) tended to the view that the Chinese pressure on India had no more than a peripheral connection with the Indo-Pakistan conflict. Sikkim, it pointed out, was once associated with Tibet and China, and the Chinese had never reconciled themselves to its inclusion in the British, and then Indian, sphere of influence.[30] In the same paper, another writer advanced the view that China's interests were largely doctrinal. She wanted to prove that her view of the world's divisions—imperialists, revisionists, and their lackeys on one side; China and the freedom-and-justice-loving Afro-Asians on the other—was correct. There seemed to be fairly general agreement that China wanted to reap popularity in Pakistan; help Pakistan by pinning down the Indian forces stationed along the Sino-Indian border;[31] humiliate India;[32] show Sikkim and Bhutan that India could not protect them; and force the United States and the Soviet Union to declare in favor of India and thus to "lure" Pakistan away from them.

China's contribution to the outcome on the field of battle must be rated as negligible or nil. Even if the Chinese were able to immobilize as many as six Indian divisions, India still had more than fifteen to fight Pakistan's five or six. More importantly, the war was much too brief to have permitted a Chinese military impact. The Chinese ultimatum was not delivered until the morning of September 17; five days later India and Pakistan agreed to a cease-fire. Consider also that the Indians would have kept some divisions on the Sino-Indian border in any case—even if the Chinese had remained entirely quiescent during the conflict.

There can be no doubt, however, that Chinese threats had a significant impact on the political-diplomatic front. Both the United States and the Soviet Union would have preferred to come down strongly on India's side. Had they been unencumbered by the Chinese factor, they would have felt free not only to aid India but also to put a great deal more pressure on Pakistan than they were actually able to do. In that event, Pakistan would have lost face, and, beyond that, she might have had to settle, in territorial terms, for something less than the status quo ante bellum. As it turned out, the two great powers, loath to see Pakistan drift closer to China, found themselves inhibited.

Further assessment of China's contribution to Pakistan's cause would depend on one's assessment of which nation won the war. If Pakistan's claim that she was winning the war is accepted, Chinese help must be assigned only a peripheral role. If India's claim that she was winning, and that with the passage of time the margin of her victory was going to expand, is accepted, the Chinese—to the extent that they were influential in bringing about a cease-fire— could be regarded as having extricated Pakistan from an unfavorable situation. But if one takes the more generally accepted view that neither side was winning and that a stalemate had soon been reached, the Chinese contribution would have to be seen primarily as a bolstering of Pakistani morale.

There can be no doubt that the vast majority of people in Pakistan deeply appreciated the Chinese support. Karachi students, carrying huge portraits of Chou En-lai and Chen Yi, called on the Chinese ambassador to thank him. Some Rawalpindi lawyers sent off a telegram to Chou En-lai thanking him and declaring: "Friendship of Pakistan and the great Chinese nation and their common struggle against Indian aggression, which has been encouraged and aided by the imperialists, is a guarantee for the final triumph of the peace loving peoples of the world."[33] Kashmiris residing in Karachi dashed off a similar telegram to Chou. Poets wrote laudatory verses about China and Indonesia. The war literature, including "histories" of the war that enterprising publishers got off the press within weeks after the cease-fire, praised China in glowing terms. She was represented as a mighty power devoted to the maintenance of peace and justice in Asia.[34] From reading this literature, the "average" Pakistani—for whom it was mainly intended, being in the vernacular—received a rather exaggerated assessment of the Chinese impact on the course of events. Western and Indian leaders were seen as feverishly seeking a cease-fire, having been reduced to a state of utter consternation by the threat of Chinese intervention.[35]

In reciprocity, Pakistanis condemned the alleged Indian provocations to China. Both China and Pakistan, wrote *Dawn* on September 18, were victims of India's "imperialist thugee." In an editorial on September 21, it praised the Chinese leaders as men "steeped in the wisdom of the sages." Peking's demand that India vacate her aggression was the "natural response of any sovereign country whose territory has been transgressed." It went on to say that during the several preceding weeks Pakistanis had come to certain important conclusions as to who their friends and foes were. "Our great neighbour China and our brotherly nation of Indonesia have stood out foremost in their support to Pakistan." President Ayub Khan sent a message of thanks to the Chinese president. In an address to the UN General Assembly on September 28, Zulfikar Ali Bhutto, Pakistan's foreign minister at the time, thanked a number of nations, including China, "who gave us full *moral* support, *and rising above ideological differences,* upheld the cause of righteousness to condemn the war of aggression launched against us by India."[36]

But it is noteworthy that official spokesmen and the major English-language newspapers in the country were inclined to be cautious. Rarely, if ever, did they single out China when acknowledging help Pakistan had received from abroad. They mentioned her along with Indonesia, Iran, Turkey, and others. While China was referred to as "our great neighbour," terms of affection such as "fraternal" and "brotherly" were reserved for Indonesia and other Muslim countries.

That China reaped enormous goodwill among the urban masses of Pakistan is undoubtedly true. But relations between the two governments did not necessarily improve further. It should be apparent that Ayub Khan wished to pursue a policy of "dual alignment"—a policy of maintaining close and profitable relations with China and the United States at the same time. The balance of relationships implicit in such a design was much too delicate to bear the strain of an Indo-Pakistan war. Moreover, the war had not gone as well as might have been expected. Neither side was able to break the stalemate and push forward. Ammunition stocks on both sides were fast depleting in what seemed to be a futile war. Both India and Pakistan desired a cease-fire; Pakistan even more desperately, for at mid-September her ammunition supplies would not last more than two weeks of fighting. All avenues to an "honorable" cease-fire required therefore to be explored.

For obvious reasons of domestic and foreign politics, Pakistani officials would prefer not to acknowledge that they were in any measure disconcerted by the excessive vigor of the Chinese role. However, some reports from Rawalpindi, London, and Washington suggested that they were disturbed. Chinese "overreaction" had encouraged the collusion theory and tended to damage what remained of Pakistan's good relations with the United States.[37] Then, inasmuch as the "average" Pakistani received the impression of all-out Chinese support for Pakistan against India, it became difficult for the government to accept a settlement that might fall short of the ideal.

Concerned by the drift of events that seemed to place his government in close alignment with China,[38] Ayub Khan moved to correct the "balance of friendships," as it were, and called upon President Johnson to take a hand in resolving the Indo-Pakistan dispute. At a well-attended press conference in Rawalpindi on September 15, more than a day before the first Chinese ultimatum to India, Ayub Khan declared: "Quite frankly, the U.S.A. has a role to play in this part of the world and they ought to play it more positively." He added: "After all, if the United States really wants this subcontinent to be solid, then the essence of that is really understanding between India and Pakistan."[39] He thought the United States could have brought about this understanding in 1962 and could still do so. According to *Dawn* of September 16, he observed also that by exercising her influence in the right measure "the United States could further its own interest of having a strong Indo-Pakistan subcontinent." And, "if only," he lamented, "India would realize how much she is losing from not having a working arrangement with Pakistan."[40] Ayub Khan went on to say that Pakistan did not aspire to playing the same role in world affairs of which India might be capable. But the Indian leaders must realize that "they could not play their due role unless they secured the help of Pakistan for it."

The Chinese could not have found much comfort in these observations. Ayub Khan had appealed to them to "do something." They had issued threats to India, but apparently these were not sufficient. The Pakistani president was now making conciliatory gestures to India and inviting the United States to play a vigorous role, not unlike that of a ward leader or a village elder, in the affairs of the subcontinent.[41] Some commentators interpreted these statements as "a virtual slap at China."[42] The Chinese must also have pondered the president's approving references to the American interest in strengthening the subcontinent and to that "due role" India might play with Pakistan's help, an idea reminiscent of Ayub Khan's earlier proposals for an Indo-Pakistan arrangement of joint defense against the "neighbor to the north." Peking's ultimatum to India came just a little more than a day after the president's press conference. It would seem that the Chinese decided to seize the initiative after the U.S. President had disdainfully declined President Ayub Khan's invitation.[43]

Chinese diplomacy during the Indo-Pakistan war did not bring Peking and Rawalpindi any closer. Ayub Khan called a halt to the "escalation" of friendliness in Pakistani-Chinese relations. Although Bhutto—one of the principals in Pakistan's normalization

Some Unintended Consequences

of relations with China and the Soviet Union—subsequently asserted that he had resigned from the government on his own initiative, it was widely believed at the time that Ayub Khan had sent him away under American pressure. But the heavily pro-Chinese sentiment of the Pakistani public inhibited this process of "deescalation." The Opposition in the National Assembly interpreted Bhutto's departure from the cabinet to mean that the government was ready to abandon its formerly independent foreign policy and accept American aid with "strings." Government spokesmen found it necessary to match the Opposition's vehemence with some of their own. They would not even "look at any amount of aid" to which strings were attached, not to speak of accepting it, declared the law minister, S. M. Zafar. He went on to assure the House that Pakistan's relations with China would remain friendly.[44]

The Chinese connection with certain unintended consequences of the war in Pakistan's foreign and domestic politics should be clarified. American military supplies to Pakistan, suspended at the outbreak of war, were never resumed on a grant basis. This amounted to an effective disruption of Pakistan's military alliance with the United States. The initial American decision to suspend the supplies was made at the beginning of the war and cannot therefore be attributed to the role the Chinese played during the war. Whether or not it had any bearing on the nonresumption of supplies after peace had been made is not equally apparent. We know that Pakistan's growing ties with China had strained her relationship with the United States. But it should be noted that the intensification of her confrontation with India, highlighted by the conflict in the Rann of Kutch earlier in 1965, also contributed to the on-going American reappraisal. It might be recalled that in the spring of that year President Johnson had disinvited both Ayub and Shastri and postponed decisions on further economic assistance to Pakistan. It would seem that these interrelated dimensions of Pakistani policy—Chinese and Indian—together influenced American calculations.

Pakistan had never stationed more than a division or so of her army in East Pakistan. In this she acted on the theory that East Pakistan's defense lay in the west, meaning that if India attacked East Pakistan, Pakistan would attack India on the western front and take substantial territory in the Indian Punjab and Kashmir. Awareness of such a Pakistani option, it was thought, would deter India from attacking East Pakistan. The 1965 war demolished this theory. India did not attack East Pakistan, fighting only on the western front, yet Pakistan was not able to take any substantial amount of significant Indian territory. This inevitably led many East Pakistanis to conclude that the central government in Rawalpindi could not defend them. Belief in the efficacy of a common defense had been an important factor in maintaining the union of East and West Pakistan. The war shattered this belief and ripped the fabric of Pakistan's national unity and integrity. In a National Assembly debate, Bhutto explained that the Indians had been deterred by a Chinese warning, conveyed to them through American channels, that an attack on East Pakistan would invite a retailatory Chinese attack on their own territory. This explanation did not alleviate the East Pakistanis' concern. They reasoned that, if they owed their safety to Peking rather than Rawalpindi, they might as well develop relations with China independently of the West Pakistani ruling elite whom, in any case, they did not like or trust. Subsequent events would show what a terrible disaster this war had been, not only for Ayub Khan personally but for Pakistani nationhood.

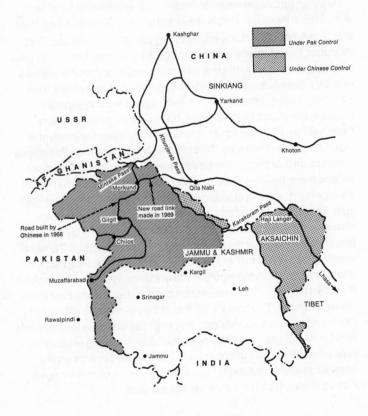

Map showing Indian version of road links (adapted from States-man, June 27, 1969)

Six

The Post-Tashkent Phase

Sino-Pakistan relations continued to expand in terms of selective political and economic cooperation during the period between the Indo-Pakistan wars of 1965 and 1971. The two countries built a system of roads linking Pakistani Kashmir with Chinese Sinkiang. China made a significant contribution to Pakistan's military capability. She made no attempt to exploit Pakistan's domestic turmoils and upheavals to her political and/or ideological advantage. Her approaches to Pakistani opinion were dominated by her concern with the Soviet and Indian opposition to her interests. But, as before, Pakistani officials were reluctant to take sides in the Sino-Soviet cold war. They wanted a mutually advantageous, but not an exclusive, relationship with China. As we will see later, the alignment of forces in the international situation relevant to Pakistan justified this basic trend of her policy.

China and the Tashkent Agreement

Pakistan and India formally ended their war when President Ayub and Prime Minister Shastri made a peace settlement following a series of meetings in the Uzbek city of Tashkent in January 1966. The Chinese were suspicious of Soviet mediation. While they did not oppose Ayub Khan's journey to Tashkent, they did caution against any precipitous capitulation, suggesting that if satisfactory terms could not be had at Tashkent, other opportunities of a more advantageous settlement might present themselves later.[1] In this connection, it is noteworthy that the Chinese maintained a degree of military pressure on the borders of Sikkim, Bhutan, and the Northeast Frontier Agency for several months following the Indo-Pakistan cease-fire with a view to strengthening Pakistan's negotiating position vis-a-vis India.[2] When the terms of the Tashkent accord became known, they were deeply disappointed.[3]

The Soviet Union took on the role of a conciliator early in the developing conflict. While she continued to send military supplies and economic aid to India, she called for peace and adopted an outward posture of neutrality. On August 24 *Pravda* urged an end to the fighting then taking place in Kashmir. Blaming the conflict on outside powers interested in weakening Afro-Asian solidarity (a typical Soviet reference to China), Moscow commended realism and restraint to Ayub and Shastri in letters made public on September 11, 1965. Soviet leaders were concerned that continuance of the war might result in the expansion of Chinese influence in Pakistan. They wanted both India and Pakistan to come closer to Moscow and, instead of fighting each other, to cooperate in expelling both China and the United States from the subcontinent. On September 19 and then again on November 21, they invited Ayub and Shastri to confer in Tashkent. The United States having declined a peace-making role, the Soviet government thought a successful meeting at Tashkent would enhance its prestige in the area, as indeed it did.

Ayub and Shastri accepted the invitation, and the conference opened on January 4, 1966, albeit in a mood of considerable skepticism. The two sides had taken rigid positions: India demanding a no-war pact and refusing to budge from her stand on Kashmir; Pakistan insisting that a meaningful peace could not be made without a mutually satisfactory Kashmir settlement—this despite the fact that neither side was able to continue the war and each had been told by the United States that peace must precede the resumption of American economic assistance. Each time the talks bogged down, Premier Kosygin traveled back and forth to the villas where Ayub and Shastri were staying to have private talks with them. He reminded Ayub that, as a result of the war, India had seized more valuable Pakistani territory than the Indian territory

Pakistan had taken. He told Shastri that Moscow had staked its prestige in sponsoring the meeting and that if India did not reciprocate the Soviet government might not always be on the Indian side of the Kashmir dispute.[4]

The Tashkent Declaration was signed on the afternoon of January 10. It contained the two governments' agreement to withdraw their forces to positions they had occupied before August 5, 1965, to repatriate prisoners of war promptly, to reestablish normal diplomatic relations, not to permit hostile propaganda against each other, to settle their disputes peacefully, and to consider measures for restoring cultural and economic relations.

Having been told that their side had been victorious on the battlefield, Pakistanis had reacted to the cease-fire on September 23 with riots in Karachi and Lahore. They were stunned by the proceedings at Tashkent, unable to understand why Ayub, the victor, was coming home without substantial Indian concessions on Kashmir. Instead of explaining the agreement to the nation immediately on his return, Ayub secluded himself in the President's House and did not speak until after riots had broken out again in Pakistan's major cities. While certain sections of the nation, especially the business community, were relieved that the war was over, the urban masses, politically aware people in rural areas, the intelligentsia, and the opposition parties generally regarded the Tashkent agreement as a betrayal and a national disgrace. The depth of public resentment was immense. It turned out to be enduring and nourished the forces that were finally to overthrow the Ayubian system. Bhutto had already become a national hero by dissociating himself from the decision to stop fighting on September 23: he had wept in the Security Council and vowed to fight India for a thousand years if necessary, before he read Ayub Khan's telegram accepting the council's cease-fire resolution. Now he let it be known that he was opposed to the settlement Ayub Khan had made with Shastri. It is in this perspective that the Chinese reaction to Tashkent should be seen.

The Chinese did not criticize the terms of the agreement, for to do so would necessarily imply a condemnation of Ayub Khan. It would also mean supporting anti-Tashkent Pakistanis against their government. Yet, they did not wish to remain completely silent. Preferring an indirect form of reproach, they found occasion to characterize the agreement as a product of Soviet-American "plotting" to weaken the united struggle of Afro-Asians against imperialism. The United States and the Soviet Union, they said, had backed India against Pakistan and made a common cause against China in pursuing their interventionist policy in Asia. The Russians wanted to apply the "Tashkent spirit" to Vietnam also, which meant bringing that area within the "orbit of U.S.-Soviet cooperation for world domination."[5] During the next few months the Chinese emphasized three themes in their contacts with Pakistanis. The Russians, they said, were no friends of Pakistan. Reacting to the suggestion that the Ayub government had been unnerved by the vigor of Chinese diplomacy during the war, they insisted that Sino-Pakistan friendship was not merely a matter of relations between the two governments but extended to the two peoples. They urged Pakistan to stand firm in face of Indian pressure.

Liu Shao-chi and Chen Yi paid a visit to Pakistan at the end of March, 1966, and were treated to an unprecedented popular welcome. The *Morning News* of Karachi printed its front-page headlines in Chinese characters greeting the visitors. Nearly a million people turned out to welcome them in Lahore. Bhutto, who was accompanying Liu and Chen, shared the applause. He expressed popular feeling when he told the Chinese that their assistance during the war had made Sino-Pakistan friendship imperishable. It did not rest on considerations of expediency; it could not be bargained away. (This expression of Pakistani gratitude and that of a belief in the permanence of Sino-Pakistan friendship became standard themes in Pakistani banquet speeches for years to come.) Ayub Khan reiterated his government's "firm" belief that China should be restored to her lawful rights at the United Nations and that any scheme to create two Chinas was bound to fail.

Liu praised the government of Pakistan for "sternly" refuting the imperialist-revisionist "nonsense" that China posed a threat to the security of the Indian subcontinent. In pursuing this course the Pakistan government was "expressing the firm will of the Pakistani people to maintain friendship with the Chinese people." A variation on this theme may be noted: Chinese officials frequently referred to an American-Soviet-Indian conspiracy to disrupt Sino-Pakistan friendship, which must, however, fail since the two peoples, whose fundamental interests were engaged in this relationship, would not countenance it. Therefore, "no force on earth" could undermine their friendship. So reasoned Chou En-lai, Chen Yi, and numerous other Chinese dignitaries.[6]

The Chinese leaders asserted that the United States and the Soviet Union had joined hands in a policy of encircling China and were using India as their agent. The Indians, being at once reactionary and expansionist, would continue to threaten Pakistan's national integrity and sovereignty as they did China's. The United States and the Soviet Union were thus enemies of both China and Pakistan, a fact which the peoples of the two countries understood quite well. In resisting Indian aggression, said Liu Shao-chi in Dacca, Pakistanis had not only upheld their own sovereignty and dignity, they had made an important contribution to the "defense of peace in this part of the world." This in itself constituted a strong support to the Chinese people. Liu went on to assure his listeners that the Chinese would aid them in defending their national independence and unity were they to be attacked by an aggressor again. Commenting on his Dacca visit, a *Renmin Ribao* editorial thus warned the Indians: "Your inexplicable concern over the friendship of the Chinese and Pakistani peoples shows precisely that you are afraid of their solidarity, because with this solidarity your aggressive schemes and expansionist plans cannot succeed."[7] The deliveries of Soviet weapons to India in the late spring and early summer of 1966, months after the Tashkent agreement, showed that the Soviets were "stoking the fires of war" and encouraging India to threaten China and Pakistan and "blackmail and browbeat her small neighbors." The Soviet action demonstrated how much the "so-called" spirit of Tashkent was worth.[8] The thought of Mao Tse-tung also confirmed the value of maintaining Sino-Pakistan friendship. Mao had said that one should support what the enemy opposed and oppose what he supported. The imperialists (U.S.), the revisionists (Soviet Union), and the expansionists (India) had all united in opposing Sino-Pakistan friendship, which proved that it had been a good thing.[9]

During the months following Tashkent a number of important visits were exchanged. Liu Shao-chi, Chou En-lai, and Chen Yi visited Pakistan. Foreign Minister Pirzada, Commerce Minister Ghulam Faruque, and Abdul Jabbar Khan, Speaker of the National Assembly, visited Peking. The Chinese were apprehensive that the Cultural Revolution—interpreted abroad as evidence of Chinese irrationality, chaos, internal debility, and possible disintegration— might give Pakistan second thoughts about the usefulness of her Chinese connection. Chen-Yi defended it at a banquet for Ghulam Faruque, saying that it was a great revolution which would enable the Chinese people to maintain their revolutionary "youthfulness, accelerate our socialist construction and strengthen our national defense so that we can more vigorously carry out [our] foreign policy . . . and better fulfil our bounden internationalist duty." Subsequently, the Chinese quoted some notable Pakistani leftist intellectuals—Ibne Insha and Shaukat Siddiqui—as praising the Cultural Revolution.[10]

Pakistani officials were cautious in responding to the Chinese rhetoric. They would not accuse any combination of powers of trying to disrupt Sino-Pakistan friendship. They limited themselves to saying that "if" attempts were made to "drive a wedge" between their two countries these would not succeed. They thanked the Chinese for their role during the war, referred to the allegedly historic links between the two peoples and the obvious fact that they were neighbors, asserted that both were peace loving and that their friendship and cooperation made for peace in the region. Sino-Pakistan friendship, they would say, was founded on their national interests and the desire of the two peoples to strengthen "good neighbor ties." They wanted to have friendly relations with *all* countries and especially with neighbors.[11] They made no references to the imperialists or the revisionists. They refrained from referring to India specifically, however gratified they might have been with the Chinese designation of Indians as reactionary expansionists who had hired themselves out to the imperialists.

From Gilgit to Kashgar: The Karakoram Friendship Highway

The substantive content of Sino-Pakistan relations continued to expand in the post-Tashkent period. The two countries were linked by a road between Gilgit in Pakistani Kashmir and the towns of Kashgar and Yarkand in Sinkiang. China's involvement in Pakistan's economic development and military preparedness also increased.

On October 21, 1967, Pakistan and China signed an agreement to facilitate "overland trade" between Gilgit and Sinkiang. Press reports at the time indicated that the agreement related to the old "silk route," extending from Gilgit through Hunza and the Mintaka Pass on to Sinkiang, which trading caravans and pilgrims had used for many centuries. It was said to span a distance of 456 miles, "being shorter and less difficult than the Leh [Ladakh] route via the Karakoram Pass to Yarkand."[12] The stretch on the Pakistani side, between Gilgit and Mintaka, was stated to be 140 miles. An official "handout" explained that the agreement would fulfill a "long felt" need for reopening the traditional land route. It envisaged a limited transit of goods that would benefit the people living in the border areas of both countries. Nothing was said of the amount of work that must be done. According to the *Times* (London) of May 14, 1968, the Chinese were to provide assistance in building the Pakistani side of the road.

The agreement was not published, and secrecy regarding its details gave rise to speculation that more than a limited passage of goods might be involved. Subsequently, two things happened. The old silk route was in fact opened. In June 1968, the two governments agreed to exchange two caravans from each side during the summer of 1969. Goods in trade would be carried by "pack animals," arrangements for whose grazing and for boarding and lodging of the traders would be made.[13] But it appears that at the same time road construction was taken in hand. In May 1968, the Indian minister of state for foreign affairs, B. R. Bhagat, told the Rajya Sabha that a motorable road was being built between Gilgit and Sinkiang, that China had already completed its portion of the road north of Mintaka, that the Pakistanis were improving an existing "jeepable" tract between Gilgit and Pasu (about seventy miles), and that they were building an additional seventy miles of new road between Pasu and Mintaka.[14]

On August 7, 1969, the two governments agreed to establish

trading organizations to handle the trade going over the "route." But by this time the route was in the process of becoming a thirty-two-foot wide highway. At a ceremony at Baltit in Hunza on February 16, 1971, the Karakoram Friendship Highway was declared open and said to have replaced the old caravan silk route. "Hewn out of rocky mountains," the road was described as an "all-weather highway capable for the most part of carrying two-way traffic." Joining with the Indus Valley road, it connected Rawalpindi with towns in Sinkiang. The *Pakistan Times* noted that its construction had involved enormous labor, perseverance, and ingenuity, of which the Pakistan engineers could be justly proud. The political and economic advantages of the undertaking were "obvious." Many hamlets had already sprung up along the highway in Gilgit. All of West Pakistan could profit from the development of overland trade routes such as this. A convoy of vehicles carrying heavy machinery had come to Karachi from Kushka in Uzbekistan in 1969. That route might be used more often. The development of similar overland trade with Iran and Turkey had been under consideration in the RCD capitals. The newspaper recommended a coherent policy regarding these trade channels.[15]

Pakistan does not claim exclusive credit for completing this extremely tortuous and hazardous feat of engineering, which at many places passes over mountains more than 15,000 feet high. At the Baltit ceremony Gen. Abdul Hamid, who represented the Pakistani side (along with Gen. Gul Hasan and Air Marshal Rahim Khan), conceded that the road could not have been built without China's "valuable assistance and cooperation." In Pakistan it is generally believed that the Chinese supplied some equipment but that Pakistani engineers and crew actually built their side of the road. Many workers are said to have met fatal accidents and others to have succumbed to the severities of the weather at the high altitudes involved. Other reports suggest, however, that Chinese engineers and road-building crew actually participated in the operation on the Pakistani side. In June 1969, the Indian government claimed to have received intelligence reports that some 12,000 Chinese technicians and workers had moved into Pakistani Kashmir. They were said to have established a camp on the Khunjerab Pass (16,000 feet), 150 miles northeast of Gilgit, and another at Mor

Kund, 90 miles north of Gilgit. According to the Indian version, Pakistan and China were linking the Gilgit-Mintaka-Sinkiang road with the Sinkiang-Tibet road. The link branched off from the Gilgit-Mintaka road at Bali, a village north of Mor Kund, and stretched some 70 miles northeast to Khunjerab. The Chinese were said to have already built a 118-mile highway from the Khunjerab Pass to "Qila Nabi" on the main road to Lhasa. Indian sources claimed that the Chinese had built the Mor Kund-Khunjerab road in 1969 and that earlier, in 1968, they had built the road between Gilgit and Mor Kund and beyond toward Mintaka.[16] Apart from the matter of Chinese assistance in the road-building operation, the Indian version suggested that a system of strategic roads, rather than just one road, had been built.

The Indians contended that the road links represented a Sino-Pakistan threat to their security. If, in the absence of these links, China wanted to put military pressure on Indian Kashmir, she would either have to pull troops away from her border with the Soviet Union 220 miles south of Mintaka or from India's northern border hundreds of miles up the Aksai Chin road all the way to Kashgar and then southward to Mintaka Pass. The distance involved had been reduced substantially with the building of the Mor Kund-Khunjerab tract linking the Tibet-Sinkiang road with the Gilgit-Sinkiang road. The Indian government protested to the Chinese and accused them of pursuing a "diabolical policy" with regard to Kashmir.[17]

The Indian interpretation is not without substance. The volume of trade going over the road must of necessity remain limited. In June 1969, *Dawn* estimated that about two million rupees' (less than $200,000) worth of goods might eventually be exchanged— Pakistan sending woolens, leather goods, garments, cutlery, and jute bags and taking Chinese tea, hides and skins, hardware, electrical equipment, and silk.[18] One need not doubt that the residents of Gilgit and Hunza, and those of the border areas on the Chinese side, would profit from the traffic. But it is clear that the economic advantages expected cannot possibly justify the initial outlay or even the recurrent cost of maintaining the roads. The reasons for building them may safely be assumed to have been political.

China's access to Pakistani Kashmir and from there to the Indian side may in certain contingencies be of some possible help to Pakistan. It may be recalled, however, that Pakistan did not want Chinese soldiers on her soil during the 1965 war. Limited quantities of Chinese military supplies may reach Pakistan through this road if effective snowplowing machinery is available and functioning on both sides. The Chinese strategy, on the other hand, is concerned not only with the possibility of conflict with India, in which Pakistan is vitally interested, but also with that of conflict with the Soviet Union, in which Pakistan cannot be directly involved. Russell Brines has written on the strategic significance of the area north of Gilgit. His interpretation, summarized below,[19] may be of interest.

In order to avoid conflict in this area, Russia and British India created a buffer zone by ceding a 40-mile wide corridor, called Wakhan, to Afghanistan in 1898. This strip separates the Soviet Pamirs from northern Kashmir. The same Anglo-Russian agreement gave the eastern portion of the buffer zone, including lands north of Mintaka Pass, to Sinkiang, then under the nominal control of China. Brines argues that an unfriendly power in control of Gilgit, which lies some 140 miles southward, can threaten the Soviet Pamirs and Central Asia. On the other hand, the Gilgit airport can be used to counter anti-Soviet military moves emanating from Sinkiang. As a result of the Sino-Pakistan border agreement in 1963, the Chinese legitimized their control of certain areas of Hunza south of the Mintaka Pass from where they could possibly dominate Gilgit. They would like to be able to outflank the Soviet Pamirs, one of their "irredentist" goals, have absolute control of the Karakoram Pass, and create a strong anti-Soviet position as well as a strategically significant position with reference to the India subcontinent. The *possibility* of an attack on their supply lines stretching all the way to Sinkiang was the weakest aspect of their position during their conflict with India. It is possible for planes taking off from Gilgit to destroy the main Chinese base at Kashgar from which most of their troops and supplies move southward. Neither the Chinese nor the Soviets, not to speak of the Indians, can calmly watch a hostile power take control of Gilgit. All of this means that, while the road links under reference may produce certain benefits, they have also placed Pakistan in a position that invites opposing Soviet and Chinese pressures. It might also be mentioned that both China and the

Soviet Union have sought to establish road link with the subcontinent. The Soviet Union has been interested in linking her Central Asian republics with Karachi through Afghanistan, a civilian project with military overtones. The Chinese obtained a contract in Nepal and built an east-west road linking Katmandu with Tibet.

Chinese Arms and Economic Assistance.

American military assistance to Pakistan stopped when the Indo-Pakistan war began in September 1965. Not only were there no supplies on a grant basis, as had been the case before, but for a time the United States would not even sell spare parts to Pakistan. She had to buy these through third countries at high prices. Her attempts to buy weapons in the world market met vigorous Indian opposition. The Indian government told prospective suppliers that, by selling arms to Pakistan, they would endanger Indian security, provoke an arms race in the subcontinent, and force India to divert funds from economic development to armaments. After the 1965 war, Iran bought ninety F86s from West Germany and sent them on to Pakistan. Indian pressure on Iran, West Germany and the United States caused their return to Iran. Pakistan came close to completing arrangements to buy M-47 tanks from some of the NATO countries, but once again Indian opposition blocked one deal after the other.[20]

Pakistan turned to the communist powers also. The Russians decided that, while India might continue to buy Soviet weapons in desired quantities, some limited supplies might be made to Pakistan also. They are reported to have sent Pakistan some ten million dollars' worth of trucks and helicopters during 1966 and 1967. In July 1966, Selig Harrison reported that the Russians were asking Pakistan to close down the American intelligence base near Peshawar as a condition for supplying arms.[21] Pakistan did ask the United States to liquidate this base, and an agreement with the Soviet Union materialized in July 1968. The USSR was then said to be willing to sell T-54 tanks or spare parts that would fit the similar Chinese T-59, 200 130mm artillery pieces, and a certain number of MIG-21 and MIG-23 fighters.[22] Pakistan does not have any of these fighters, but she does have 200 130mm guns and 100 T-54 tanks.[23] Whether these were supplied by the Soviet Union is not altogether clear.

The Western armament-producing nations and the Soviet Union were all, in varying degrees, hesitant to sell arms to Pakistan for fear of alienating India. China was not so inhibited. Pakistan turned to her even though her production and stockpile capabilities were modest as compared to those of the Western powers or the Soviet Union. Pakistan received a token supply of Chinese weapons during, or shortly after, the 1965 war. Since then China has continued to be a major source of arms supplies to Pakistan. The International Institute of Strategic Studies reports that as of July 1971, Pakistan had 16 Il-28 light bombers and 64 MIG-19 interceptors out of a total of 285 combat aircraft. She had 50 T-55 and 225 T-59 medium tanks in a total tank force of 870. (If the 100 T-54s came not from the Soviet Union but from China, which too has an inventory of these tanks supplied to her by the Soviet Union before 1960, the Chinese element would increase to 375.) Pakistan also has a variety of smaller Chinese arms. In the spring of 1972 she received an additional 60 MIG 19s and 100 T-59 tanks, an undisclosed number of surface-to-air missiles, patrol boats, and other weapons. These supplies would partly make up the losses sustained during the 1971 war.[24]

The terms on which Chinese weapons have been made available are not precisely known. It is generally assumed that initially they were supplied on favorable prices and easy credit terms. In the final analysis they would appear to have cost Pakistan little or nothing. During Bhutto's most recent visit to Peking (January 31 to February 2, 1972), the Chinese government converted four previous interest-free loans, amounting to $110 million, into outright grants. According to the *New York Times* (February 3, 1972), the new deliveries of MIG-19s and T-59s were part of a $300 million military and economic development loan Bhutto had secured during his visit; but the day before the same paper had quoted Chou En-lai as saying to Bhutto: "We are not ammunition merchants. Whatever your defense requirements are, they will be met gratis." In any case, it now transpires that the Chinese have converted all their previous loans to Pakistan into grants.[25]

The dimensions of Sino-Pakistan trade remained modest. In 1969-70 Pakistan exported approximately 138 million rupees' worth of goods—jute manufactures, raw jute, raw cotton, and "other" articles—to China. This figure formed a little over 4 percent of her total exports for that year. She imported some 95 million rupees' worth of Chinese chemicals, coal, cotton, yarn, drugs and medicines, iron and steel, paper and pasteboard, spices, and "other" articles, representing less than 2 percent of her total import trade. The year 1966-67 would seem to have been the busiest for Sino-Pakistan trade: Pakistani imports from China stood at 159,248,000 rupees, and her exports to China reached 221,730,000 rupees. Imports were the lowest, less than 2 million rupees, during 1955-56, and exports the lowest, less than 11 million rupees, during 1961-62.[26] With the departure of East Pakistan from the union, Pakistani trade has suffered some severe dislocations. She must look for alternative markets for her textiles and other surpluses. It is likely that her exports to China will expand. But on China's part this will be more an act of political accommodation than economic necessity. In the past Pakistani exports have included surgical instruments, sports goods, fruit juices, cutlery, and medicinal herbs. Larger quantities of these products plus shoes and cotton and woolen textiles might go to China. Not only business calculation but political considerations influence Chinese trade policy. In November 1968, for instance, she offered to pay higher freight rates to Pakistani vessels carrying cargo between Pakistani and Chinese ports. The rate from Karachi went up from 90 shillings per ton to 130 shillings, that from Chittagong from 70 to 116. There were to be a minimum of 12 sailings between Pakistani and Chinese ports. Peking also offered to negotiate the establishment of a joint Sino-Pakistan shipping corporation that would expand their trade and advance Pakistan's industrialization.[27]

The actual dimensions of Chinese assistance to Pakistan—military, economic or technical—are difficult to ascertain, partly because of the secrecy surrounding some of its components, and partly because of a propagandistic element in the Pakistani and Chinese advertisement of others. The same act of assistance or friendship may, for instance, be announced in the press several times as it goes through various stages of implementation. In the absence of background information, successive versions may convey the impression of additional assistance. This procedure may serve to exaggerate the level and intensity of Sino-Pakistani interaction at times when interaction is in fact sluggish. The figures for Chinese assistance provided in *Pakistan Economic Survey 1972-1973,* a publication of the Ministry of Finance, may be of interest. According to this source, China had, up to March 1973, given Pakistan a total of $110.369 million in grants and pledged $220.536 million in loans as *capital aid.* These figures do not include other types of Chinese assistance. Nor, according to some government officials, do they include the cost of Chinese equipment or technical advice. The grants were made on three occasions: $60 million during the Second Five-Year Plan; $47.485 million during the Third Plan; and $2.884 Million during the fiscal year 1970-71. The entire amount of the loan was pledged during the same fiscal year. But note also that until June 30, 1972 only $5.994 million out of the $220.536 million pledged had actually been disbursed; the rest being in ''pipeline'' or in the realm of intention. With the recent conversion of Chinese loans into grants, Chinese grants for capital development in Pakistan would come to $330.9 million out of which more than $214 million was still to be disbursed when the fiscal year 1971-72 closed.[28] The cost of Chinese military equipment and amounts of assistance other than capital aid, currently unavailable to this writer, would have to be taken into account to get a fuller picture of Chinese aid to Pakistan.

Some of the Chinese assistance has been given for designated development projects, the most notable being the sprawling heavy mechanical complex at Taxila, capable of producing machines that would make cement, sugar, textiles, boilers, road-building equipment, and railway engines. The Chinese supplied some 1,300 mechanical units and sent technicians to help Pakistani engineers build the plant and install these machines. They trained 300 Pakistani technicians to work in the plant. Thirty Pakistani engineers and some business executives connected with the project received training at Chinese institutes lasting, in some cases, more than two years. The presence of Chinese overseers on the scene made for efficient and expeditious proceedings, and the plant began "trial production" in September 1970. The project was estimated to cost 176 million rupees.[29] The Chinese have also undertaken to build a heavy foundry and forge at Taxila that will produce steel castings, steel ingots, iron castings, press forgings, forged billets, and copper and aluminum castings. This project will also cost about 176 million rupees, of which the Chinese will meet the foreign exchange component, estimated at 55.29 million rupees. They helped build an ordnance factory in East Pakistan where they trained Pakistanis in relevant skills.

A variety of professional Pakistanis have visited China over the years and have brought back word of her willingness to share her scientific and technical knowledge. Pakistani diplomats believe the Chinese do not wish to keep Pakistan dependent upon themselves: their policy is to enable her to become self-sufficient. In discussions with their Pakistani counterparts, they have repeatedly emphasized the theme of self-reliance. For instance, they have helped Pakistan develop the capability of servicing and overhauling MIG aircraft engines in her own workshops instead of sending them to China. Pakistani engineers, on their part, have made some needed adjustments to improve the performance and range of these aircraft and have been equally willing to share their findings with the Chinese.[30]

It should, however, be added that intellectual interaction between Pakistan and China, as compared to that between Pakistan and the West, remains extremely limited. Other than trainees connected with Chinese-aided projects, few Pakistanis have ever gone to China in pursuit of higher learning. The language barrier, among others, precludes any large-scale exchange. In 1973 the Chinese offered seven scholarships for prospective Pakistani students, three of them for learning the Chinese language and four for technical education. But apparently there has been no great rush of applicants for them. In turn Pakistan offered *one* scholarship to

China for someone interested in learning Urdu. In both China and Pakistan language competence necessary for studying each other's culture is modest. Chinese is not taught in Pakistani universities. About twenty Pakistan military officers are said to be moderately proficient in reading and speaking the language. Only three Pakistan Foreign Service officers have the same capability. On the other hand, one official in the Pakistan section of the Chinese Foreign Office is said to be able to speak Urdu.[31] The Chinese are better situated with regard to English, which is the language of Pakistani diplomacy. But as they expand their contact and relations with the outside world, a communication crisis may be developing: the supply of English-speaking Chinese interpreters is not increasing commensurately with the fast-growing need for their talent. The number of foreign visitors must therefore be adjusted to the availability of interpreters and some kind of a rationing system worked out to accommodate the nations desiring to make contact with China. The number of nonofficial Pakistani delegations visiting China, and Chinese delegations visiting Pakistan, may actually decline over the next few years while China overcomes this communication lag.

Pakistan and the Sino-American Detente

This may be as good a place as any to refer to Pakistan's role in facilitating the Sino-American detente.[32] It appears that when President Nixon visited Pakistan in July 1969 he requested President Yahya Khan's assistance in removing "misunderstandings" between China and the United States. Yahya responded affirmatively. The two presidents met again in October 1970 in Washington where the Pakistani president arrived after a visit to the United Nations, which would seem to have been undertaken to give him an excuse for visiting Nixon. (Here it might be recalled that he was scheduled to visit Peking the following month.) Nixon asked Yahya to see if the Chinese would be willing to receive an important American official. Yahya had two private meetings with Chou En-lai in Peking the next month and found, among other things, that the Chinese would rather receive the proposed American official openly than secretly. After that numerous messages between China and the United States passed through Yahya. This does not mean that he was merely delivering letters in Peking and Washington: Nixon and Chou En-lai were still not talking to each other. The messages were addressed to Yahya Khan, who then conveyed them, in his own words, to the party concerned. He often gave each side his own comments, evaluation, or recommendation but was careful to separate these from the message itself, which he conveyed without permitting any distortion in the process of transmittal.

The message, and Yahya Khan's comments if any, were placed in a sealed envelope and carried by special courier to the Pakistani ambassador in Peking or Washington, as the case might be. In Washington the ambassador delivered the package personally to Henry Kissinger; in Peking to Chou En-lai. On occasion Yahya Khan conveyed the message orally to the Chinese ambassador in Islamabad who then transmitted it to Chou En-lai.

In addition to the principals and their top advisors or associates (in the American case, Henry Kissinger), only a small number of individuals—the Chinese ambassador in Islamabad, the Pakistani foreign secretary and ambassadors in Peking and Washington—knew that exchanges between China and the United States were proceeding through Yahya Khan. But the contents of the messages were, at the time, known only to Nixon, Kissinger, Yahya Khan, Chou En-lai and, in some cases, the Chinese ambassador in Islamabad. Yahya Khan's confidential secretary typed them out. Pakistani officials who have since seen the files, report that some were written in Yahya Khan's own hand.

The rest of this great adventure in secret diplomacy is now well known. In July 1971, Henry Kissinger, ostensibly on a tour of several Asian countries, stopped in Pakistan for a brief visit. The day after his arrival in Rawalpindi, he was said to be ill and resting in Nathiagali, a mountain resort in the North West Frontier Province. The government of Pakistan made elaborate arrangements to make it appear that Kissinger was indeed ill and resting. In fact a PIA plane had taken him to Peking where he talked with Chou En-lai and arranged for President Nixon to visit China the following year. The same plane brought him back to Rawalpindi just as secretly.

China and the United States are no doubt appreciative of Pakistan's role in bringing them together. But some Pakistani diplomats submit that this role may have contributed to her defeat and dismemberment later the same year. The Soviet Union is said to have been greatly angered by the fact that Pakistan helped her two great adversaries travel towards a detente. The fact of this detente, and in India's case also the manner of its coming about, alarmed Moscow and New Delhi and hurried them toward a treaty of "friendship" including mutual defense assistance provisions. Needless to say, it was Yahya Khan's responsibility, not that of Nixon or Chou En-lai, to calculate the consequences that the role asked of him might have for his own country.

One may refer to a similar, though less spectacular, Pakistani role in bringing about the establishment of diplomatic relations between Iran and the People's Republic of China in 1971. As early as 1954 the Chinese had asked Ambassador Raza, who was leaving Peking to head the Pakistani embassy in Tehran, to convey their desire for friendly relations to the Iranian government. But at this time Iran was much too apprehensive of communism and communist powers to respond favorably to the Chinese suggestion. At the beginning of the 1970s this threat perception had considerably declined all over the "free world." Some key Iranian officials were still suspicious of China. But despite their skepticism, Pakistani diplomats were able to convince the Shah that the Chinese harbored no unfriendly designs toward Iran. With the Shah's consent, they arranged for Princesses Ashraf and Fatima to visit Peking, where the Chinese government accorded them a warm and cordial welcome. These visits paved the way for the normalization of Sino-Iranian relations.[33]

China and the Political Upheavals in Pakistan

The first decade of Sino-Pakistan amity must be perplexing to the ideologue. On the one hand, he sees Mao's China, representing a brand of communism more militant than the Soviet. On the other, he sees a coalition of feudal landlords, exploitative big business, imperious bureaucrats, and military notables ruling Pakistan. But Chinese behavior in international politics is not ideologically governed to any significantly greater degree than that of other nations. Her leaders have often declared that ideological differences do not preclude mutually beneficial relations with other countries. A commitment to nonintervention in the domestic affairs of their friends is a recurring theme in the speeches they make and the communiqués they sign with their guests and hosts. The significant thing is not that these declarations are made but rather that they have been observed. As far as any one knows, the Chinese have made no attempt to disrupt the established political and social order in Pakistan, this despite the fact that a pro-Peking political organization, Maulana Bhashani's National Awami party (NAP), functioned in East Pakistan. The Chinese may even be said to have put their influence on the side of governmental stability rather than revolutionary change.

In 1963 Bhashani led a Pakistani delegation to the October celebrations in Peking where he met Mao Tse-tung and Chou En-lai. They told him that they would welcome a rapprochement between his party and the Ayub regime. In a tape-recorded interview, Bhashani told Tariq Ali:

Mao said to me that at the present time China's relationship with Pakistan was extremely fragile and that the United States, Russia and India would do their utmost to break this relationship. He said, "You are our friends, and if at the present moment you continue your struggle against the Ayub government it will only strengthen the hand of Russia, America and India. It is against our principles to interfere with your work, but we would advise you to proceed slowly and carefully. Give us a chance to deepen our friendship with your government."[34]

The Maulana agreed and kept his word for almost six years. He and his associates refrained from opposing or embarrassing the Ayub government, even though they continued to blast at capitalism and imperialism. They reasoned that Ayub was making an opening to the left. In time Pakistani industrialists would have to establish economic ties with socialist countries, and this would help break the hold of Western imperialism on Pakistan. Ayub's China policy showed that he too was an opponet of imperialism. The NAP did join a coalition of parties to oppose Ayub Khan's reelection in 1965, but its support for the opposition candidate, Miss Fatima Jinnah, remained lukewarm. Bhashani did not actively campaign for her. There were allegations that some of his lieutenants had secretly urged their followers to vote for Ayub. In rural East Pakistan, where the Maulana's influence was said to be high, the president won with a substantial margin. As I said earlier, the 1965 war with India had left many East Pakistanis deeply disturbed. But Bhashani's secretary, Anwar Zahid, characterized the conflict as a "people's war." Some of the NAP leaders thought Pakistan should have continued to fight, although they later endorsed the settlement Ayub had made at Tashkent. On his part, Ayub let the Maulana and his party do their political work unmolested.

The Chinese leaders said or did nothing to support the popular movement against Ayub Khan during 1968-69. In West Pakistan the pro-Peking NAP remained uninvolved for a whole month. Initially, Bhashani too remained aloof; he changed his stance only after the movement had developed into a massive and general uprising. In the first week of December 1968, he apparently concluded that his continued aloofness would destroy his party's credibility. Overruling those who would still opt for passivity, he responded to the appeal of Dacca's rickshaw drivers, addressed a public meeting at Paltan Maidan on December 6, denounced the Ayub regime, supported the East Pakistani demand for autonomy, and called for a general strike. Thereafter he was to call for many more strikes and *gheraos* of government and industrial establishments and homes of civil servants. He aroused the countryside of East Pakistan and visited the major cities of West Pakistan. But even now his chief target remained Pakistan's capitalistic order. Food, clothing, housing, and other basic necessities of the masses were more important issues than parliamentary democracy or regional autonomy. Bread before franchise. If the capitalists did not provide bread to the people, the people, he thundered, would literally eat the capitalists.[35]

The Pakistani civil war in 1971 placed the Chinese on the horns of a most disagreeable dilemma. They disapproved Yahya Khan's military action in East Pakistan, and they also disapproved the East Pakistani rebels' links with India. They were considerably more apprehensive of the consequences of this conflict than Yahya Khan would seem to have been. In private communications, the first of them as early as April 9, they urged him to work through East Pakistan's own leaders toward a political settlement. When refugees, in large numbers, started moving into India, they warned that this development would internationalize the conflict by giving India a reason, or excuse, for becoming openly involved.[36] Publicly, they supported the government in Islamabad, albeit with moderation. In a note to Yahya Khan, Chou En-lai characterized the crisis as an internal affair of Pakistan, whose unity a "handful of persons," unsupported by the broad masses of East Pakistan, were trying to disrupt. The unity of East and West Pakistan, he said, were vital to Pakistan's attainment of prosperity and strength. He condemned India, the Soviet Union, and for good measure the United States for their "gross interference" in Pakistan's domestic affairs. He assured Chinese support should the "Indian expansionists dare to launch aggression against Pakistan."[37] In response to an Indian demonstration outside the Chinese embassy in Delhi protesting Chinese aid of Yahya Khan against the "freedom-loving people of East Bengal," a Chinese note of April 6, 1971, accused the Indian government of "flagrantly interfering in the internal affairs of Pakistan."[38] In May the Chinese offered Pakistan a substantial loan to alleviate her tight foreign-exchange situation resulting from the disruption of East Pakistani exports. In the subsequent months Chinese media gave regular coverage to Pakistani charges of Indian infiltration and subversion in East Pakistan. But otherwise they remained prudently silent. Yahya Khan's campaign in East Pakistan was not easy to praise; it has since been condemned by Bhutto and other Pakistani leaders.

East Pakistan's problems are stupendous, and no government, however dedicated or competent, can solve them in a hurry. In the

absence of any significant number of capitalists and great industrial entrepreneurs, an independent East Pakistan could not rely on
private enterprise as a major strategy of economic organization
and development. It would probably go beyond the petit bourgeois
ethos represented by the Awami League and adopt a variey of
"socialism" more advanced than the Indian. In other words, there
were opportunities for the Chinese to exploit. There can be several
explanations of why they did not do so. Initially they may have
thought the Pakistan army would be able to quell the uprising. By
the time it transpired that the uprising was massive and that India
was deeply involved on the side of the rebels, China's options were
all disagreeable. Continuous and emphatic backing of the Yahya
government would mean endorsing its use of terror in East Pakistan. Supporting the rebels would not only mean endorsing Pakistan's formal or virtual breakup, it would mean supporting India
against Pakistan. Beyond these lay the equally obnoxious proba
bility that such a support role would, in terms of impact on East
Pakistani sentiment, remain secondary to that of India. True, as
East Pakistan become independent with Indian military assistance
might fall under the sway of forces hostile to China; but in the
absence of viable alternatives the possibility of such a reverse had
to be accepted. Given the severity of its problems, East Pakistani
gratitude toward India might dissipate fairly rapidly so that there
would be opportunity again to cultivate influence in that quarter. In
the meantime, it would be unwise to alienate West Pakistan where
the only counter, even if limited, to the Indian military position in the
subcontinent resided. Another consideration is also relevant.

The Chinese concern over their own national integrity has made
them reluctant to support separatism elsewhere. They haye pulled
Tibet into the fold of Chinese nationhood. They wish to recover
some other areas that were once part of China but were subsequently lost to outside powers, notably czarist Russia, through
"unequal" treaties. Their sensitivity to the idea that Taiwan might
permanently be a separate and independent entity is well known;
they have denounced it time and again as an imperialist-revisionist
plot. It is then understandable that they did not wish to go on record
as favoring East Pakistani separatism and thus create a precedent

that might subsequently be quoted to their own disadvantage.

Chinese support of Pakistan during the 1971 war remained subdued as compared to that in 1965. On the day General Niazi surrendered in Dacca (December 16) and then again on December 27, the Chinese charged Indian incursions into Tibet and violations of their air space. Eight Indian soldiers, they said, had crossed into Tibet and carried out reconnaissance for a half hour! But there were no ultimatums this time. Only denunciations and some sermonizing such as that "he who plays with fire will be consumed by fire," and not necessarily a Chinese fire but one of the player's own making: India had her own nationality problems that might flare up.

The Chinese denunciations were directed as much at the Soviet Union as at India. Once again they accused India of subversion, military provocation, and then "brazen" aggression. They supported Pakistan's right to defend her state sovereignty, territorial integrity, and national unity. During the Security Council debates on the war, they insisted, as did the United States, that a cease-fire resolution should also call for mutual withdrawal of forces behind the international frontiers. They referred to the Indo-Soviet treaty of 1971 as a military alliance and accused the Soviet Union of planning to extend her imperialist control over the Indian subcontinent. "The present armed aggression by the Indian government against Pakistan," said Huang Hua, the chief Chinese delegate, " is being carried out with the connivance, support and protection of the Soviet Union."[39] He likened it to the Soviet invasion of Czechoslovakia in 1968 and referred to the Soviet delegate, Yakov Malik, as "Mister" instead of "comrade," a supreme insult to a fellow communist.

The Pakistani public had expected that the Chinese would put some kind of military pressure on India as they had done in 1965. This expectation was heightened by Bhutto's claim, on his return from Peking on November 8, 1971, that his visit, undertaken as Yahya Khan's personal emissary, had been a "complete success" and that the results were "tangible" and "concrete." After seeing Bhutto, Yahya announced that in the event of an Indian attack the Chinese would intervene and help Pakistan as much as they could.[40]

In a banquet speech the acting foreign minister, Chi Peng-fei, had indeed assured "resolute" Chinese support in case of Indian aggression. But this need not have been seen as anything more than a routine and generalized type of assurance typical of Chinese speeches before Pakistani audiences since the 1965 war. On the basis of my interviews with Pakistani officials, I would submit that in private conversations with visiting Pakistani dignitaries on this and a previous occasion the Chinese had made it quite clear that they were not in a position to intervene in an Indo-Pakistan war or provide military assistance sufficient to repel a Soviet-backed Indian offensive. They urged Pakistan to avoid war with India and, if it could not be averted, to contain it in as small an area as possible. Pakistani diplomats assert also that these Chinese representations were conveyed to Yahya Khan in no uncertain terms. But note that beyond these private communications, some public indications of the Chinese position were also available. Chou En-lai, while present, did not speak at the banquet for Bhutto. Nor is it without significance that during Bhutto's two days in Peking he was taken to see the underground shelters the Chinese had built for protection from a possible Soviet attack.

Outside Pakistan few, if any, expected Chinese intervention. There was the problem not only of snow on the Himalayan passes into India but that this time the Soviet Union had taken India's side. Claiming that the Indo-Pakistan war engaged its own security interests, Moscow warned Pakistani leaders that they were taking a "grave responsibility" by pursuing a "dangerous course" of conflict with India. Nor could the Chinese overlook the fact that a quarter of the Soviet army, including forces equipped with nuclear weapons, remained poised along the Sino-Soviet border. Furthermore, they had barely recovered from a deadly confrontation between their party leadership loyal to Mao and their army leadership loyal to Lin Piao. Along with Lin, Huang Yung-sheng (chief of staff of the armed forces), Wu Fa-hsien (the air force commander), and forty other top military men had recently been purged. These disabilities were presumably known to Bhutto and Yahya.

Pakistan had gone into the 1965 war in the name of Kashmir's right to self-determination. In 1971 the major part of her own population had revolted against the existing political order. Pakistanis had slaughtered Pakistanis. The roles were reversed: This time India claimed to be fighting in aid of East Pakistan's right to self-determination. However dismayed or angered the Chinese might have been at India's role, they could not have been enthusiastic about the Yahya regime. Their state of mind can be seen in an observation Chou En-lai made while entertaining President Bhutto in the Great Hall of the People on February 1, 1972. Explaining the limited nature of China's response to the events of 1971, he said: "Our assistance is for repelling aggression and not for suppressing the people."[44] Yet it would be wrong to assume that China would have done much more had Pakistan's cause been free of blame. We will see in the next chapter that there are limitations on what China can do, and this is beginning to be realized in Pakistan. In an editorial comment on February 4, 1972, *Dawn* wrote:

Had we ... not presumed that we would get unlimited Chinese support, regardless of our objectives and conduct, the country might have been saved from humiliation and defeat. ... The People's Republic of China has been a great friend of Pakistan. Let us honour this friendship by being rational and realistic and by not imposing unnecessary burdens and strain on the friendship. Objective reality must be measured by its own size and not by the length of its shadow.

Seven

Pakistan and China: A Futuristic View

Pakistan's relations with China have been more political than economic or ideological. Even if the Chinese have evangelistic goals, they are evidently in no great hurry to see communism come to Pakistan. They are a patient people with a long view of historical development. In the meantime, they have been a source of valuable support to Pakistan in her efforts to resist Indian pressure. Pakistan's security problems has always been difficult. Despite frequent references by her own spokesman and others to a "balance of power" in the subcontinent, no such thing in the sense of an equality of power between India and Pakistan has ever existed. Militarily India has always been much stronger. The idea of the balance in fact referred only to a level of Pakistani military capability sufficient to hold an Indian invading force at the border, away from her urban centers, long enough for great-power diplomacy to bring about a disengagement and a return to the status quo ante bellum. But the balance even in this limited sense has broken down as a result of the events of 1971, which neither China nor America was able to prevent. Consequently, Pakistan's security problem would appear to have worsened. Any contribution that China could make toward its alleviation must depend, as before, on the nature of Indian, American, and Soviet policies toward Pakistan. A futuristic analysis of the underlying premises, and likely course, of these policies is necessary before a prognosis of Sino-Pakistan relations may be made.

The Outlook for an Indo-Pakistan Rapprochement

Let us first see if Indian and Pakistani hostility toward each other can be mitigated and Pakistan's security problem thus eased. The Indian dismemberment of Pakistan in 1971 has hardened Pakistani perceptions of India, discussed earlier, and aggravated her sense of insecurity. India's sense of threat from Pakistan, on the other hand, has virtually disappeared after her victory and the resulting fact that Pakistan is now only about one tenth the size of India. Consequently, Indian attitudes toward Pakistan may conceivably loosen and become less hostile. But this development, at the level of government policy, still belongs to the future.

India and Pakistan have not yet completed the process of making a peace settlement. From the Pakistani standpoint, India ought to be more than content with having detached East Pakistan from the West. She should have promptly returned the Pakistani prisoners of war, offered a "just" settlement of the Kashmir dispute, and then left Pakistan alone. The Indians, on the other hand, wanted Pakistan to accept a package deal containing the following elements: Pakistani recognition of Bangladesh; a revision of the Kashmir cease-fire line, presumably to India's strategic if not territorial advantage, and its acceptance as the international frontier between the two countries; a no-war pact and a commitment to solve all disputes bilaterally, that is, without the intervention or participation of third parties; a quiescent and modest role in international politics consistent with India's vital interests.

A beginning toward a settlement was made when President Bhutto and Prime Minister Indira Gandhi concluded their meetings at Simla on July 3, 1972. Since then the two governments have withdrawn their forces behind their international border and delineated a new line of actual control in Kashmir. Under the Simla agreement they are to respect each other's national unity, territorial integrity, political independence, and sovereign equality; refrain from the threat or the use of force against each other and settle their disputes by peaceful means; discourage hostile propaganda against each other and prevent acts detrimental to peaceful and harmonious relations between them. The repatriation of prisoners and a a final settlement in Kashmir were left to be negotiated in subsequent meetings.[1]

Then came the "Delhi Agreement" in the summer of 1973, as a result of which India is returning the Pakistani prisoners she has been holding. One hundred and ninety five of them, whom Bangladesh accuses of "war crimes," will be detained longer and their fate decided in a round of tripartite negotiations among Pakistan, India, and Bangladesh. The "spirit" of Simla and Delhi appears to be just as fragile as the "Spirit of Tashkent" seven years earlier. Both governments continue to speak, in the same breath, as it were, of their desire for peace and their increasing preparedness for defense. An incredible amount of wrangling preceded the delineation of the new "line of control" in Kashmir and the withdrawal of troops behind their respective frontiers.

The negotiations leading to the Delhi Agreement were just as difficult. To date Pakistan has not recognized Bangladesh. India is in no hurry to reestablish diplomatic relations with Pakistan, which is her way of saying that she will not recognize the "new Pakistan" until the latter has recognized Bangladesh. At Pakistan's urging, China is keeping Bangladesh out of the United Nations. Pakistan accuses India, Afganistan, and the Soviet Union of formenting subversion and issurrection in her frontier regions. As recently as early January 1974, Prime Minister Bhutto complained that there was more foreign intervention in Pakistan than in any other Afro-Asian country. Responding to this situation, he threatened to issue a call for a strike in Indian Kashmir whereby the Kashmiris might demonstrate their solidarity with Pakistan. It is clear that the present state of Indo-Pakistan relations is still charged with considerable tension. The main difficulty appears to be that Pakistani leaders are unwilling to accommodate themselves to the Indian view of an acceptable Pakistani role in South Asia and in international politics. This Indian view, crucial to the future of Indo-Pakistan relations, merits more than a passing reference.

The Indians are asking Pakistan to accept the "new realities" in southern Asia; her own weakened position after the 1971 war; the emergence of Bangladesh as an independent state; and the emergence of India as the "dominant" power in the area. There are several dimensions to this Indian position. Mrs. Gandhi asserts that if Indo-Pakistan relations are to be "normal" Pakistan must not rearm so as to be able to threaten India.[2] The Indian Foreign Minister Swaran Singh, has interpreted Pakistan's acquisition of Chinese aircraft and tanks to supply her war losses as evidence of a continued "posture of confrontation." Such moves on her part, he warns, will hinder the "speedy normalization of relations" between the two countries.[3]

Indian spokesmen argue also that Pakistan belongs to the Indian subcontinent and should make friends there, not on the outside. This demand is expressed variously. Mrs. Gandhi says India will not tolerate the interference of outside powers in the affairs of the subcontinent and will not permit them to "use" Pakistan as, allegedly, they have done in the past. Swaran Singh hopes Pakistan has learned the "lesson thet help from other countries can at best be marginal" and will not be "misled" by them.[4] Satish Kumar, a former official in the Indian Ministry of Information, has spelled out this thesis:

Another requirement of the situation, as regards Pakistan, is that it should stop looking outwards for friends and partners, and establish such a relationship with countries of the region, namely India and Bangla Desh. Hitherto Pakistan has been cultivating the Muslim countries, in addition to some major powers, as allies in fulfilment of its national objectives.... But such an approach proved to be of no special advantage to Pakistan in the past. Therefore, Pakistan must now identify and utilise the areas and opportunities of cooperation within the region.[5]

In the Indian government's view, the idea of an external role, even such as Soviet mediation at Tashkent or the judicial arbitration of the Rann of Kutch dispute, has been "thrown overboard."[6] Mrs. Gandhi, while publicly disowning any desire for hegemony on India's part, asserts nevertheless that, in the interest of peace and economic development, "foreigners should withdraw from this region."[7] Her officials have been more outspoken. Swaran Singh recently called upon the United States to recognize the "new realities" in the subcontinent, which, according to a senior Foreign Ministry official, meant that Washington "should recognize and treat India as the dominant power in South Asia."[8]

Some of India's opinion makers see her emerging role on a grand scale, as a role in which she enforces not only peace but a congenial political order in the region. Inder Malhotra, noted journalist and author, says India must increase her military might if she is to play her "rightful" role in South Asia, "for it takes power to be a power." Pakistan will be restrained only if it sees plainly that India is powerful enough to "cut it to pieces." India should also be able to deter any Chinese "nonsense" in NEFA (Northeast Frontier Agency) or Ladakh. A. B. Shah, editor of *Quest,* thinks India should "reassure the people in the disaffected areas of Pakistan about their future" were they to break away from a "militarist dictatorship." Harji Malik speaks of India's "natural obligation" to help people free themselves from military rule and political or economic exploitation "wherever it may be." On the other hand, G. S. Bhargawa urges Pakistan to reconcile itself "forever . . . to its present size and importance in Asian and international affairs.[9]

Even those who write about Pakistan from sympathetic understanding, such as B. G. Verghese, are not content with peaceableness on her part. They want to bring her back into the fold. Verghese hopes Bangladesh, Pakistan, and India will eventually come together in a "common market, commonwealth, or a loose confederation," which Sikkim, Bhutan, Nepal, Ceylon—and perhaps Burma and Afghanistan—might in time join.[10]

These role images call for a militarily ineffective and politically isolated Pakistan that has ceased to be an independent or dynamic international actor. To use an Indian mode of thought and expression, they envisage the role of a younger brother for Pakistan. In the Indian tradition, the younger brother may be protected and loved, but he is not treated as an equal or conceded independence. As might be expected, President Bhutto has declined the station and role the Indians would seem to have in mind for Pakistan. He regards India's demand that she be treated as the "dominant" power in South Asia as a provocation. "The friendship of India," he says, "we are prepared to accept. But the hegemony of India we will never accept." And again: "The present reality, according to Swaran Singh, is that India is the only dominant power in the subcontinent... which means that India wants to keep Pakistan under its shadow and hegemony. When India wants that its hegemony be recognized by the foreign countries, we will have to make ourselves strong to protect the sacred soil of Pakistan.''[11] It follows that while India insists on being the dominant power in southern Asia the prospect of Indo-Pakistan amity will remain bleak. In that case, Pakistan's security problem remains severe.

Limitations of a Military Deterrent

Let me now say a word about the possibility of assembling a Pakistani military deterrent to Indian pressure. This will require a level of military capability sufficient to insure that India's cost of a victory over Pakistan will be intolerably high. Apart from imponderables such as the relative quality of training, internal cohesion and coordination, strategy-making skills, and leadership characteristics of the two military establishments at the time of conflict, the performance of Pakistan's weapons must match or surpass that of India's best in some crucial categories even if her inventories are numerically smaller. Disregarding each side's war losses in 1971, let us take the case of air power, which India's defense planners now regard as decisive.[12] Pakistan cannot rely on her F-86s and MIG-19s to repel India's MIG-21 and SU-7 planes, which are counted among the Soviet Union's more notable high-performance aircraft and of which India has eight and six squadrons respectively. According to figures published in 1972, Pakistan had one squadron of F-104A interceptors and two squadrons of Mirage IIIE fighter-bombers. She had two squadrons of Mirage Vs on order[13] which would give her the means of dealing effectively with the MIG-21, India's best interceptor with some ground-support and attack capability.[14] A Pakistani squadron normally consists of 16 planes. This means that of high-performance aircraft Pakistan had 48 and expected to have 32 more. India had about 160 MIG-21s and 72 to 150 SU-7s. Both sides had other types of combat planes also,

The totals being: for India, 650; for Pakistan, 200 and possibly 260. The picture of relative air power emerging from these figures cannot be comforting to Pakistani defense planners, and the situation is not much different with regard to the army and the navy.

Modern warfare can break the financial back of a developing country. Manpower expenses could conceivably be reduced to tolerable limits through organizational adjustments: the volunteer army might, for instance, be augmented by a draft system that trains a substantial part of the adult population in the use of modern weapons. But the weapons, or rather the weapon systems, are prohibitively expensive. The so-called cheap F-5 costs $1.5 million. The United States has been selling F-4 Phantoms to Israel at $4.5 million each and has sold them to Iran at $5 million. The Soviet Union has sold SU-7 fighter-bombers to India at $1 million each, payable in rupees, which appears to have been a special price.[15] Prices of naval craft are even more staggering. A patrol boat can cost a quarter of a million dollars and a Daphne submarine $11 million. A few years ago a frigate cost 5 million British pounds and a 30,000-ton aircraft carrier, without the aircraft, 50 to 60 million pounds. Armament prices keep rising not only because of inflation but because of the increasing sophistication of weapons. According to one estimate, it cost six times as much to equip a British infantry battalion in 1968 as it had five years earlier.[16]

India assembles and/or produces many types of weapons in her own plants. These include MIG-21, HF-24, and Gnat interceptors, HS-748 transports used for dropping paratroops, trainers, and helicopters; medium tanks, antitank guided weapons, some artillery and a variety of small arms; naval escorts and patrol boats.[17] In the business of making weapons, time is not on Pakistan's side.

During the last several years Pakistan has been spending between 3 and 4 percent of her GNP on defense. This does not seem to be high. Corresponding figures for the United States, the Soviet Union, and India for 1970 are 7.8, 11, and 3.4.[18] But some additional considerations may afford a fuller understanding of these percentages. In the case of a developed country such as the United States, a higher proportion of the GNP committed to defense might result in nothing worse than a thinning of the prover-

bial icing on the cake. In a developing country it may cause the cake
virtually to disappear by precipitating a sharp decline in the availability of essential supplies and services that were already at a
depressed level. A GNP percentage may be especially unreveal-
ing of the burden it represents if the country's tax system is regres-
sive. It may therefore be more instructive to place Pakistan's
defense appropriations alongside the national government's total
revenue receipts (not including domestic borrowings or foreign
aid), as shown in table 1.

Table 1

	Total Revenue Receipts	Defense Approp.	Defense Appropriation as Percentage of Total Revenue
	(In Millions of Rupees)		
1970-71 (revised)	7,873.0	3,200	approx. 40.6
1971-72 (estimated)	8,773.4	3,400	approx. 38.7
1972-73 (estimated)	8,510.0	4,240	approx. 49.8

Sources: The figures for 1970-71 and 1971-72 may be seen in Embassy of
Pakistan, Washington, D.C., "Pakistan's Fourth Five Year Plan: Interim
Report Series," June-July 1971. For the 1972-73 figures see the *Times* (London), June 19, 1972. *Pakistan Economic* Survey (Karachi: Manager of Publications, 1972), pp. 94-95, places defense expenditure at 56.17, 59.33, and
56.89 percent of the national govermnent's total expenditure for the years
1970-71, 1971-72, and 1972-73.

Pakistani defense spending for 1972-73 thus absorbed nearly
50 percent of the national government's total revenue receipts.
This is not a level that the society and economy can easily sustain.
The breakaway of East Pakistan and the subsequent nation-
alization measures of Prime Minister Bhutto's government have
disrupted the economy, and it will be some years before the resulting dislocations can be overcome. There are other constraints, too.
The serious beginning toward social reform and distributive justice
promised by the ruling parties will require a larger share of public

funds than that which programs of social amelioration have traditionally received; yet this endeavor cannot long be deferred without inviting social upheaval and political turmoil. On the other
hand, if the military is once again to be subordinated to civil authority presided over by the people's representatives, its share of
national resources will have to be rationalized. The current defense
spending should be viewed partly as the government's response to
a situation of uneasy cease-fire arising from a war that was lost and
a peace that is still to be made.

As Pakistani democracy advances, and with it the people's aspirations, Pakistan's own resources will not suffice to provide both
guns and butter: butter enough to keep the people in reasonably
good humor, and guns that will deter Indian military pressure. The
prospect of assistance from external sources will turn on two factors: the degree of external interest in the maintenance of Pakistan's independence, and the production and stockpile
capabilities of countries willing to assist her.

Pakistan and Her Muslim Neighbors

Pakistan is attempting to augment her defense capabilities through
a network of bilateral arrangements with friendly nations other than
the superpowers. There are indications that a Mirage aircraft plant
may be set up in Pakistan with French and Arab assistance: France
would supply the equipment and the more sophisticated technical
competence; emirates of the Persian Gulf would put up the money;
and Pakistan would provide land, needed and available manpower,
and other facilities. The project is said to be under consideration by
the governments concerned.[19] Pakistani military personnel, especially pilots, have from time to time been loaned to Arab nations, for
instance, Saudi Arabia, Jordan, Libya, and, more recently, Syria.
They have trained Arab personnel in the handling of combat aircraft and other weapons. Reports that Abu Dhabi has ordered two
squadrons of Mirage fighters have occasioned speculation, and in
New Delhi protest, that these aircraft might become available to
Pakistan since at this time Abu Dhabi has neither airfields nor pilots

of her own to use them. Reference has already been made to Iran's large scale purchases of sophisticated American weapons and her interest in Pakistani security.

Pakistani officials are aware that these prospects are subject to numerous inhibitions. There is first the familiar factor of Indian opposition and, in that context, the following facts may be relevant. Neither Iran nor any of the Arab countries with whom Pakistan is building cooperative relations has any fundamental conflict of interests with India at the present time. An Indian attempt to dominate the Persian Gulf neighborhood may arouse Iranian, and possibly also Arab, hostility and resistance, but that development belongs to the future. In the meantime, India is not without some influence in these countries: her economic and commercial relations with them are much more extensive than those of Pakistan. Furthermore, the appeal of Pakistan's Muslim personality is somewhat reduced by the fact that India contains within her borders the third largest Muslim community in the world, larger than the present population of Pakistan.

As I said earlier, Iran is conscious of a stake in Pakistan's continued existence as an independent state separating her from India. Nevertheless, Iranian assistance in Pakistan's defense would raise some difficult problems. Ever since her establishment, Pakistan has sought fraternal ties with Arab countries, but Iran's relations with some of them, most notably Iraq, are marked by conflicts of interest and tension. This policy difference with regard to the Arabs has often been an irritant in Iranian-Pakistani relations. But if Pakistan were to expect substantial military help from Iran, her Arab policy might have to be harmonized with Iranian requirements. This would not only involve a traumatic realignment of Pakistani policy but would arouse considerable opposition within the country. Iranian-Pakistani consultations in dealing with their common Baluchi problem have already brought forth charges of Iranian interference in Pakistan's domestic affairs from Wali Khan's NAP. It should be noted also that Iran is not prepared to give Pakistan military equipment free of cost. As her new American weapons begin to arrive, she would be willing to *sell* spare parts and even whole units from her old inventories; but Pakistan may not have the money to buy them. On the other hand, if Iran were to be expected to intervene in a conflict involving Pakistan, such as another war with India, she would most likely demand a role in determining how the conflict was to be waged and ended. She would also wish to be consulted in the formulation of Pakistani policies towards countries with whom the latter was likely to have military conflict. In other words, Pakistan could not have Iran's protection, assuming Iran had the capability of providing it, without incurring some loss of her freedom of choice and action.

The contribution Pakistan's Muslim neighbors might make to her defense is still in the nature of a potential. The next few years will tell us to what extent, and on what terms, it can, if at all, materialize.

United States and Southern Asia

Being the largest producer of modern armaments in the world, the United States has the capability not only of supplying arms to Pakistan but even of intervening in an Indo-Pakistan conflict should such a course of action appear to her to be imperative. But capability does not necessarily imply willingness. Several considerations, including her "new" Asia policy, are relevant to a prognosis of her likely disposition toward Pakistan.

The prime objective of her earlier policy was to maintain an American imperial role in Asia, which meant that the territorial status quo, and possibly the balance of power and influence, in the area might not be changed without her consent. Containment of communism, and particularly the containment of China, were among her more specific goals. But two decades of involvement and intervention in Asian politics have convinced a growing number of Americans that this policy has been intolerably expensive and counterproductive. That it will be abandoned is by no means certain.[20] The new Asia policy does, however, seem to call for a period of recuperation from the exhaustions of Vietnam. Two other elements in it are striking. First, it envisages for the United States, at least for the period of recuperation, the less expensive role of a balancer in a balance-of-power system in which the Soviet Union, China, and subsequently Japan may be the other actors. (In power political terms, India is not considered to be ready to play the role of a principal in such a system.) Second, President Nixon and Dr. Kissinger appear to have determined that, despite the relatively moderate quality of Moscow's anti-American rhetoric, it is the Soviet Union, not China, that poses the greater threat to American interests in Asia and elsewhere, mainly because the USSR is militarily and economically the more powerful.

A balance-of-power system can transcend ideological distinctions, operating from the premise that capitalists can do business with communists and that communists—or democracies—can have conflicts of interest and fights among themselves. It assumes that politics have a rationality of their own so that, after ideological fervor has had time to cool, political actors everywhere will respond to similar drives. The Soviet Union now has considerable influence in Afghanistan, India, Bangladesh, and North Vietnam. If and when the American presence recedes from Southeast Asia, Moscow will doubtless attempt to enlarge its influence in the area. The Chinese are likely to resist such a move. The idea of a Chinese brake on the advance of Soviet influence is quite satisfactory to the United States. Hence the declaration, in the Shanghai communiqué of February 27, 1972, of Sino-American opposition to the "efforts of any other country or group of countries" to establish hegemony in the Asia-Pacific region.

The earlier Soviet-American collaboration against China would now seem to have been imprudent: it is an elementary rule of power politics that a great power ought not to join another great power against a smaller power. Were China to collapse, it would be the Soviet Union, the power in China's neighborhood, and not the United States, who would profit from such a turn of events. Her capabilities augmented, she would pose an even greater threat to American interests than she was able to do before. Hence, China's advancement to a position of power where she is no longer subject to Soviet intimidation is a necessary condition for her effectiveness as an actor in the balance-of-power system envisaged in America's new Asia policy.[21] It follows that Washington will no longer be interested in an Indian counterpoise to China. Nor does the United States stand to gain from India's rise to a hegemonious position in South Asia. That India is democratic is irrelevant. More important is the fact that in international politics she is allied with the Soviet Union. On major issues between the two superpowers she has hardly ever seen fit to side with the United States. America's interest, or perception of stake, in India's advancement as an international actor is therefore likely to decline.

How does Pakistan figure in all of this? The loss or serious weakening of Pakistan's independence under Indian or Indian-Soviet pressure will further strengthen the forces opposed to an American imperial or balancing role in Asia. In this sense the maintenance of Pakistani independence is an American interest. But the dimensions of this interest are modest, as a review of the U.S. response to the Indian invasion of Pakistan in 1971 will show.

Indian troops moved into East Pakistan on November 22, and war came to the western front on December 3. In Washington, the Anderson papers reveal,[22] the National Security Council's Special Action Group, meeting on December 3, 4, and 6, anticipated, without any feeling of alarm, that Pakistan's resistance in the East would collapse within two weeks and that her forces there would be trapped. On the other hand, Henry Kissinger told the group that the president was not inclined to let the "Paks" (meaning West Pakistan) be "extinguished." Yet by this date (December 6) the matter of sending emergency military assistance to Pakistan had not received the president's attention.[23]

The United States took no military action to help Pakistan. Washington's actions were diplomatic and political in nature, and their impact on the course of events remains problematic. The administration called India the aggressor in the war. It canceled Indian licenses for military purchases in this country and suspended some economic assistance to India. At the UN Security Council it called for a cease-fire and withdrawal of forces behind their respective frontiers, knowing that the Soviet Union would veto these resolutions. The Nixon administration has claimed, and President Bhutto has acknowledged, that it saved West Pakistan by taking the following actions: (1) proceeding from intelligence reports that India fully intended to push into West Pakistan as hard as she could after taking the East, it advised the Yahya government to surrender in the East and accept a cease-fire in the West. (2) it advised the Soviets that if they did not restrain India on the western front, President Nixon's scheduled visit to Moscow might be reconsidered. (3) the president ordered a naval task force led by the *Enterprise,* a nuclear-powered aircraft carrier, to move from Singapore into the Bay of Bengal to demonstrate the seriousness of American interest in the survival of West Pakistan.

A threat is effective only if the party to whom it is addressed fears that noncompliance on his part will cause the party issuing the threat to carry it out. The Moscow visit would have been an item of leverage if the issues to be negotiated there were vital to the Soviet Union but not to the United States. Since this was not the case, the threat of cancellation could not have carried a high degree of credibility. Whether the naval move deterred India on the western front would depend on how New Delhi interpreted it. Considering American disenchantment with military action in Asia and the generally pro-India, anti-Pakistan mood of the media, academia, and Congress, it is altogether unlikely that the ships would have attacked Indian targets in case India drove deeply into West Pakistan. If they were not to attack, their presence in the Bay of Bengal accomplished nothing beyond an affront to Mrs. Gandhi's government.[24]

It seems to me that the *Enterprise* mission, the resolutions in the Security Council, the naming of India as the aggressor, and the public expressions of dissatisfaction with Soviet policy during the crisis were addressed as much to China and Pakistan as to India and the Soviet Union. The Nixon administration was plainly dismayed by the Indian invasion, and it had an interest in the survival of West Pakistan. But, beyond these, it wanted to convey to China its disapproval of Indian actions. To appear to have abandoned Pakistan, its own ally and China's friend, under attack from India with Soviet help—both China's enemies—would hardly encourage the Chinese to trust American engagements or inspire confidence in American understanding of Soviet designs in Asia. The administration also wanted to have a talking point in its approach to the future government of Pakistan. The *Enterprise,* the UN resolutions, the signals to Delhi and Moscow would be cited to show that the United States had defeated India's objective of annihilating Pakistan. The Anderson papers would seem to support this interpretation. The officials gathered in the Situation Room at the White House thought it did not matter that the American resolutions in the Security Council would fail. The important thing was to go on record, "to make clear our position relative to our greater strategy."[25] In their public comment on the suspension of American aid to India, they were to emphasize aid that was cut off and not aid that would be continued. The administration took a harder line toward India publicly than it had taken privately. This unusual posture cannot be understood except with reference to the necessity, thought to be overriding, of conveying certain impressions to Pakistan and China.

After the détente with China, the United States is not likely to view southern Asia as an area engaging her vital interests. In view of the continuing Indian and Soviet confrontation with China, and China's Pakistani connection, she may take a lively interest in Pakistani security, stability, and economic development. But this interest will not be such that she might intervene on Pakistan's side in a future Indo-Pakistan war. Nor can Pakistan expect the revival of a large-scale grant of American weapons such as she enjoyed between 1954 and 1965. The Cold War strategy of which that policy was a part has long since been discarded. There is much impatience in Congress with the whole idea of foreign aid, especially military aid. There are tasks of social reconstruction within the American polity, and money is tight.[26] On the other hand, the Nixon administration is not conceding India the role, and the prerogatives, of the "dominant" power in the region. The logic of dominance implies that outside powers should consult India in making their policies with respect to the other states of the subcontinent and submit to an Indian veto if she were to find that their policies were inconsistent with her own role and interests. It is likely that Washington will continue to assert its independence of New Delhi in dealing with the states of southern Asia in order to have the necessary flexibility in pursuing the developing strategies and goals of its new Asia policy, not to speak of the fact that the Indian demand is repugnant to American sovereignty and that of the other states concerned. Pakistan should then be able to buy limited quantities of sophisticated American weapons if she has the money to pay for them. Add to this, if you will, a certain amount of goodwill, economic aid (mostly loans), and diplomatic support from time to time depending on the specifics of the case and the general international situation. In functional terms, this is likely to be the extent of American interest in Pakistan.

The Soviet Union and Southern Asia

The Soviet Union assisted India in dismembering Pakistan. Now that that has happened and East Pakistan has become Bangladesh, what will Moscow's policy be? Without doubt the Soviets will want to retain influence in the area. They could adopt one of two approaches. They might choose to work through the intermediary agency of India, that is, concede India the preponderant role in the region and hope that under Indian dominance its governments will pursue foreign and domestic policies congenial to the USSR.[27] Alternatively, they might wish to reach these governments and peoples independently of India. The matter of approaches is relevant because India is eager to be recognized as the dominant South Asian power. At this particular time, while her relations with the Soviet Union are those of mutual assistance and cooperation, her desire for dominance might not seem to be prejudicial to Soviet interests. But India is too large to be a Soviet satellite or stooge. Over time her posture toward the USSR may change; she may include the Soviets in the list of foreigners no longer welcome in her neighborhood. It follows that in the long run the Soviet Union will not tolerate the prospect of an Indian veto on her relations with the smaller states in the region. It follows also that further enlargement of India's size or power at the cost of Pakistan need not be a Soviet interest.

In Bangladesh Moscow's strategy remains undefined except for the conclusion of aid and trade agreements. The Communist party (pro-Moscow faction) has surfaced and opened offices all over the land. In May 1972, pro-Moscow leftists won sweeping victories in Student Union elections at the University of Dacca and two other Bangladesh universities. India, not the Soviet Union, has made a twenty-year treaty with Bangladesh including mutual-defense assistance clauses similar to those in the Indo-Soviet treaty of August 1971—thus linking the new state with the Soviet Union in defense matters, albeit indirectly.

The present Soviet posture toward Pakistan is firm, almost hard. The USSR is careful not to cause anxiety to India. During Bhutto's visit to Moscow in March 1972, the Soviets agreed to restore aid and trade relations that had been suspended in 1971. At his luncheon for Soviet dignitaries, Bhutto made a most conciliatory speech. He recalled his own contribution to the development of Soviet-Pakistan relations when he was Ayub Khan's minister. He praised the excellence of Soviet technology and the USSR's "revolutionary social justice." He appealed for Soviet understanding of Pakistan's concern regarding her men and territory held by India and the "disastrous situation" of the Biharis in Bangladesh. In return Kosygin went out of his way to justify his government's policy toward Pakistan during the events of 1971 and delivered a warning. The "recent crisis," he said, had involved a clash between the "forces of national liberation" and "an antipopular military dictatorship that had joined ranks with external aggressive circles hostile to the people of 'Hindustan,' including the Pakistani people." He added that "if history were to repeat itself, we would again take the same position, because we are convinced it was correct."[28]

Bhutto's speech implied a recognition of the Soviet Union as an arbiter of international disputes in southern Asia. Twice he expressed the hope that his talks with Soviet leaders would bring peace to "our part of the world." Kosygin agreed, but not the way Bhutto might have wished. He linked the improvement of Soviet-Pakistan relations with the normalization of relations among Pakistan, India, and Bangladesh. He called for an end to the era of confrontation and a commitment to the principle of peaceful resolution of disputes between the countries of "Hindustan." He said nothing about the concerns Bhutto had mentioned. Instead, he wondered what was preventing progress on agreement to hold talks among Pakistan, India, and Bangladesh and asked Pakistan to "display a realistic approach" to this matter.

It is apparent that the Soviet leaders declined to use their good offices to bring about an Indo-Pakistan peace settlement as they had at Tashkent in 1966. They endorsed Mrs. Gandhi's position that Pakistan would have to negotiate a settlement directly with India and Bangladesh. Moscow did not wish to interfere with India's opportunity to obtain whatever concessions she could from Pakistan, while showing that any concessions she might make in return were determined of her own accord without external pressure. The joint communiqué issued at the end of Bhutto's visit is almost barren from the Pakistani point of view. It announces agreement on matters far removed from Pakistan's urgent and immediate concerns at the time: the desirability of ending Israeli occupation of Arab territories, withdrawing foreign troops from Indochina, complete and general disarmament, banning bacteriological warfare, eliminating colonialism, respecting the UN and its charter.

Pakistani officials refer to evidence of Soviet attempts to build secessionist movements in Baluchistan and the North West Frontier Province of Pakistan.[29] A "Radio Free Baluchistan" is said to broadcast from somewhere in Iraq, where Soviet influence is now considerable. In February, 1973, Pakistani police entered the Iraqi embassy in Islamabad and, in the presence of foreign and local newsmen, seized over sixty crates of Soviet weapons including, among other things, 331 automatic submachine guns.

The Soviet Union has always wanted, understandably, to weaken Pakistan's links with anti-Soviet powers, first the United States, then China. Moscow and Delhi probably expected that, after the disasters of 1971, Pakistan would conclude that her Chinese connection had been worthless and, in a state of depressed morale, would accept India's terms for a peace settlement. Neither of these developments has taken place. The Soviets may then be expected to continue their earlier diplomacy of combining pressure and promises with a view to pulling Pakistan away from China and into a collaborative relationship with Moscow and Delhi. In the foreseeable future, the best Pakistan can expect is that the Soviets will not sponsor subversion within her territory or encourage another Indian invasion. Even for such self-restraint they will expect Pakistani reciprocity. They will not tolerate Pakistan seeking a "special relationship" with either China or the United States or offering herself as an American-Chinese outpost against the Soviet Union. There are many lessons for Pakistan to learn from her recent defeat and dismemberment. One of them indubitably is that she cannot invite Soviet hostility except at her peril. Neither the United States nor China will protect her from its consequences.

The Soviets do have greater freedom of action with respect to South Asia than either the United States or China. They are not subject to another power's nuclear intimidation as China is to theirs. They are not tired of Asian involvements as the United States is. The pressures of public and legislative opinion do not bear on their government as heavily as they do on the American administration. They are physically located next door to Pakistan and India. They have an abundance of modern sophisticated weapons. All of this means that they are in a position to guarantee Pakistan's frontiers should they so desire. Having helped India to detach East Pakistan from the West and thus having eliminated any Pakistani threat to Indian security, they could now call a halt to India's further harassment or nibbling of Pakistan. Such a policy would imply the assertion, on their part, of an imperial role in the area. Whether they will play this role remains to be seen.

It appears that at this time Moscow would like Islamabad to do the following:[30] support its Asian security project; participate in a transit system which would permit Soviet goods, and those of its trading partners, notably India and possibly also the countries of Indo-China, to travel over Pakistani roads and railways; negotiate its differences with Afghanistan; reach an accommodation with its own dissident groups in Baluchistan and the North West Frontier Province, especially Wali Khan's pro-Moscow NAP; recognize Bangladesh and make peace with India. These goals need not be regarded as nonnegotiable demands. Partial concessions on Pakistan's part—for instance, participation in the transit plan (which, incidentally, has the support of Iran and Turkey also), and a settlement with domestic dissidents—might suffice to mollify the Soviet

Union. Recognition of Bangladesh is, in any case, on Bhutto's calendar. Peacemaking with India will go through its slow and tortuous course.

The Soviets are not necessarily committed to a further break-up of Pakistan. Their current harassment, such as covert support of Baluchi and Pathan separatists, is a pressure tactic which may, however, be intensified if Pakistan appears to be wholly unreceptive to their goals. It is partly their response to Bhutto's unfortunate suggestion, soon after coming to power, that the United States and China had a common interest in containing Soviet influence in Asia and that Pakistan might have a role to play in such an enterprise.[31] The subjects of Soviet expansionism and the concomitant Soviet-supported threats to Pakistani security and territorial integrity continue to figure importantly in Pakistani representations to China and the United States. An indication of Soviet displeasure with this Pakistani approach appeared in the Kosygin speech mentioned above. He denounced "external aggressive circles," meaning China, and "imperialism," meaning the United States, which, he said, were "sowing discord and animosity" among the nations of South Asia.

Pakistan and China: A Prognosis

The Chinese have been among Pakistan's more important friends for over a decade. They have provided her significant economic and military assistance and given her political and diplomatic support during her conflicts with India. They have a strategic interest in Pakistan's northern areas. The political party currently ruling Pakistan, Bhutto's PPP, claims to be not only socialistic but pro-Peking. China's relations with India have been strained since before the Sino-Indian border conflict in 1962. It would seem to follow that China has a positive interest in preventing the extension of India's control over Pakistan. But while China may have an interest in containing India, India and the Soviet Union have a common interest in containing China. The Indo-Soviet treaty of 1971 became operative during India's last war with Pakistan and will doubtless be invoked in case of a Sino-Indian conflict. Then what can, or will, China do to relieve Pakistan's security problem?

It is probable that she will continue to supply weapons to Pakistan on generous terms. But at this time she cannot match the high-performance Soviet weapons India has and may receive. China produces the MIG-19 in substantial numbers but, as we saw above, it is inferior to the MIG-21. Chinese armament production is going forward. She now produces the Tu-16 medium bomber, the MIG-21, the T-59 medium and T-62 light tanks, and armored personnel carriers (APC). She has developed and put on the assembly line since April, 1971, a new fighter, designated the F-9, which can fly at twice the speed of sound (Mach 2.0). These fighters are being produced at the rate of about ten a month.[32] It will be several years before the Chinese build an F-9 inventory sufficient for their own needs and can begin to supply them to friendly countries in any significant number. The same may be said of their MIG-21 and Tu-16, whose production rate is no higher, and is possibly smaller, than that of F-9.

China has a severe security problem of her own vis-à-vis the Soviet Union, one quarter of whose army (forty-four divisions) is posted along, or close to, the Sino-Soviet border. The Soviet forces are said to be equipped with nuclear weapons and have far greater air support, fire power, and mobility than do the Chinese. Soviet IRBMs and MRBMs cover about seventy targets in China and Japan.[33] China might, in any case, be reluctant to intervene in an Indo-Pakistan war to relieve pressure on Pakistan. She did not do this in 1965 or 1971. But even if the Chinese wished to take such an action, were able to surmount the problems of terrain and logistics, and were willing to absorb the cost, they would have to be able to deter a Soviet retaliatory attack on their territory and installations before they could seriously consider it. Could the Chinese deter such a Soviet attack by threatening a nuclear response?

The Chinese are believed to be capable of fabricating about twenty H-bombs a year, probably of the three-megaton variety. By contrast the Russian stockpiles (as also the American) of nuclear weapons are reckoned in the tens of thousands. The Chinese have

reportedly developed a new intermediate-range missle capable of
carrying nuclear warheads to a distance of 1,500 to 2,500 miles.
Launched from Sinkiang it could reach Soviet cities beyond the
Urals and possibly Moscow. Chinese progress on ICBMs remains
unclear: according to some estimates they could have ten to
twenty-five operational ICBMs by the mid or late 1970s. It would
seem then that over the next several years the Chinese are able to
launch a limited, but only a limited, nuclear attack on Soviet targets.
But it is clear also that the Soviets could absorb such an attack and
retaliate with hundreds of nuclear warheads on Chinese targets virtually obliterating China.[34]

Will the Chinese attack India if India invades Pakistan? Will the
Soviets attack China if China attacks India to relieve pressure on
Pakistan? Can the Chinese make a credible nuclear threat to the
Soviet Union, deterring a Soviet attack upon themselves while they
attack India? These questions cannot be answered with any reasonable degree of assurance. The Chinese are a cautious people
and so are the Soviets. It follows that, while the Sino-Soviet conflict
of interests remains acute and Soviet-Indian amity continues, Pakistani policy makers cannot assume that in the event of another
Indo-Pakistan war the Chinese will intervene in their behalf.

None of the great powers is likely to guarantee Pakistan's security. Their politics seem to be in a transitional phase. The era of the
Cold War has ended, but the governing premises of their interaction in an era of competitive coexistence in a multipolar world
have not fully emerged. The most powerful of them, the United
States, is likely to be engaged during the next few years in rethink-
ing her national purpose and role with respect to the outside world.
In any case, American interest in southern Asia is not likely to return
to the high point where it was before the Sino-American détente
began to develop. The Chinese do not suffer from gnawing doubts
about their policy goals. But they are restrained by Soviet opposition. The Soviets themselves stand in an interlude between two policy periods. The breakup of Pakistan closes one fairly long era of
Soviet policy toward the Indian subcontinent. Their broader
strategy for the next phase is not quite apparent yet.

The current disposition, alignments, and relative power positions of the great powers will some day change again, and when

that happens Pakistan's options may change also. But the present situation, while it lasts, suggests a certain setting for Pakistan, a setting in which she concentrates on mutually profitable economic relations with the great powers, avoids political connection with all of them, and devotes herself to the domestic tasks of economic and social reconstruction. Where does this leave her security problem vis-à-vis India?

Given the relative insufficiency of her military capability and that of her foreign connections, Pakistan will have to strengthen the political and other nonmilitary elements of her defense. On the diplomatic front, she must take care not to arouse Soviet hostility. Pakistanis will be loath to accept the role of India's younger brother, but they will have to do their part in ending the politics of confrontation with India. For instance, they will have to leave it to the Indian Muslims and Kashmiris to work out their own destiny. This may even further their interest in these people: it may help release the Indian Muslims from the frequent and humiliating call to prove their loyalty to India and thus enable them to assert their rights within the Indian polity more vigorously. Again, where her own vital interests are not engaged, Pakistan need not be the standard-bearer of opposition to India in international forums and elsewhere, the challenger of India's claims to higher virtue at home and abroad. There are others who will play this role.

It needs to be borne in mind that the alternative to confrontation is not necessarily romance and marriage or even "friendship." A limited relationship—modest trade, occasional cultural exchanges, easier travel, and a halt to hostile propaganda against each other—may also be possible. India will probably press Pakistan for larger and deeper "cooperation" between the nations of the subcontinent. But Pakistan's unwillingness to join these ventures need not become a casus belli. In the actual day-to-day workings of diplomacy, smaller nations do have some leeway. A peaceable Pakistan under Indian pressure will evoke considerable international sympathy. She may evoke some sympathy even in India. However, her ability to resist Indian pressure will derive mainly from her domestic political cohesion and vigor. If India wishes to coerce Pakistan, she is not likely to begin with a frontal military attack. She will first exploit Pakistan's domestic divisions.

But she can subvert Pakistan only if Pakistanis, in large enough numbers, are disaffected with the prevailing political order. The East Pakistani secession has shown that Pakistan cannot be defended unless the people of her various regions are determined to remain together as one independent nation. They will be so determined if they feel that their participatory urges will be fulfilled and their access to the means of well-being will be larger by remaining together.

The Chinese will probably continue to make a significant, though limited, contribution toward Pakistan's military and economic capabilities. It seems to me that, at the same time, they would welcome such Pakistani domestic and foreign policies as might have the effect of easing her security problem. Contrary to the prevailing impression in some Pakistani quarters, a normalization of Pakistan's relations with India and the Soviet Union, as distinguished from an extensive collaborative relationship, would not be uncongenial to them. They would be content with a Pakistani policy of equidistance in relation to the great powers. In this their calculations are no different from those of other great powers. They are not anxious to commit a disproportionately large share of their aid-giving capacities to Pakistan. They are beginning to assume the role of a world power and have interest in other areas also. It might be recalled that the Soviets were quite satisfied to see the United States and other Western powers meet most of India's development assistance needs.

The Pakistani connection has had no more than a peripheral relevance to China's own security problem. The greater threat to her comes not from India but from Russia, and in that context Pakistan cannot be helpful. At this time India's role as a competitor of China is only in the nature of a potential. She has no significant influence anywhere in South and Southeast Asia other than Bangladesh and the tiny Himalayan kingdoms of Sikkim and Bhutan. Pakistan, Nepal, Ceylon, Burma, the states of Indochina, Malaysia, Indonesia, and the Philippines have never shown any inclination to look to India for leadership. Nor is the Indian "model" of political and economic development a shining success. Until 1971 Pakistan acted as a brake on Indian "expansionism" inasmuch as Indian capabilities were largely committed to opposing Pakistan. But if Indo-Pakistan relations are normalized so that Pakistan does not play such a role in the future, Peking will not necessarily view this as a major loss. While there is no prospect of Sino-Indian friendship in the foreseeable future, a normalization of Sino-Indian relations is possible, and this need not have an adverse effect on China's relations with Pakistan.

My interviews with senior Pakistani diplomats, including Prime Minister Bhutto, confirm these interpretations. These officials assert that China does not stand in the way of normal relations between Pakistan and India, and that China would like to normalize her own relations with India. There has been no Chinese ambassador in New Delhi and no Indian ambassador in Peking for the last several years, each nation's mission in the other's capital being headed by a chargé d'affairs. The Indians would like to upgrade the missions but so far the Chinese have not responded favorably. Their coolness to this Indian proposal, their continued nonrecognition of Bangladesh, and their vetoes of resolutions seeking to place Bangladesh at the United Nations are calculated to strengthen Pakistan's negotiating position in making a peace settlement with India and Bangladesh. But these measures are not indicative of a long-term policy. The Chinese would like to be able to counter Soviet influence in India and Bangladesh as far as possible, and normalization of relations with these countries is a necessary step in that direction. At the same time, they wish to avoid the appearance of "indecent haste": they are waiting for Pakistan, their "friend," to normalize relations with India and Bangladesh before they do the same.

Nor do the Chinese wish to control the extent to which Pakistan's relations with India might develop. In this connection, certain observations Prime Minister Bhutto made during my interview with him on November 4, 1973, should be of considerable interest. He stated that as a result of a series of long meetings with Premier Chou En-lai before and after the Indian victory in East Pakistan, the Pakistani ambassador in Peking at the time, K. M. Kaiser, an East Pakistani who defected to Bangladesh in the spring of 1972, was able to persuade the Chinese leader that the problems of the subcontinent would be best resolved, and presumably the Chinese interests safeguarded, if Bangladesh, India, and Pakistan were not only to make peace but to come together in some sort of a "commonwealth." Chou En-lai conveyed Kaiser's idea to Zulfikar Ali Bhutto in approving terms. The latter responded by despatching Aziz Ahmad, his chief foreign policy aide, to Peking, where, after four hours of plain speaking, he was able to rid Chou En-lai of "this preposterous idea."

Security considerations do not exhaust the rationale of Sino-Pakistan relations. Both nations have reaped other significant advantages. Moscow's decision to support India against China disappointed and angered the Chinese leaders. Later when Moscow began collaborating with Washington to isolate Peking from the world community, Pakistani friendship, along with that of a small but slowly growing number of other nations, enabled Chinese leaders to show both at home and abroad that they were not quite so isolated after all. The Sino-Pakistan air-travel agreement in 1963 symbolized their success in breaching the wall their adversaries were trying to build around them. That Pakistan, a capitalist country and an American ally, was a friend of China proved also that the American rhetoric about the Chinese threat to the security, stability, and good order of Asia was not to be believed. Pakistan facilitated the improvement of China's relations with some countries in the Muslim world and, as mentioned above, made a valuable contribution toward the earnest beginning of a Sino-American détente.

Washington's decision to arm India against China dramatized its relative unconcern with Pakistani security and gave the Pakistani people a sense of isolation. The Chinese connection had a remedial effect: it lifted their morale and gave them the reassuring feeling that they were not alone, that the largest nation in Asia was on their side. It also enabled them to project a "nonaligned" image, reinforce their Asian and third-world personality, and gain greater respectability in Afro-Asian circles. Pakistan's growing cordiality with China kept the United States and the Soviet Union from a thorough alignment with India and induced them to maintain a balance of affections as between India and Pakistan. In other words, the connection with China served, both directly and indirectly, to

advance Pakistan's economic development, her military capability, and her political role in international relations. Pakistan's
relationship with China has been one of the few policy questions on
which something approaching a national consensus has come to
exist. The Jamat-e-Islami and Wali Khan's NAP might wish to tone it
down somewhat, but none advocate its abandonment. If the new
Pakistan pulls herself up and keeps herself together, so that she is a
reasonably free agent (as free as most nations in an interdependent
world are) in making her policy choices, a cordial and mutually
advantageous relationship will continue to commend itself to both
Pakistan and China. However, it cannot be an exclusive relationship. The exigencies of Pakistan's relations with China, the United
States, and the Soviet Union—and in the long-term perspective,
possibly even India—will define the outer limits beyond which her
relations with any one of these countries could not develop without
disrupting her relations with the others.

Eight

Toward a Theory of Pakistani Foreign Policy

While international politics are dominated, as they often are, by calculations of the relative coercive capabilities and self-interest of nations and the elite who speak and act for them, the options of a relatively small state, such as Pakistan, contending with the hostility of a much larger neighbor and the cross pressures of mutually antagonistic global powers, tend to be narrowly circumscribed. Not all small states are under pressure or harassment from the great powers. Pakistan invites their interest partly because of her physical proximity to two of them—China and Russia—and partly because of her extended confrontation with India, so that, in formulating policies toward India, the powers have had to take account of her.

A theory of Pakistani foreign policy would almost necessarily be a theory of small-nation behavior. Students of this subject, of whom there are not many, agree that the small state lives a perilous existence. Threatened by a great power and lacking the support of a rival great power, it cannot defend itself by military means. David Vital goes so far as to say that since, in all likelihood, a small nation cannot bear the financial burden of maintaining a modern and sufficient military capability it is useless for her to build a halfway modern or partially effective establishment. It is safer to rely exclusively on political, psychological, legal, and moral factors inhibiting great-power aggression or making it difficult for the aggressor to hold the small state even if the initial act of aggression could not be prevented.[1] V. V. Sveics has given the small state similar advice.[2] Both concede also that the nonmilitary means are not always efficacious. Alliances of small states against a great power are said to be ineffective, for no combination of "squirrels" will add up to an "elephant" in international politics, the sum of their power still being weakness.[3]

In the great majority of cases and over extended periods of time, small states have not followed the courses of action recommended by Sveics and Vital. They have instead played the game of power politics as best as they could, depending upon options and constraints implicit in the international situation and the ingenuity of their policy makers. They were participants in power politics even when they claimed to be nonaligned, for nonalignment is nothing other than a "tactical principle" designed to obtain the greatest possible advantage from a given power configuration. It will work when the state concerned may assume that, if and when it is threatened by a great power, rival great powers will come to its assistance. The experience of small states over time might justify the following general statement.[4]

For purposes of analysis, a small state may be defined as one which recognizes, as do others, that it cannot safeguard its security "primarily by the use of its own capabilities, and that it must rely fundamentally on the aid of other states, institutions, processes, or developments to do so."[5] Its stakes in the game of international politics are enormous, involving national survival in a basic sense. Foreign policy may often dominate its political process to the relative neglect of domestic concerns.

When a balance of power has prevailed, small states within its operation have tried to be its beneficiaries, often by placing themselves on the heavier side. When the balance was even, or nearly so, their allegiance was actively sought. Great powers were reluctant to molest a small state enjoying the protection of another great power for fear of generating a larger conflict. But when they acted in concert and made decisions affecting the small states, the latter had to comply. In our own times, small states had more leverage during the years of tight bipolarity when the Cold War tensions were high. Their fortunes declined when the superpowers began to pursue détente.

It has been recognized at least since the time of Machiavelli that alliances between small states and great powers can be dangerous to the former and bothersome to the latter. The small state wants to be protected from all threats to its security. Its ally, the great power, is unwilling to make such a wide-ranging commitment. The small state worries about the balance of power in its own neighborhood. The great power, having global interests, is concerned with the balance of a much larger international system to whose preservation the security interests of its small ally may, at times, become irrelevant. They may even have to be sacrificed. There is also the danger that the alliance may turn the small state into a satellite of the great power, without alleviating its insecurity. Depending on availability, small states may prefer to rely on a less powerful ally or a combination of lesser states.

The pattern of small-nation behavior outlined above would explain the more important characteristics and shifts of Pakistani foreign policy: her overriding concern with security; the advantages and frustrations resulting to both Pakistan and the United States from their alliance; her desire to retain American support and mollify the Soviet Union at the same time that she cultivated the Chinese. The decision to turn to China can also be viewed as an attempt to align with a power that shared her disposition toward India and, being a lesser power than her former ally, the United States, would be more inclined to treat her as a partner rather than as a satellite. It recalls to mind Richelieu's advice that small states should seek an alliance at the rear of their potential enemy so as to pin down some of its forces in a distant area.

Developing societies reveal a mix of modernity and tradition in their ways of doing things. Pakistan's alliances may also be seen from the perspective of her own cultural tradition. Accustomed, as many developing nations are, to "patron-client" roles, Pakistan has, since the early 1950s, looked for a patron who would protect her interests from Indian encroachment or usurpation and thus put "justice" back on her throne. In return she would give such a patron virtually unlimited loyalty and cooperation. The two nations powerful enough to be patrons—America and Russia—have been anxious to have Pakistan as a client without having to assume the obligations of a patron. They have desired Pakistan's cooperation in expelling the rival power or powers from South Asia, but they have been reluctant to identify themselves with Pakistani goals in relation to India. During the 1950s this was true of China also.

Pakistani reliance on the value of friendship—which, in her own culture, tends to be a relationship of much more extensive mutual obligation than it is in "modern" societies—has been likewise unavailing. It has produced anguish and a sense of betrayal among Pakistani masses, even the intelligentsia. The realization has been slow in coming that the ideas of imperialistic dominance and exploitation, and of limited businesslike relationships when exploitation is not a goal, are more congenial to the "modern" ethos of great powers. In their approaches to Pakistan, the Chinese, also a developing nation, have repeatedly stressed the theme of friendship. Their rhetoric gave their Pakistani listeners the impression that the Chinese notion of friendship was essentially the same as their own (the sort of friendship found in Alexander Dumas's *The Three Musketeers*). But even if the two notions were similar, the logic of the relative coercive capabilities of the powers interested and willing to act in South Asia actually prevailed.

Of Pakistan's own intellectuals, Prime Minister Bhutto alone has written what may be called a prescriptive theory of small-nation behavior. His book, *The Myth of Independence,* is addressed to the problem of how a small state may preserve its independence and protect its interests in the face of a global power's hostile pressure. As Ayub Khan's minister between 1958 and 1966, Mr. Bhutto had the opportunity to influence the direction and substance of Pakistani foreign policy. He is now Pakistan's chief executive, and it is likely that he will continue to direct Pakistani policy in the foreseeable future. It should be instructive to examine his argument.

In the unequal relationship between a global power and a small nation, writes Mr. Bhutto, the former is often able to impose its will on the latter and exact one-sided concessions. Guided by its own national interests, it is unreceptive to the small nation's pleas of justice or righteousness or reminders of past services. Yet, a smaller nation should not, as a matter of course, submit to a global power's dictation. She should attempt to isolate the area of conflict and propose that neither side coerce or call upon the other to change its position on disputed matters. If such "segregation" of conflicting interests has been effected, the global power and the small nation may have mutually advantageous relations in areas where their interests are compatible.

The small nation should avoid conflict with a global power, but if the latter does not agree to the above model of bilateral relations, it is better to take a stand, to have "one sharp crisis," than to let a series of capitulations erode her independence. "Pressure is both a worm and a monster. It is a worm if you stamp on it, but it becomes a monster if you recoil."[6] The small nation's chances of survival in such unequal confrontations will improve if her own resolve to resist pressure is supplemented by the support of other small nations in the third world and the support of those global and great powers with whom she does not have conflicts of interest. "It is largely by the compulsion of these outside forces that the state concerned can bring about a change in the [hostile] Global Power's attitude on the points of difference."[7]

Mr. Bhutto noted that the global powers were engaged in a struggle for hegemony in the world. The Sino-American confrontation, he thought, must one day end, for otherwise it would bring about Asia's ruin. The Sino-Soviet rift, on the other hand, while also regrettable in some ways, might be something of a blessing in disguise for the third world. In its absence, the United States and the Soviet Union would have been inclined to divide the world into spheres of influence, offering China only a secondary role. Such a role China has not accepted. Her insistence on equality of status with the United States and the Soviet Union has acted as a brake on Soviet and American expansionism. This clash at the summit aggravates tensions in world politics, but it also offers "opportunites, which small powers can ill afford to ignore, for the protection of their own vital interests and, indeed, sovereignty."[8] But in exploiting these opportunities, they should proceed with caution: they should adopt a noncommittal attitude and refrain from aligning with one global power against another.

According to Mr. Bhutto, a small nation under pressure from a great or global power should handle her affairs adroitly; propose a limited cooperative relationship to the hostile power and thus dissuade it from being hostile; muster the support of other small nations and sympathetic great and global powers to resist the hostile power if it persists in its policy of pressure; see and take such opportunities as the current conflict among the global powers themselves seems to offer; be more cordial with those who support her causes than with those who do not, without aligning with one global power against another.

In other words, a small nation should make the best of a bad situation and mitigate, as far as possible, the disadvantages implicit in her relative weakness. This is good advice to the extent that it can be followed in the actual conduct of affairs. But global powers, and others, having the requisite means of coercion, are often unwilling to isolate, *and thus abandon,* interests and positions merely because they conflict with those of another state. The noncommittal posture Mr. Bhutto endorses will commend itself to many states to which a small nation under pressure might look for support against a global power. We have seen also that global and great powers are often unwilling, or unable, to translate their sympathy for a small friendly nation into effective support against another global power. It should be noted that in *The Myth of Independence* Mr. Bhutto was responding mainly to American pressure on Pakistan to cooperate with India against China. He was not considering the possibility that harsher pressures might be directed against Pakistan by a Soviet-Indian combination.

Segregation of conflicting interests, bilateralism, and reciprocity are viable strategies of interaction among powers of roughly equal rank, such as the United States and the Soviet Union or, let us say, Pakistan and Yugoslavia. They will work in the relationship between a great power and a small nation if the former's coercive capabilities cannot, for one reason or another,[9] be applied upon the latter. But while means of coercion are available, the expectation that they will not be employed calls for a degree of self-restraint and self-denial on the part of great powers that ought not to be taken for granted. In this connection, Pakistan's own experience in 1971 is instructive.

Mr. Bhutto's note of caution regarding a small state's opportunities arising from the rivalry of great powers is important. A balance-of-power system among the great powers, if and when it prevails, may operate to protect the independence and territorial integrity of smaller states. But great powers are known to have devoured their smaller neighbors through a system of mutual compensations during the heyday of the balance-of-power system in Europe. In more recent times, while a balance of terror prevailed, neither superpower saw fit to interfere with the other's handling of smaller states in its area of influence. But the thaw in the Cold War, and America's developing withdrawal from Asia, are likely to return the smaller states of this region to the life of insecurity generally characteristic of their size. These developments may also increase the freedom of action of major powers, such as India, in their dealings with their smaller neighbors. The foreign-policy makers of smaller states, such as Pakistan, will thus need all the adroitness they can bring to bear on their task. They may also have to redefine their national interests so as to disengage the global or great powers' hostile attention.

Mr. Bhutto wrote that, while Pakistan fervently sought peace, peaceful coexistence with India would remain "out of the question" until India stopped suppressing the cultural, linguistic, and religious identity of her Muslim population and agreed to settle her disputes with Pakistan on the basis of equality and "recognized international merit."[10] The most important of the disputes related to Kashmir, "the handsome head of the body of Pakistan," a Muslim-majority area whose continued inclusion in India negated the two-nation theory and thus the raison d'être of Pakistan![11] Bhutto recognized that India was more powerful but argued that this relative inequality was counterbalanced by the following factors:

... the justice of Pakistan's cause, the spirit of her people, the collaboration of the people of Jammu and Kashmir who resent India's occupation of their land and seek to join Pakistan in a common brotherhood, and the overwhelming support she has received from other countries, including that of the People's Republic of China.[12]

This argument and the model of small-nation behavior outlined above were made in 1967. Subsequent events—the civil war and the war with India in 1971—were to show that Mr. Bhutto's estimates of the Pakistani national resolve, the relative power positions of Pakistan and India, and the prospect of external assistance were less than cautious. Since he became the chief executive in December 1971, he has repeatedly called for an end to the era of confrontation with India. But he insists also that Pakistan's foreign policy is based on principles which his government will uphold. This apparently moralistic position is more than an expression of his own predisposition to defiance in face of adversity. It accommodates the insight, well known to political theorists, that resort to principles, and the implicit appeal to the conscience of mankind, may at times be of some supplemental use to small states in unequal confrontations. In a recent interview with this writer, Prime Minister Bhutto expressed the view that insistence on moral principles of international behavior was vital to Pakistan's defense. Thus it is that he continues to call for a "just and honorable" settlement in Kashmir.

Some aspects of the Kashmir problem need to be spelled out. India has the larger and the more attractive part of this territory and has no intention of giving it up. Pakistan does not have the capability of taking it away by force. In a bargaining situation, if one were to materialize, Pakistan's only talking point—other than the moral necessity of keeping one's covenants, to which India is not receptive—is that in the absence of a "just" settlement Indo-Pakistan "amity" will not come about. While India desires such amity, possibly with a view to blunting the sharp edge of the partition of 1947, she is not willing to trade Kashmir for Pakistani goodwill the prospect of which, in her calculation, is in any case uncertain. It might appear then that Pakistan would not gain from perpetuating the dispute. At the same time, it would be an oversimplification to suggest that the ruling elite in Pakistan have maintained the confrontation with India and kept up the Kashmir dispute as tactics of their own political survival. On these matters mass opinion in Pakistan, especially in the Punjab, which has more than 60 percent of the nation's population, is much more inflexible than elite attitudes. Nevertheless, it must indeed be surprising to students of politics that few Pakistani commentators, if any, have argued that a Kashmir settlement made on the basis of the best obtainable terms at a given time need not preclude the possibility of reopening the issue when relevant circumstances have changed. Countless examples from the experience of various nations, including that of India in her dealings with Pakistan, can be found to show that international engagements are not eternally binding.

The argument that India's continued possession of Kashmir, a Muslim-majority area, negates the two-nation theory and thus the raison d'être of Pakistan is disastrous for the Pakistani psyche, for it places the rationale of Pakistani nationhood within India's will and power to destroy. In some ways, the two-nation theory[13] has become a millstone around the Pakistani nation's neck. Indian commentators have recently argued that East Pakistan's secession has invalidated the two-nation theory and abolished the justification for Pakistan's continued existence. Many rightist Pakistani politicians and intellectuals, alarmed and confused by the Indian taunt, have in effect embraced the Indian interpretation and insisted that Pakistan's recognition of Bangladesh will destroy the two-nation theory and dismantle the remaining Pakistan.

Yet, some nation-preserving perspectives are also possible. The two-nation theory may be viewed as a representation of the Indian Muslims' state of mind during a given historical period that intensified their struggle for achieving political separation from a Hindu-dominated polity. But after the separation was achieved and Pakistan established, its work done, this ideological midwife should have been discharged and the doctors called in to prescribe for the new nation's growth and development. If pressed into continued service, the theory would function as an ideology of confrontation with India. But it lacked the capacity to lead the infant nation toward adulthood and maturity. After independence centrifugal forces were bound to assert themselves. The bonds of unity forged during the struggle for independence would begin to loosen. Pakistan needed an egalitarian ideology that would give her diverse people a powerful stake in remaining united in a common nationhood.

Nationalism and nationhood are, first and foremost, states of mind. Pakistan's continued existence as a nation does not, any longer, depend on the merits of the two-nation theory. It depends on whether Punjabis, Sindhis, Pathans, and Baluchis desire, despite their regional loyalties, to remain together as a nation. No American will seriously contend that the United States should dissolve herself as an independent nation because certain propositions in the Declaration of Independence, which provided the ideological justification for America's separation from Britain in 1776, are "wrong." Three cheers for the Declaration, one might indeed say, even if it was wrong, for it brought independence and countless blessings to succeeding generations of Americans. Pakistanis might usefully adopt a similar approach.

No overall foreign or domestic policy design can be viable without a balancing of ends and means. It is precisely the difficulty of striking such a balance that makes the survival of small states precarious. Specific foreign policies may temporarily correct the imbalance by supplementing domestic resources with foreign assistance. But such advantage may be offset by losses at home if heavy reliance on foreign policy has produced neglect of domestic concerns. In the scale of means, as I have argued above, one must reckon domestic cohesion—no less than weapons of war—as an essential ingredient of a nation's capacity to resist external pressure. The events of 1971 showed how fragile Pakistan's nationhood had been. They showed also that the nationhood of a culturally diverse people coming into a federal union cannot be taken for granted. Consolidation must be pursued as a high priority goal of public policy to which political and economic resources commensurate with the magnitude of the task must be committed.[14]

In Pakistan participatory and egalitarian urges were denied for a long time on the reasoning that a foreign enemy stood at the door. But the more these urges were neglected and, consequently, national cohesion weakened, the greater the potential for foreign intervention and pressure became. In other words, domestic repression and foreign pressure interacted in something like a vicious circle. This problem persists: reference has already been made to the existence of separatist movements in Baluchistan and the North West Frontier Province and related external pressures. One does not have to choose between domestic and foreign policy approaches to the problem of national security. But the question of focus is relevant. A Pakistani policy of limited accommodation with India and the Soviet Union, not inconsistent with her relationship with China, may reduce the dimensions of her security problem and thus reduce the imbalance between her ends and means. But such a corrective would be all too transient if the domestic resource base continued to erode, making the scale of means progressively lighter. In the long run, no amount of concession to the foreigner will ensure Pakistani security and independence if domestic cohesion and a national resolve to defend and maintain her territorial integrity are wanting.

Appendix 1

A Biographical Note

Many of the Pakistani names mentioned in the text are likely to be unfamiliar to the reader. Some biographical detail may enlarge his perspective on the issues involved, even if causal connections between the actors' backgrounds and their policy roles cannot be made.

Pakistani leaders have been singularly uncommunicative about their personal lives and professional careers. With the exception of Ayub Khan, Firoz Khan Noon, and Zulfikar Ali Bhutto, whose writings were cited earlier, none of the notables mentioned in this volume has written of his role. A disposition to taciturnity on the part of career officials might be attributed to the norm which requires them to be self-effacing. But that does not apply to politicians or retired officials. Nor is the Official Secrets Act so thoroughly forbidding. A better explanation might be found in the essentially antiintellectual biases of Pakistan's bureaucratic tradition, which pervades even nongovernmental institutions with intimidating effect.

Pakistani scholars have also shied away from the subject of political or bureaucratic leadership—but not the sycophants or genuine admirers. Several men wrote poetic prose in praise of Ayub Khan: Col. Mohammad Ahmad, *My Chief* (Lahore: Longmans, Green, 1960); S. A. Saeed, *President without Precedent* (Lahore: Lahore Book Depot, n.d.); M. H. Bhatti, *The Saviour of Pakistan,* (Lahore: Star Book Depot, 1960). A number of books on Bhutto have already appeared: Mahmood Sham, *Larkana Se Peking* [Urdu] (Karachi: National Forum, 1972); Khalid Kasmiri, *Awam Ka Sadar* [Urdu] (Lahore: Munib Publications, 1972); Yunas Adeeb, *Quaid-e-Awam* [Urdu] (Lahore: Makataba-e-Pakistan, 1972); Qazi Zulfikar Ahmad and Rana Mahmood-ul-Ahsan, *Zulfikar Ali Bhutto* [Urdu] (Lahore: Moallam Publishing House, 1973); Rana Rahman Zafar, *Zulfikar Ali Bhutto [Urdu] (Lahore: Khyber Publishers, 1973); Fakhar Zaman and Akhtar Aman, Z. A. Bhutto: The Political Thinker* (Lahore: The People's Publications, 1973).

Two less enthusiastic accounts of Bhutto's career have been published in India. His old friend, Piloo Mody, now president of the Swatantra party, has written *Zulfi My Friend* (Delhi: Thomson, 1973). An Indian journalist, Dilip Mukerjee, has produced *Zulfikar Ali Bhutto: Quest for Power* (Delhi: Vikas, 1972). More objective analyses of Ayub Khan and Bhutto will be found in Lawrence Ziring, *Ayub Khan Era: Politics in Pakistan, 1958–1969* (Syracuse: Syracuse University Press, 1971) and Herbert Feldman, *From Crisis to Crisis: Pakistan 1962–1969* (London: Oxford, 1972).

The following short notes on individuals who were influential in the making of Pakistani policy—the policy of alignment with the United States and then the policy of an entente cordiale with China—may be helpful.

Aziz Ahmad (1906–), minister of state for defense and foreign affairs—formerly foreign secretary, ambassador to the United States, secretary-general to the government of Pakistan, chief secretary to the government of East Pakistan—was educated at the University of the Punjab in Lahore and later at Cambridge University. He entered the Indian Civil Service (ICS) in 1930 and has been known for the qualities—both attractive and unattractive—typically associated with that elite class of colonial civil servants. During the early 1960s he, as foreign secretary, carried forward Pakistan's developing relationship with China. Currently, he is Pakistan's principal negotiator with India.

Chaudhuri Mohammad Ali (1905–), prime minister of Pakistan (1955–56) and finance minister (1951–54), received a master's degree in chemistry from the University of the Punjab in 1926. Two years later he entered the Indian Audit and Accounts Service and, after serving in various posts in the field of financial administration, became secretary-general to the government of Pakistan in 1947, a position which he held until 1951. A mild and moderate person, a perfect gentleman, justly famous for his administrative talent, sincerity of purpose, and patriotism, Chaudhuri Mohammad Ali was never much of a politician. The adoption of the 1956 constitution must be reckoned as the only significant event of his prime ministership. He gave no indication of entertaining any innovative ideas regarding Pakistan's foreign policy.

Maulana Abdul Hamid Khan Bhashani (1885-), Born in Pabna and once a primary school teacher in Mymensingh, president of the pro-Peking National Awami Party, which he formed in 1957—has been, for decades, a most influential peasant leader in East Pakistan (now Bangladesh). A son of the soil, without a trace of westernization in his bearing or life style, educated in a local madrasah and partly at the famous seminary of Deoband, the Maulana has devoted his life to the development of political consciousness among the poor and the oppressed. A great admirer of Mao Tsetung and his revolution, he refrained from opposing Ayub Khan's exploitative despotism, reportedly because of the latter's policy of establishing friendly relations with China. Bhashani never held governmental office.

Zulfikar Ali Bhutto (1928-), prime minister of Pakistan, chairman of the ruling Pakistan People's Party (PPP)—formerly Ayub Khan's foreign minister (1963-66) and minister holding other portfolios (1958-63)—was educated at the Cathedral and John Connon School in Bombay, University of California at Berkeley, and Oxford University and was called to the bar from Lincoln's Inn (London) in 1952. Bhutto became immensely popular in West Pakistan as a result of his tough posture toward India, his dissociation with the Indo-Pakistan agreement at Tashkent in January, 1966, his vigorous opposition to the Ayubian order, and his espousal of "Islamic socialism." Young, vivacious, dynamic, exceedingly well read, articulate, fluent, controversial, Bhutto is the first mass leader, commanding a large following, to have appeared on West Pakistan's political scene during the last quarter century. He claims to have been the main initiator, if not the sole author, of Pakistan's trend toward an "independent" foreign policy and her policy of seeking cordial relations with China.

Mohammad Ali Bogra (1901–63)—Pakistan's prime minister (1953–55), foreign minister (1962–63), twice ambassador to the United States and, earlier, ambassador to Burma and Canada—graduated from Calcutta University in 1930. A member of the Bengal Legislative Assembly (1937–47), he served briefly as a minister in the preindependence Bengal government. As a politician his talent and support base were modest. He owed his appointment to, and dismissal from, the office of prime minister to the arbitrary will of a bureaucratic governor-general, namely, Ghulam Mohammad. Bogra's honesty, forthrightness, and personal warmth inspired confidence and endeared him to many at home and abroad. He was Pakistan's most popular ambassador in Washington. He was also the first Pakistani leader to have opened a dialogue with China's Chou En-lai.

S. K. Dehlavi (1913–) foreign secretary (1961-63), was educated at the University of Bombay and Oxford University, entered the Indian Civil Service in 1938, and transferred to the Pakistan Foreign Service soon after independence. Convinced that India meant to harm Pakistan and that the United States would not aid her against India, he became, during his tenure as foreign secretary, the most vigorous and effective Foreign Office spokesman for a policy of delinking Pakistan from America's global strategy and seeking a cordial relationship with China.

Mohammad Ikramullah (1903–63), foreign secretary (1947–51, 1959–60), was educated at the University of Allahabad and Cambridge University and entered the Indian Civil Service in 1926. Before coming to the Pakistan Foreign Office, he had represented the government of British India at numerous international forums and conferences.

Mohammad Ayub Khan (1907–)—president of Pakistan (1958–69), commander in chief of the Pakistan army (1951–58), and defense minister (1954–56)—was educated at the Aligarh Muslim University and the Royal Military Academy at Sandhurst. In collaboration with President Iskander Mirza, whom he soon sent away to exile in London, Ayub Khan seized power in a coup d'état in October, 1958. He hated the craft of politics and, ideally, would have liked to make Pakistan into a politics-free society. The despotism, corruption, and arbitrariness associated with his rule destroyed its legitimacy. A popular uprising overthrew him in March, 1969.

Ayub Khan possessed considerable organizing ability. An impressive appearance, a congenial personality, and a much advertised "no-nonsense" directness of approach won him a reasonably good press abroad. While basically antiintellectual, he had plenty of common sense. He knew how to attach individuals to himself and did so. During much of his rule, he commanded the loyalty of the propertied classes in Pakistan, including the higher bureaucracy. According to some observers, he was much troubled by the awareness that his social origins had been modest: he was the son of a noncommissioned officer in the Indian army, a mere "risaldar-major." Behind the apparent firmness and affability, there stood a lonely man "who, in essence, kept his own counsel and made his own decisions." In the end, he fell because power had corrupted him, because "the fibre of the man did not correspond to the manner of his address and was unequal to the necessities of his mission" (Feldman, *From Crisis to Crisis, p. 296*).

Ayub Khan claimed that he himself had been the author of independence, "bilateralism," and a shift toward China in Pakistani foreign policy. (In the two chapters on foreign policy in his book, *Friends Not Masters,* Bhutto, his foreign minister, is not mentioned.) But note that in the early 1950s he had been among the principal advocates of a military alliance with the United States, a connection he was always loath to break.

Sir Muhammad Zafrullah Khan (1893–), Pakistan's first foreign minister (1947–54) and more recently president of the International Court of Justice at The Hague, was educated at Government College, Lahore, and King's College, London. Called to the bar from Lincoln's Inn (London), he became one of the more distinguished lawyers and jurists in British India. He served as a judge of the Federal Court, attended the Round Table Conferences on India in 1930, 1931, and 1932, and represented the government of British

India at numerous international conferences. He was a member of the viceroy's Executive Council from 1935 to 1941 and in 1942 served as his agent-general in China. Much more of a jurist than politician, Sir Muhammad shared the pro-Western orientation of his colleagues in the government of Pakistan while he was foreign minister.

Sultan Mohammad Khan (1919–), Pakistan's ambassador to the United States, formerly foreign secretary (1970–72) and ambassador to China (1966–68), was educated at Allahabad University. He received a commission in the Indian army in 1942, entered the Indian Political Service in 1946 and the Pakistan Foreign Service in 1949. One of Pakistan's ablest diplomats, he too, in his turn and time, served to advance friendly relations between Pakistan and China.

Gen. Agha Mohammad Yahya Khan (1917–)—currently under house arrest for bungling the East Pakistan crisis and the war with India in 1971, president of Pakistan (1969–71), commander in chief of the army (1966–69), division commander during the 1965 war with India, general officer commanding in East Pakistan (1962–64), chief of the army General Staff (1957–62)—was educated at the University of the Punjab and the Indian Military Academy in Dheradun. Yahya Khan can claim the distinction of having held, in 1970, the one and only general election in Pakistan's history and, by all accounts, an honest and fair one. During 1971 he acted as an "honest broker" to facilitate Henry Kissinger's mission to Peking. With regard to the East Pakistan crisis and the war with India, his own side of the story remains to be told.

Iskander Mirza (1890–1970), president of Pakistan (1956–58), was educated at Elphinstone College, Bombay, and the Royal Military Academy at Sandhurst. After a few years in the Indian army, he entered the Indian Political Service in 1926 and served in the North West Frontier Province as a political agent and district officer. He rose to be a joint secretary in the Indian Ministry of Defense (1946–47), defense secretary in the government of Pakistan (1947–54), governor of East Pakistan (1954), interior minister (1954–55), and governor-general of Pakistan (1955–56). One of the early advocates of Pakistan's military alliance with the United States, Mirza was the more notable for his contempt for politics and politicians, his espousal of "controlled democracy," his blatant and unconstitutional interference in party politics, his making and unmaking of prime ministers through political intrigue, his self-aggrandizement, and his abrogation of constitutional government in 1958.

Ghulam Mohammad (1895–56), governor-general of Pakistan (1951–55) and finance minister (1947–51), was educated at Aligarh Muslim University, entered the Indian Audit and Accounts Service in 1920 and served the government of British India and the princely states of Bhopal and Hyderabad in various posts connected with financial administration. A man of exceptional administrative ability and an immense will to power, Ghulam Mohammad, as governor-general, subverted the constitution, dismissed a prime minister who commanded majority support in Parliament, dismissed Parliament itself, appointed a puppet prime minister, and ruled Pakistan despite a semiparalytic condition. A bureaucrat himself, he had the support of the higher bureaucracy and at least the acquiescence of the army in his suppression of constitutional government. Contemptuous of democratic politics, he was the first of a train of tyrants with whom Pakistan was to be afflicted. Along with Ayub Khan and Iskander Mirza, he was the moving spirit behind Pakistan's quest for a military alliance with the United States.

Malik Firoz Khan Noon (1893–1971)—Knight Bachelor, Knight of St. John of Jerusalem, K.C.I.E., K.C.S.I., Pakistan's last prime minister (1957–58) under the 1956 constitution, and foreign minister (1956–57)—came from a family of great landlords in the Sargodha district of Punjab. He was educated at Aitchison College in Lahore (popularly known as the Chiefs' College) and at Wadham College, Oxford, of which he later became an honorary fellow. A barrister-at-law of the Inner Temple (London), he preferred politics, which, at the time, were dominated by landed aristocrats loyal to British rule. He served as a minister in the Punjab government (1927–36), as the Indian high commissioner in London (1941–45), and as a member of the viceroy's Executive Council (1941–45). In Pakistan he served as governor of East Pakistan (1950–53), chief minister of Punjab (1953–55), and foreign minister (1956–57). One of the few Pakistani politicians to have written books, some of which were published in England, his memoirs—*From Memory* (Lahore: Ferozsons, 1969)—make interesting reading. An aristocratic gentleman, and essentially a drawing-room politician, Noon once threatened an "agonizing reappraisal" of Pakistan's pro-western policy, but this was generally regarded as a bluff.

Manzur Qadir (1913–), foreign minister of Pakistan (1958-62), was educated at the University of the Punjab and Oxford University and was called to the bar from Lincoln's Inn (London) in 1935. Brilliant, articulate, eloquent, he is one of Pakistan's most eminent jurists. It was during his term of office at the Foreign Ministry that a Pakistani proposal for a border agreement was first made to Peking.

Nawabzada A. M. Raza (1905–)—foreign secretary in charge of administration, twice ambassador to China—comes from an aristocratic Persian-speaking family of Kizilbash nawabs in Lahore. Educated at Bishop Cotton's School in Simla and the Royal Military Academy in Sandhurst, he was commissioned in the Indian army in 1927. A major general when he entered the Foreign Service in 1951, he is said to have had personal rapport with Chou En-lai. He aided Prime Minister Bogra's talks with the Chinese premier at Bandung in 1955 and, in 1962, negotiated the border agreement with Chinese officials. Frankness, sincerity, and personal warmth—enhanced by an apparent incapacity for deviousness—are among his more attractive qualifications.

Agha Shahi (1920–), foreign secretary, briefly ambassador in Peking, and Pakistan's permanent representative at the United Nations (1967–72), graduated from Madras University in 1941 and received a law degree from Allahabad University in 1943. He joined the Indian Civil Service the same year (1943) and, after serving in various capacities in the cadre, entered the Pakistan Foreign Service in 1951. He accompanied Prime Minister Bogra to the Bandung Conference in 1955. In the early 1960s he was one of those in the Foreign Office who argued for a new, and more friendly, China policy.

Husain Shaheed Suhrawardy (1893–1963), prime minister of Pakistan (1956–57) and law minister (1954–55), came from an aristocratic Bengali family long renowned for its learning and public service. He was educated at St. Xavier's College in Calcutta and at Oxford University. Before independence he had been chief minister of Bengal (1946-47) and, before that, a minister holding various portfolios. Suhrawardy was among the nation's most outstanding lawyers and ablest politicians. The greater part of his political career in Pakistan was spent in opposing the government of the day. He founded the Awami League in 1949, which prospered in East Pakistan but not in West Pakistan. A truly well-educated man, a fluent speaker, and a powerful advocate, Suhrawardy was given to certain frivolities in personal life that detracted from his political effectiveness. In foreign policy he was strongly pro-Western.

Appendix 2

A Chronology of Sino-Pakistan Relations 1955-72*

1955

Prime Minister Bogra of Pakistan tells reporters that the five principles of peaceful coexistence announced by Nehru and Chou En-lai are not adequate (Apr. 17).

Bogra and Chou En-lai have meetings in Bandung (Apr. 19–22).

At an independence day reception in the Pakistan Embassy in Peking, Chou En-lai says economic and cultural ties between the two countries are growing "with each passing day" (Aug. 14).

A delegation of Chinese women, led by Health Minister Madam Li Teh Chaun, visits Pakistan (Nov.).

A Chinese trade delegation discusses a possible trade agreement with the government of East Pakistan (Nov.).

The prime minister of Pakistan accepts an invitation to visit China (Dec. 1).

1956

Vice-Chairman Madam Soong Ching Ling arrives in Karachi on an eight–day visit (Jan. 24).

*Pakistan recognized the People's Republic of China on January 4, 1950, but significant interaction between them did not begin until 1955. This chronology should be read as a supplement, not as a "capsule" version of the preceding text. Most of the entries have been taken from a much larger chronology of national and international affairs printed in each issue of *Pakistan Horizon*, Journal of the Pakistan Institute of International Affairs.

Vice-Chairman Marshal Ho Lung attends the inauguration of the Islamic Republic of Pakistan (Mar. 23-25).

Prime Minister Mohammad Ali says his intended visit to China does·not indicate any change in his foreign policy (May 2).

Pakistan arranges to buy 300,000 tons of Chinese coal (May 10).

A Pakistan-China Friendship Association is formed (May).

Prime Minister Mohammad Ali cancels his visit to China, scheduled for June 2, because of "illness" (May 30).

Sixteen Pakistani newspaper editors visit China at the invitation of the All-China Journalists' Federation. Addressing them, Chou En-lai reaffirms his desire for closer and friendlier relations with Pakistan and asserts there is a historic link between the two peoples (June 15).

An exhibition of Chinese Arts and Crafts opens in Dacca (Sept.).

Prime Minister Suhrawardy arrives in Peking for a twelve–day official visit (Oct. 18).

Chou En-lai, accompanied by Marshal Ho Lung, arrives in Karachi for a state visit (Dec. 20).

1957

Chou En-lai appeals to Pakistan and India to settle their Kashmir dispute through bilateral negotiations (Feb. 5).

Prime Minister Suhrawardy of Pakistan turns down Chou's suggestion (Feb. 15).

A ten–member Pakistani group of Parliamentarians goes on a goodwill visit to China (June).

Pakistan welcomes Mao's reported statement that China would not take sides in the Kashmir dispute (July 20).

1958

A seven–member team of Pakistani labor leaders goes on a three–week tour of China at the invitation of the All China Trade Union Federation (Apr.-May).

China offers to supply Pakistan machinery and capital equipment in exchange for Pakistani cotton and other raw materials
(Apr. 28).

Pakistan signs a barter trade agreement with China (Aug. 8).

1959

A parcel post service between Pakistan and China is introduced
(Oct.).

Manzur Qadir wonders why Nehru takes "slap after slap" from
the Chinese (Oct. 14).

President Ayub warns the Western democracies that a Soviet-
Chinese drive to the Indian Ocean is a "major aim in the Communist drive for world domination" (Nov. 18).

Pakistan says she will not accept the creation of a "no-man's
land" in Ladakh as proposed by Nehru to Chou En-lai (Nov 23).

1960

Manzur Qadir says China's admission to the U. N. would not mitigate her expansionist urges (May 30).

Z.A. Bhutto tells reporters at the U. N. that China has made
"incursions" into Kashmir (Oct. 21).

1961

Manzur Qadir reports China has, in principle, agreed to discuss
border demarcation with Pakistan (Jan. 15).

President Ayub says in London that Pakistan would probably
vote for China's admission to the U. N. at the next General
Assembly session (Mar. 18).

Pakistan's ambassador to the U. N. says China should be seated
in the U. N. (Aug. 17).

Pakistan votes in favor of seating China at the U. N. (Dec.).

1962

Pakistan and China announce agreement to negotiate border demarcation (May 3).

Pakistani press reports suggest the possibility of a treaty of friendship between China and Pakistan (May 25).

Sino-Pakistan border demarcation talks open in Peking (Oct. 12).

The Pakistani press reports that China has offered Pakistan a nonaggression pact (Nov. 23).

Z.A. Bhutto assures the National Assembly that Pakistan will continue to develop friendly ties with China (Dec. 4).

Pakistan and China announce agreement in principle regarding the alignment of their common border (Dec. 28).

1963

Pakistan and China sign trade agreement based on "most-favored nation treatment" in trade, commerce and shipping. Chinese delegation offers Pakistan long–term credit and technical assistance for setting up small and medium sized industries (Jan. 6).

Pakistan and China conclude an agreement in Peking provisionally delimiting their common border (Mar. 2).

A joint communiqué in Peking declares Chinese appreciation of Pakistan's stand in the Kashmir dispute with India (Mar. 4).

Chinese survey experts arrive in Pakistan to discuss boundary demarcation arrangement with the surveyor-general of Pakistan (June 8).

A joint China-Pakistan Boundary Commission agrees on procedure and method of work in relation to boundary demarcation (June 13).

Pakistan and China sign an air transport agreement allowing their airlines, PIA and CAAC, to operate over each other's territory with landing and other facilities. They also agree to establish, if and when necessary, an air link between Lahore and Sinkiang (Aug. 29).

A direct radio–photo telegraph service is inaugurated between Karachi and Peking (Sept. 16).

Pakistan and China sign a barter trade agreement for the exchange of Pakistani raw jute with coal and cement from China (Sept. 30).

Pakistan supports a General Assembly move to seat China in the U. N. (Oct. 17).

1964

Chou En-lai, with a party of 48 members, including Vice-premier and Foreign Minister Chen Yi, arrives on an eight–day official visit to Pakistan (Feb 18).

President Ayub accepts an invitation to visit China (Feb. 23).

Pakistan National Assembly speaker is invited to lead a parliamèntary delegation to China (Mar. 7).

PIA inaugural flight to China arrives in Shanghai (Apr. 29).

Mao Tse-tung receives the Pakistan Commerce Minister in Peking (July 16).

China offers a $60 million interest–free, long–term loan to Pakistan (July 31).

Pakistan announces that the old caravan route between Sinkiang and Gilgit might be reopened (Sept. 30).

A Pakistani delegation visits China to negotiate utilization of the $60 million Chinese loan (Oct. 27).

The Chinese foreign minister, during a stopover in Karachi, states that he favors a Kashmir plebescite (Oct. 30).

China indicates the possibility of additional interest–free credit to Pakistan (Nov. 3).

It is announced that a regular shipping service between Pakistan and China will begin in March 1965 (Dec. 14).

1965

It is announced that President Ayub Khan will pay a state visit to China beginning March 2, 1965 (Feb. 9).

President Ayub Kahn and other officials leave for Peking on an eight-day visit to China (Mar. 2).

Pakistan and China sign a boundary protocol and a cultural agreement (Mar. 25).

Chou En-lai arrives in Karachi for an official visit (Apr. 2).

Pakistan and China agree to issue free visas to each other's citizens (May 10).

Chou En-lai arrives in Rawalpindi (June 2).

Chou En-lai describes Sino-Pakistan friendship as a factor for world peace, since both are opposed to war and aggression (June 19).

President Ayub meets Chou En-lai in Cairo. (June 28).

China promises interest-free loans for Pakistan's heavy engineering projects (Aug. 3).

During a stopover in Karachi Marshal Chen Yi reaffirms his government's support for Kashmiris' right of self-determination (Sept. 4).

China condemns India's "criminal aggression" against Pakistan (Sept. 7). During the following weeks numerous condemnations of India and accusations of Indian violations of Chinese territory, including two ultimata, are issued from Peking.

A Pakistani civil aviation team and a friendship mission visit Peking (Sept. 29).

China and Pakistan sign an agreement regarding the production program and other technical details of a proposed heavy mechanical complex in Pakistan (Nov. 14).

Marshal Chen Yi warns India against launching another armed aggression against Pakistan and reiterates Chinese intention to "support Pakistan in her just struggle against Indian aggression" (Dec. 2).

1966

Bhutto denies that China poses a threat to the Indo–Pakistan subcontinent (Feb. 20).

Liu Shao-Chi arrives in Pakistan for a five-day state visit (Mar. 26).

Liu Shao-Chi arrives in Dacca for a two-day state visit (Apr. 15).

Pakistan and China adopt an annual program of scientific and cultural exchange (June 1).

Chou En-lai arrives in Rawalpindi on a two-day unofficial visit to Pakistan (June 28).

Pakistan and China sign a trade protocol (July 4).

China and Pakistan sign a barter agreement for Pakistan to import 100,000 tons of Chinese rice (Aug. 2).

Pakistan and China conclude a shipping agreement (Oct. 21).

Bhutto pays a goodwill visit to China (Oct. 22).

1967

China agrees to supply 150,000 tons of foodgrains to Pakistan over the next five months (Jan. 17).

Pakistan and China sign an accord whereby China agrees to supply 600,000 rupees worth of equipment for a training institute to be attached to the projected heavy mechanical complex at Taxila (Mar. 3).

China successfully explodes her first hydrogen bomb (June 17).

China agrees to supply 100,000 tons of rice to Pakistan (Aug. 2).

Chinese Red Cross donates 50,000 Yuans to the Pakistani Red Cross for relief of the "rain-stricken" people of Karachi (Aug. 12).

Entertaining a visiting Pakistani delegation in Peking, Vice-Premier Nieh Jung Chen assures Chinese support for Pakistan's struggle against foreign aggression and interference (Sept. 29).

Pakistan and China sign an agreement to facilitate overland trade between Pakistini Gilgit and Chinese Sinkiang (Oct. 21).

Pakistan calls for the restoration of China's rights in the U. N. (Nov. 17).

At a Pakistan embassy dinner in Peking Chen Yi says Sino–Pakistan friendship is based on "mutual cooperation and respect" (Dec. 20).

1968

Pakistan and China sign a barter agreement for exchanging goods worth 11 million rupees during the following year (April 27).

China agrees to provide technical help to Pakistan for projects in the Fourth Five–Year Plan (May 22).

Pakistan announces China is helping build an ordnance factory in East Pakistan (June 24).

A Chinese–aided training school and a workshop at the heavy mechanical complex in Taxila are inaugurated (June 25).

Pakistan declares that friendship with China is a cardinal principle of her foreign policy (June 29).

China agrees to supply machinery worth 15 million rupees for the heavy mechanical complex in Taxila (July 26).

The Pakistan foreign minister announces that China is willing to assist in the control of floods in East Pakistan (Aug. 10).

Presidential advisor Fida Hasan, heading a goodwill mission, arrives in China (Sept. 28).

A Pakistani delegation goes to Kashgar to discuss exchange of goods between Sinkiang and the northern areas of Pakistan through the old caravan route (Nov. 3).

A Pakistani military delegation, led by General A. M. Yahya Khan, visits China (Nov. 7).

China extends a 200–million rupees credit to Pakistan (Dec. 26).

1969

China reaffirms support for the Kashmiri people's right of self–determination (May 5).

At Chou En-lai's dinner in his honor in Peking, Pakistan's Air Marshal Nur Khan says U. N. effectiveness will remain limited until China is properly represented (July 13).

The arrival of a Chinese trade caravan in Misgar on the Pakistan border marks the reopening of the historic "Silk Route" between China and Pakistan. The caravan leader reiterates firm Chinese support for the people of Kashmir (Aug. 14).

Pakistan Army Chief of Staff General Abdul Hamid Khan arrives for the People's Republic's anniversary celebrations and meets Chou En-lai (Oct. 2).

Pakistan asks for the restoration of China's lawful right of representation in the U. N. (Nov. 19).

1970

Kuo Mo-jo, a standing committee vice-chairman of China's National Peoples Congress, meets President Yahya Khan while visiting Pakistan (Mar. 11).

China offers assistance for Pakistan's Fourth Five-Year Plan (Mar. 22).

A Chinese economic mission arrives in Pakistan (Apr. 4).

Pakistan and China sign an agreement providing for Chinese assistance to four development projects in Pakistan (Apr. 9).

Pakistan and China sign in Peking the Third General Barter Trade Agreement, which provides for exchange of goods worth 116 million rupees on a self-balancing basis (May 5).

A Chinese trade delegation headed by Lien Cheng-Hsien, member of the Revolutionary Committee of Sinkiang, arrives in Pakistan (May 15).

Pakistan and China sign an agreement for further development of trade among the border areas of Gilgit and Baltistan and Sinkiang during 1970-71 (May 21).

Pakistan's Air Marshall A. Rahim arrives in Peking (May 31).

Pakistan announces a plan to import 100,000 tons of Chinese rice in exchange for Pakistani commodities (June 6).

Pakistan's navy chief arrives in Peking (Sept. 19).

President Yahya Khan arrives in Peking on a five-day state visit (Nov. 10).

Pakistan and China sign an agreement for an interest-free Chinese loan of over $200 million for Pakistan's Fourth Five-Year Plan (Nov. 14).

1971

A Chinese delegation, headed by Communications Minister Yang Chieh, arrives in Pakistan to attend the opening of the Karakorum highway linking Gilgit with Sinkiang (Feb. 12).

China accuses India of "flagrantly interfering in the internal affairs of Pakistan" (Apr. 6).

In a message to President Yahya Khan of Pakistan Premier Chou En-lai assures support "should the Indians dare to launch aggression against Pakistan" (Apr. 12).

Pakistani sources report that to date China has pledged a total of $307 million in economic assistance to Pakistan, including the $200 million pledge announced in November 1970 (May 15).

A Sino-Pakistan border trade agreement is signed in Sinkiang (May 29).

Pakistan and China sign a new trade agreement for exchange of goods between Gilgit and Sinkiang via the ancient Silk Route (July 12).

China transfers to Pakistan ownership of two branches of the Bank of China situated in Karachi and Chittagong (Aug. 5).

Air Vice-Marshal Zafar Ahmad Chaudhury, managing director PIA, announces his intended visit to Peking to negotiate a new air route linking West Pakistan and China over the Karakorum mountains (Aug. 10).

China agrees to supply 100,000 metric tons of rice to East Pakistan (Sept. 4).

Z.A. Bhutto, PPP chairman, arrives in Peking as personal representative of the president of Pakistan. He is accompanied by a large delegation of military leaders and top officials including the commanders in chief of the army, navy and air force (Nov. 5).

A delegation led by Chinese Minister for Machine Building Li Shui-Ching arrives in Pakistan (Nov. 24).

The Chinese acting foreign minister reiterates support for Pakistan in her struggle against India. The Chinese premier makes a similar statement in an interview with the *Sunday Times* (Dec. 4).

Authoritative diplomatic sources reveal in Peking that Chinese officials are maintaining an hour-by-hour contact with Pakistani diplomats in Peking in view of the Indian invasion of Pakistan (Dec. 5).

In an official statement China pledges continued political support and "material assistance" to the Pakistan government and people in their struggle against "aggression, division and subversion" (Dec. 16).

1972

The president of Pakistan, Z.A. Bhutto, arrives in Peking (Jan. 31).

Pakistan and China sign a new border trade agreement (May 7).

Pakistan and China sign a trade agreement for 1972–73 (June 23).

The Chinese minister for foreign trade arrives in Lahore (June 25).

President Bhutto declares that China will veto any attempt to seat Bangladesh at the U. N. until Bangladesh and India implement the U. N. resolutions of December 7 and 21, 1971 (Aug. 10).

Pakistan's minister for production expresses the hope that a steel mill set up with Chinese assistance will start production in three years (Aug. 12).

In the U. N. Security Council China vetoes Bangladesh's application for U. N. membership (Aug. 25).

Chinese Vice Foreign Minister Chiao Kuan-hua arrives in Islamabad for a two–day visit (Aug. 28).

It is officially announced that China will help in setting up two medium–sized steel mills in Pakistan (Nov. 17).

China and Pakistan sign an agreement under which Pakistan will export 40 million rupees worth of cotton yarn, textiles, and hosiery goods to China (Dec. 29).

Appendix 3 Pakistan's External Indebtedness and Commitment of Foreign Aid

Outstanding External Indebtedness of Pakistan as on June 30, 1972 (U.S. $ million)

Lending country / agency	Disbursed and out-standing	Undis-bursed	Total Debt
1	2	3	4
I. Consortium			
Belgium			
Capital Aid	5.293	0.843	6.136
Export Credit	2.828	—	2.828
Sub-total (Belgium)	8.121	0.843	8.964
Canada			
Capital Aid	114.900	8.831	123.731
France			
Export Credit	36.325	15.854	52.089
Germany			
Capital Aid	276.789	29.885	306.674
Export Credit	57.992	6.393	64.385
Sub-total (Germany)	334.781	36.278	371.059
Italy			
Export Credit	70.166	28.202	98.368
Japan			
Capital Aid	234.209	29.724	263.933
Export Credit	8.702	—	8.702
Sub-total (Japan)	242.911	29.724	272.635
Netherlands			
Capital Aid	20.229	8.741	28.970
Export Credit	6.648	3.806	10.454
Sub-total (Netherlands)	26.877	12.547	39.424
Sweden			
Capital Aid	7.257	0.015	7.272
Export Credit	0.138	—	0.138
Sub-total (Sweden)	7.395	0.015	7.410
U.K.			
Capital Aid	194.696	5.822	200.518
Export Credit	25.073	—	25.073
Sub-total (U.K.)	219.769	5.822	225.591
U.S. Aid			
Capital Aid	1,361.129	39.062	1,400.191
U.S. Eximbank			
Capital Aid	48.111	1.911	50.022
U.S.A.			
Export Credit	6.471	—	6.471
Singer Manufacturing Co.	0.194	—	0.194
NGB Euro-Dollar Loan	20.370	0.288	20.658
Sub-total (U.S.A.)	1,436.275	41.261	1,477.536

Source: Government of Pakistan, Ministry of Finance, *Pakistan Economic Survey 1972-1973*, pp. 104-11.

			(U.S. $ million)
Lending country / agency	Disbursed and out-standing	Undis-bursed	Total Debt
1	2	3	4
I.B.R.D.	269.929	23.528	293.457
I.D.A.	262.468	170.232	432.700
A.D.B.	11.447	35.403	46.850
I.F.C.	7.174	1.000	8.174
Sub-total (Consortium)	3,048.448	409.540	3,457.988
II. Non-Consortium			
China	5.994	214.542	220.536
Czechoslovakia			
Export Credit	28.269	4.510	32.779
Denmark			
Capital Aid	2.609	5.270	7.879
Export Credit	2.493	—	2.493
Sub-total (Denmark)	5.102	5.270	10.372
Kuwait			
Capital Aid	3.920	0.048	3.968
Poland			
Export Credit	5.477	1.824	7.301
Switzerland			
Export Credit	15.924	11.116	27.040
U.S.S.R.			
Capital Aid	26.286	5.065	31.351
Export Credit	22.278	4.196	26.474
Sub-total (U.S.S.R.)	48.564	9.261	57.825
Yugoslavia			
Export Credit	22.950	2.804	25.754
Sub-total (Non-Consortium)	136.200	249.375	385.575
Sub-total (I + II)	3,184.648	658.915	3,843.563
III. Indus Basin/Tarbela*			
France	32.645	—	32.645
Italy	42.992	—	42.992
U.K.	15.915	3.896	19.811
U.S. Aid	31.729	0.001	31.730
U.S. Eximbank	47.500	—	47.500
I.B.R.D.	66.466	43.540	110.006
I.D.A.	63.557	—	63.557
Sub-total (Indus/Tarbela)	300.804	47.437	348.241
Grand Total (I + II + III)	3,485.452	706.352	4,191.804

*Does not include $4.888 million (disbursed and outstanding $1.693 million and undisbursed $3.195 million) reported by the Administrator of Tarbela Development Fund.

Country/Agency	Pre 1st Plan		1st Plan		2nd Plan	
	Grants	Loans	Grants	Loans	Grants	Loans
1	2	3	4	5	6	7
Australia						
Capital Aid	26.342	—	2.790	—	7.090	—
Austria						
Export Credit	—	—	—	—	—	—
Belgium						
Capital Aid	—	—	—	—	—	—
Export Credit	—	—	—	—	—	0.517
Sub-total (Belgium)	—	—	—	—	—	0.517
Canada						
Capital Aid	42.340	—	62.850	—	65.515	11.315
Non-project	—	—	—	—	—	—
China						
Capital Aid	—	—	—	—	60.000	—
Czechoslovakia						
Export Credit	—	—	—	—	—	—
Denmark						
Capital Aid	—	—	—	—	—	—
Export Credit	—	—	—	—	—	7.409
Sub-total (Denmark)	—	—	—	—	—	7.409
France						
Export Credit	—	—	—	23.045	—	32.041
Germany						
Capital Aid	—	—	—	—	—	131.283
Export Credit	—	—	—	—	—	90.022
Sub-total (Germany)	—	—	—	—	—	221.305
Italy						
Export Credit	—	—	—	—	—	5.908
Japan						
Capital Aid	—	—	0.192	—	0.837	103.199
Export Credit	—	—	—	25.211	—	42.585
Sub-total (Japan)	—	—	0.192	25.211	0.837	145.784
Kuwait						
Capital Aid	—	—	—	—	—	—
Netherlands						
Capital Aid	—	—	—	—	—	6.630
Export Credit	—	—	—	6.160	—	8.183
Sub-total (Netherlands)	—	—	—	6.160	—	14.813

3rd Plan		1970-71		1971-72		July 1972 to March 1973		Grand Total	
Grants	Loans	Grants	Loans	Grants	Loans	Grants	Loans	Grants	Loans
8	9	10	11	12	13	14	15	16	17
4.440	—	0.170	—	—	—	—	—	40.832	—
—	5.484	—	—	—	—	—	—	—	5.484
—	4.000	—	1.500	—	—	—	2.231	—	7.731
—	5.483	—	—	—	—	—	—	—	6.000
—	9.483	—	1.500	—	—	—	2.231	—	13.731
53.798	140.615	7.509	17.899	7.000	—	10.000	10.000	249.012	179.829
—	—	—	—	—	—	—	—	—	—
47.485	—	2.884	220.00	—	—	—	—	110.369	220.000
—	51.528	—	—	—	—	—	—	—	51.528
—	2.000	—	5.731	—	—	—	—	—	7.731
—	—	—	—	—	—	—	—	—	7.409
—	2.000	—	5.731	--	—	—	—	—	15.140
—	67.464	—	16.567	—	—	—	19.548	—	158.665
—	149.077	—	35.655	—	—	—	24.025	—	340.040
—	55.742	—	2.732	—	2.907	—	—	—	151.403
—	204.819	—	38.387	—	2.907	—	24,025	—	491.443
—	98.282	—	34.791	—	1.974	—	0.036	—	140.991
0.240	148.714	—	—	—	—	—	31.097	1.269	283.010
—	9.089	—	—	—	—	—	—	—	76.885
0.240	157.803	—	—	—	1.974	—	31.097	1.269	359.895
—	4.958	—	—	—	—	—	—	—	4.958
—	14.917	—	4.420	—	—	—	4.931	—	30.898
—	5.841	—	—	—	3.412	—	—	—	23.596
—	20.758	—	4.420	--	3.412	—	4.931	—	54.494

Country/Agency	Pre 1st Plan		1st Plan		2nd Plan	
	Grants	Loans	Grants	Loans	Grants	Loans
1	2	3	4	5	6	7
Norway						
Capital Aid	—	—	—	—	—	—
New Zealand						
Capital Aid	3.130	—	2.490	—	1.112	—
Poland						
Export Credit	--	—	—	—	—	—
Romania						
Capital Aid	—	—	—	—	—	—
Switzerland						
Export Credit	—	—	—	—	—	0.114
Sweden						
Capital Aid	0.369	—	—	—	1.103	—
Export Credit	—	—	—	—	—	—
Sub-total (Sweden)	0.369	—	—	—	1.103	—
Turkey						
Export Credit	—	—	—	—	—	—
U.K.						
Capital Aid	1.151	28.000	3.633	28.000	5.697	124.603
Financial Institutions and suppliers	—	—	—	—	—	26.533
Sub-total (U.K.)	1.151	28.000	3.633	28.000	5.697	150.569
U.S.A.						
Grants	88.121	—	401.527	—	160.410	—
DLF Loans	—	—	—	123.825	—	92.358
US AID Loans	—	—	—	—	—	683.364
US Financial Institutions and Suppliers	—	—	—	3.610	—	28.148
Sub-total (U.S.A.)	88.121	—	401.527	127.435	160.410	803.870
U. S. Exim Bank						
@	—	15.000	—	2.827	—	45.479
*	—	20.000	—	68.000	—	—
Sub-total (Exim Bank)	—	35.000	—	70.827	—	45.479
PL-480						
Title I	29.086	—	340.620	—	638.754	—
Title II	84.559	—	36.841	—	49.267	—
Title III	1.207	—	29.741	—	20.808	—
Sub-total (PL-480)	114.852	—	407.202	—	708.829	—

3rd Plan		1970-71		1971-72		July 1972 to March 1973		Grand Total	
Grants	Loans	Grants	Loans	Grants	Loans	Grants	Loans	Grants	Loans
8	9	10	11	12	13	14	15	16	17
5.026	—	1.001	—	—	—	—	—	6.027	—
0.078	—	—	—	—	—	—	—	6.810	—
—	11.326	—	—	—	—	—	—	—	11.326
—	—	—	9.407	—	—	—	—	—	9.407
—	26.647	—	0.040	—	—	—	—	—	26.801
13.941	17.707	1.114	—	—	—	—	—	16.527	17.707
—	0.318	—	—	—	—	—	—	—	0.318
13.941	18.025	1.114	—	—	—	—	—	16.527	18.025
—	3.646	—	—	—	—	—	—	—	3.646
3.954	111.674	—	15.228	—	—	—	10.423	14.435	317.361
—	57.070	—	47.772	—	—	—	—	—	131.375
3.954	168.744	—	63.000	—	—	—	10.423	14.435	448.736
59.934	—	4.880	—	0.908	—	0.282	—	716.062	—
—	—	—	—	—	—	—	—	—	216.183
—	589.113	—	9.500	—	—	—	120.000	—	1401.977
—	19.752	—	24.445	—	—	—	—	75.955	—
59.934	608.865	4.880	33.945	0.908	—	0.282	120.000	792.017	1618.160
—	74.081	—	16.100	—	—	—	—	—	133.487
—	—	—	—	—	—	—	—	—	88.000
—	74.081	—	16.100	—	—	—	—	—	221.487
307.280	91.100	21.100	59.600	15.300	43.100	—	78.500	1352.140	272.300
19.419	—	11.981	—	—	—	—	—	202.067	—
3.474	—	—	—	—	—	—	—	55.230	—
330.171	91.100	33.081	59.600	15.300	43.100	—	78.500	1609.437	272.300

Country/Agency	Pre 1st Plan		1st Plan		2nd Plan	
	Grants	Loans	Grants	Loans	Grants	Loans
1	2	3	4	5	6	7
U.S.S.R.						
State Credit	—	—	—	—	—	30.000
Export Credit	—	—	—	—	—	11.000
Sub-total (USSR)	—	—	—	—	—	41.000
Yugoslavia						
Export Credit	—	—	—	—	—	29.562
Suppliers Credits	—	—	—	42.285	—	—
Asian Development Bank.	—	—	—	—	—	—
IBRD	—	58.226	—	92.655	—	208.888
I.D.A.	—	—	—	—	—	235.444
I.F.C.	—	—	—	1.380	—	9.352
UN and Specialized	3.940	—	5.177	—	4.488	—
Agencies:						
UNDP-Special Fund	—	—	8.175	—	9.743	—
Ford Foundation	—	—	17.230	—	19.329	—
Others	0.015	—	5.313	—	0.040	—
Total (All Loans)	280.260	121.226	916.579	416.998	1044.193	1963.370

@Loans repayable in US Dollars.
*Loans repayable in Pak. Rupees.
Note — PL-480 Title I also includes grant portion.

3rd Plan		1970-71		1971-72		July 1972 to March 1973		Grand Total	
Grants	Loans	Grants	Loans	Grants	Loans	Grants	Loans	Grants	Loans
8	9	10	11	12	13	14	15	16	17
—	21.111	—	—	—	—	—	—	—	51.111
—	74.486	—	0.351	—	—	—	—	—	85.837
—	95.597	—	0.351	—	—	—	—	—	136.948
—	87.431	—	15.562	—	—	—	—	—	132.555
—	—	—	—	—	—	—	—	—	42.285
—	10.000	—	36.850	—	—	—	38.500	—	46.850
—	273.700	—	—	—	—	—	—	—	633.469
—	220.150	—	48.000	—	—	—	50.000	—	533.594
—	7.119	—	—	—	—	—	—	—	17.851
2.812	—	—	—	—	—	—	—	16.417	—
11.851	—	—	—	—	—	—	—	29.769	—
14.116	—	1.744	—	—	—	—	—	52.419	—
0.013	—	—	—	—	—	—	—	5.381	—
547.861	2459.625	52.383	622.150	23.208	51.393	10.282	350.791	2950.721	5889.598

Appendix 4 Pakistan and her Neighbors: A Comparative Profile

Country	Area in thousand kms.	Population million	Density, per sq. km.	Percentage of literacy	Percentage of labor force employed in agriculture	Percentage of labor force employed in industry	GNP at market prices (millions of $)	Per capita income ($)	Contribution of agriculture to GNP	Contribution of industry to GNP
Egypt	1,001[5]	33.3[5]	34[5]	30[6c]	56.67g[*]	26[7g*]	6,870[5]	210[5]	N.A.	N.A.
India	3,268[5]	538[5]	168[5]	29.35[4f]	72[7a]	11[7a]	57,270[5]	110[5]	52[1]	15[1]
Iran	1,648[5]	28.7[5]	18[5]	40[4h]	41.8[7e]	17[7e]	10,800[5]	380[5]	30[7e]	13[7e]
Iraq	435[5]	9.7[5]	23[5]	50[6a]	55.8[7f]	3.2[7f*]	3,090[5]	320[5]	19[7f 10]	9[7f]
Pakistan	804[8]	64.9[8]	79[8]	19.2[9]	54.89[2]	15.69[2]	7,450[8]	90[8]	42[8]	17[8]
Saudi Arabia	2,150[5]	7.4[5]	4[5]	10[6b]	N.A.	N.A.	3,220[5]	440[5]	15[7d]	N.A.
Turkey	781[5]	35.2[5]	45[5]	49[4i]	72.3[7c]	10.4[7c]	10,860[5]	310[5]	31.2[7c]	20.4[7c]
Afghanistan	647[5]	14.3[5]	27[5]	10[4g]	N.A.	N.A.	1,070[5]	80[5]	N.A.	N.A.

Country	Net food supply per capita		Telephones per 100 inhabitants	Circulation of daily newspapers per 1000 inhabitants	Population per hospital bed	Population per physician	Total route mileage railways (kms.)	Total road mileage (hard-surfaced) (kms.)
	Calories per day	Proteins (grams) per day						
Egypt	2960[3a]	76[3a]	1.1[3b]	23[3c]	472[3d]	2004[3d]	4510[j]	22,142[j]*
India	1940[3a]	48[3a]	0.2[3b]	14[3c]	1671[3d]	4610[3d]	60,000[4a]	324,940[4a]
Iran	2030[3a]	55[3a]	1.1[3b]	8[3c]	778[3d]	3297[3d]	3480[4c]	4907[4c]
Iraq	2050[3a]	58[3a]	1.2[3b]	N.A.	540[3d]	5301[3d]	2352[4d]	4550[4d,11]
Pakistan	2350[3a,13]	54[3a,13]	0.314*	9.28[1]*	2000[1]*	12,168[1]*	5334*	25,042[11,12]*
Saudi Arabia	2080[3a]	56[3a]	0.6[3b]	10[3c]	1162[3d]	14,041[3d]	....	N.A.
Turkey	2766[3a]	78[3a]	1.7[3b]	41[3c]	489[3d]	2222[3d]	7,985[4b]	15,000[4b]
Afghanistan	2060[3a]	65[3a]	0.1[3b]	6[3c]	6756[3d]	20,668[3d]	....	2,000[4e]

Sources

1. *Asia Yearbook* 1973 (Hong Kong: Far Eastern Economic Review, 1973), pp. 241-42.

2. Government of Pakistan, *25 Years of Pakistan in Statistics 1947–1972* (Karachi: Central Statistical Office, 1972).

3. United Nations, *Statistical Yearbook 1971* (New York, 1972, 23rd issue), pp. (a) 504-9; (b) 487-90; (c) 796-99; (d) 711-15.

4. *The Statesman Yearbook 1972–73* (London: Macmillian, 1972), pp. (a) 350-51; (b) 1388; (c) 1053; (d) 1061; (e) 730; (f) 335; (g) 728; (h) 1048; (i) 1383; (j) 885.

5. World Bank, *Trends in Developing Countries* (Washington, D. C., 1973), tables 1.1-1.4.

6. *The Encyclopedia of Education* (London: Macmillian and Free Press, 1971), (a) 5:218; (b) 8:12; (c) 9:303.

7. *World Mark Encyclopedia of the Nations* (New York: Harper and Row, 1971), (a) 4:91-95); (b) 4:6-7; (c) 4:356-58; (d) 4:295-97; (e) 4:121-24; (f) 4:131-34; (g) 2:335-36.

8. Viqar Ahmad, *R.C.D.—A Study in Regional Economic Cooperation* (Lahore: Pakistan Administrative Staff College, 1973).

9. According to the 1961 census.

10. Percentage of gross domestic product.

11. Roads and tracks.

12. Motorable roads.

13. Figures pertain to pre-1972 Pakistan.

14. Figures obtained from official sources.

   *Computed.

(This table was prepared by Iftikhar Ahmad, Lecturer, South Asia Institute, University of the Punjab, Lahore.)

Notes

Chapter 1

1. The following list may be useful. First, the pronouncements and writings of some of the chief policy makers: Muhammad Zafrullah Khan, *Pakistan's Foreign Relations* (Karachi: Pakistan Institute of International Affairs, 1951); H. S. Suhrawardy, "Foreign Relations and Defense," *Pakistan Quarterly,* Spring 1957, and "Political Stability and Democracy in Pakistan," *Foreign Affairs,* April 1957; Aziz Ahmad, "American Alliances with Asian Countries," *Annals,* July 1960; Mohammad Ayub Khan, *Friends Not Masters: A Political Autobiography* (New York: Oxford, 1965), *Speeches and Statements,* 7 vols. (Karachi: Pakistan Publications, n.d.), "Pakistan Perspective," *Foreign Affairs,* July 1960, "The Pakistan-American Alliance: Stresses and Strains," *Foreign Affairs,* January 1964, "Pakistan's Approach to World Problems," *United Asia,* November 1962, "Strategic Problems of the Middle East," *Asian Review,* July 1958. Zulfikar Ali Bhutto's statements, speeches, and articles, many of them on foreign policy, have been collected and edited by Hamid Jalal and Khalid Hasan and published in three volumes in Politics of the People series. They are entitled *Reshaping Foreign Policy 1948-66, Awakening the People 1966-1969,* and *Marching Towards Democracy* (Rawalpindi: Pakistan Publications, n.d.). Since these volumes are not really inclusive, the following volumes of speeches should also be consulted: *Foreign Policy of Pakistan: A Compendium of Speeches Made in the National Assembly of Pakistan 1962-64* (Karachi: Pakistan Institute of International Affairs, 1964); *The Quest for Peace: Selections from Speeches and Writings, 1963-65* (Karachi: Pakistan Institute of International Affairs, 1966); Bhutto's *The Myth of Independence* (London: Oxford, 1969), and a pamphlet, *Pakistan and the*

Alliances (Lahore: Pakistan People's Party, 1969), are important reading. In addition to the above, the following works may be helpful: Keith Callard, *Pakistan's Foreign Policy: An Interpretation* (New York: Institute of Pacific Relations, 1959); Mohammad Ahsen Chaudhri, *Pakistan and the Great Powers* (Karachi: Council for Pakistan Studies, 1970), and *Pakistan and the Regional Pacts* (Karachi: East Publications, 1958); K. Sarwar Hasan, *Pakistan and the United Nations* (New York: institute of Pacific Relations, 1964); Arif Hussain, *Pakistan: Its Ideology and Foreign Policy* (London, Frank Cass, 1966); Shaheen Irshad, *Rejection Alliance* (Lahore: Ferozsons, 1972); Norman D. Palmer, *South Asia and United States Policy* (Boston: Houghton Mifflin, 1966); Latif Ahmad Sherwani et al., *Foreign Policy of Pakistan: An Analysis* (Karachi: Allies Book Corporation, 1964); Aslam Siddiqi, *Pakistan Seeks Security* (Lahore: Longmans, Green, 1960), and *A Path for Pakistan* (Karachi: Pakistan Publishing House, 1964); Wayne Wilcox, *Asia and United States Policy* (Englewood Cliffs, N. J.: Prentice-Hall, 1967), and *"India and Pakistan,"* in Kenneth Waltz and Steven Spiegel, eds., *International Conflict in the Nuclear Age* (Cambridge: Winthrop, 1971).

2. For a listing of these and many other works on various aspects of Pakistani politics, including periodical literature, see Lawrence Ziring's bibliographical essay, "Political Science and Pakistan," one of the State of the Art papers presented to the National Seminar on Pakistan and Bangladesh at Southern Asian Institute, Columbia University (May 1972), and likely to be published, along with others, under its auspices.

3. *Pakistan's Foreign Policy: An Historical Analysis* (London: Oxford, 1973).

4. Pakistan's relations with China are explained and defended in the pronouncements and writings of Ayub Khan and Z. A. Bhutto cited above. B. L. Sharma's *Pakistan-China Axis* (Bombay: Asia, 1968) is largely propagandistic and therefore worthless. In addition to the other materials cited in the text above, one may consult: Mohammad Ayoob; "India as a factor in Sino-Pakistani Relations," *International Studies,* Bombay, January 1968. S. M. Burke, "Sino-Pakistan Relations," *Orbis,* Summer 1964; W. M. Dobell, "Ramifications of the China-Pakistan Boundary Treaty," *Pacific Affairs,* Fall 1962; K. Sarwar Hasan, ed., *Documents on the Foreign Relations of Pakistan: China, India, Pakistan* (Karachi: Pakistan Institute of International Affairs, 1966); Khalida Qureshi, "Pakistan and the Sino-Indian Dispute," *Pakistan Horizon, 1962,* no. 4, and 1963, no. 1; Latif Ahmad Sherwani, *India, China, and Paki-*

stan (Karachi: Council for Pakistan Studies, 1967); Sheldon Simon, "The Kashmir Dispute in Sino-Soviet Perspective," *Asian Survey*, March 1967; Wayne Wilcox, "China's Strategic Alternatives in South Asia," in Tang Tson, ed, *China in Crisis: China's Policies in Asia and American Alternatives*, vol. 2 (Chicago: University of Chicago Press, 1968).

5. A senior Pakistani diplomat gave this explanation in an address at the Pakistan Administrative Staff College at Lahore on November 13, 1973.

6. During 1972–73 Pakistan's exports to Iran and Turkey were less than 1 percent of her total exports, and her imports from them were less than 1.5 percent of her total imports. Viqar Ahmad, *RCD: A Study in Regional Economic Cooperation* (Lahore: Pakistan Administrative Staff College, 1973), p. 56.

7. The matter of possible Iranian assistance in Pakistan's defense is discussed in chapter 7 below.

8. In a recent interview with me, Prime Minister Bhutto described Sukarno as a dynamic leader, a great freedom-fighter and patriot.

9. Statements of Daoud and Bhutto may be seen in *Musawat, Nawa-e-Waqt* [Urdu], and *Pakistan Times,* Nov. 15, 1973.

10. *The Myth of Independence, p. 148.*

11. During the course of my interviews at the Foreign Office in Islamabad in the fall of 1973, Paki-

stani diplomats were unanimous on this point.

12. In 1972, months after the Pakistani surrender in East Pakistan, a Chinese volleyball team went to play a match in Sialkot, a large town close to the Indian border, which had suffered war damage during the previous December. Men, women, and children from the neighboring villages lined the road, raining flowers on the players all the way to Sialkot, which, in the words of interviewees, looked as if it had been clothed in red. Even the conservative Jamat-e-Islami participated in the welcoming ceremonies (interviews with Chaudhury Anwar Aziz, lawyer, businessman, and former legislator from Sialkot district, and Mr. Nawab Ali, a Communist worker of Sialkot, who also happened to be on the reception committee; these interviews were held in October 1973).

13. The linkage between foreign–policy choices and the personal backgrounds of the choice makers is tenuous. This is further illustrated by the following list of the men who held the office of foreign secretary in Pakistan at various times. Their professional background, before entering the Pakistan Foreign Service, is also indicated: Ikram-Ullah, former ICS (Indian Civil Service); M. O. A. Baig, former IPS (Indian Political Service); J. A. Rahim, Akhtar Hussain, M. S. A. Baig, S. K. Dehlavi, Aziz Ahmad, S. M. Yusaf—all former ICS; Sultan Mohammad

Khan, Iftikhar Ali, Mumtaz Ali Alvie—Indian army and then Indian Foreign Service (shortly before independence); Agha Shahi (present foreign secretary), ICS. In other words, all these men belonged to an elite service during British rule, a fact from which it may safely be inferred that their social and educational backgrounds had been, at least roughly, similar. Yet, in their turn and time, they supported different policy positions.

14. See, for instance, Michael Brecher, *The New States of Asia: A Political Analysis* (New York: Oxford, 1966), p. 97-105.

Chapter 2

1. Cf. Krishan Bhatia, quoted on pp. 32–33.

2. Jamil-ud-Din Ahmad, ed., *Speeches and Writings of Mr. Jinnah* (Lahore: Ashraf, 1960), 1:67-84, 90-91, 98-99, and passim.

3. *Speeches and Writings of Mr. Jinnah,* 1:98-99. Jinnah's assessments of the Congress and its leadership are shared by most Pakistani historians. See, for instance, Abdul Hamid, *Muslim Separatism in India* (Lahore: Oxford, 1967), pp. 215-24; Ishtiaq Hussain Qureshi, *The Struggle for Pakistan* (Karachi: University

of Karachi, 1965), pp. 96-109; K. K. Aziz, *The Making of Pakistan* (London: Chatto and Windus, 1967), pp. 100-102, 186.

4. These Indian statements and actions are cited in most Pakistani discussions of Indian policy. See Sherwani, *India, China, and Pakistan,* pp. 14-21; Sharif al-Munjahid in Sherwani, et al., *Foreign Policy of Pakistan,* pp. 32-36; Bhutto, *Foreign Policy of Pakistan,* pp. 34-35. See also a reputable Indian source, J. B. Das Gupta, *Indo-Pakistan Relations 1947-1955* (Amsterdam: Djambatan, 1958), pp. 46-51, 223-29.

5. See T. N. Dupuy, *Almanac of World Military Power* (New York: T. N. Dupuy Associates and Stackpole Books. 1970), p. 299. Nirad C. Chaudhuri attributed India's anger at American military aid to Pakistan "to the check given by it to India's policy of keeping the latter country weak and isolated" *(The Continent of Circe* [London: Chatto and Windus, 1965], p. 245).

6. See Mushtaq Ahmad, *Pakistan's Foreign Policy* (Karachi: Space Publishers, 1968), pp. 10-13; Sherwani, *India, China, and Pakistan,* pp. 14-15.

7. *Dawn* (Karachi), editorials of July 23, 1951, Aug. 22, 1958, Mar. 1 and Nov. 10, 1962.

8. *Morning News (Karachi), editorials of Jan. 2 and 25, Apr. 24, May 8, and Nov. 2, 1962; Pakistan Times* (Lahore), editorials of Jan. 24 and 25, 1962.

9. *Dawn,* Mar. 7, 10, and 11, 1958. Also see Firoz Khan Noon,

From Memory (Lahore: Feroz-sons, 1969), pp. 288-89. Noon had the understanding that Nehru often read Chanakys's *Arthashastra* before going to bed.

10. Ayub Khan, *Friends Not Masters*, pp. 42, 47-48, 115-17, 183, and passim, and his "Pakistan-American Alliance: Stresses and Strains," p. 199; Bhutto, *Foreign Policy of Pakistan*, pp. 6-7, 34; and his *The Myth of Independence*, chaps. 7-8, 17-18, and passim.

11. *The Autobiography of an Unknown Indian* (New York: Macmillan, 1951), pp. 427, 212-13, 401-2, 405-7, 428-34, 440-42, 471, 480, 492.

12. Ibid., pp. 226-27.

13. Ibid., p. 408.

14. Rajni Kothari, *Politics in India* (Boston: Little, Brown, 1970), pp. 21-22, 32-35.

15. *Dawn*, editorial of Mar. 11, 1958.

16. *Friends Not Masters*, pp. 172, 214.

17. Reported in *Pakistan Times*, May 13, 1958.

18. Overseas *Hindustan Times*, May 23, 1970.

19. Ibid., May 30, June 27, 1970.

20. Upendra Vajpeyi, "Lessons of the Riots," in ibid., June 13, 1970.

21. *Uncertain India* (Cambridge: MIT Press, 1968), pp. 250-51.

22. Verghese, "Bangla Desh and the Crisis of Identity," Overseas *Hindustan Times*, July 3, 1971.

23. "The Meos," *Illustrated Weekly of India*, Jan. 30, 1972, pp. 40-47.

24. "How Secular Is Secular India?" *Illustrated Weekly of India*, Jan. 30, 1972, pp. 14-19, and Feb. 6, 1972, pp. 20-23. For still another perceptive analysis of the Muslim community's depressed status and isolation in independent India, see Chaudhuri, *The Continent of Circe*, Chap. 12.

25. Cf. Das Gupta, *Indo-Pakistan Relations;* Bhabani Sen Gupta, *The Fulcrum of Asia* (New York: Pegasus, 1970); Krishan Bhatia, *The Ordeal of Nationalhood* (New York: Atheneum, 1971).

26. *Times of India*, Apr. 1, 1958.

27. Jawaharlal Nehru, *Toward Freedom* (New York: John Day, 1941), pp. 291-93.

28. Ibid.

29. Sri Prakasa, *Pakistan: Birth and Early Days* (Meerut: Meenakshi Prakashan, 1965), pp. 8, 54, 78, 97, 141-43, 155; J. N. Sahni, *Fifty Years of Indian Politics* (New Delhi: Allied Publishers, 1971), p. 290.

30. S. K. Majumdar, *Jinnah and Gandhi: Their Role in India's Quest for Freedom* (Calcutta: K. L. Mukhopadhyay, 1966), pp. xvii-xviii.

31. See, for instance, V. B. Kulkarni, *The Indian Triumvirate* (Bombay: Bharatiya Vidya Bhavan, 1969), pp. 103-6 and passim; V. D. Mahajan, *Fifty Years of Modern India, 1919-1969* (Delhi:

S. Chand and Co., 1970), p. 276; Sri Prakasa, *Pakistan: Birth and Early Days,* p. 6; K. C. Saxena, *Pakistan: Her Relations with India.* (New Delhi: Vir Publishing House, 1966), pp. 1-2; Sangat Singh, *Pakistan's Foreign Policy* (New York: Asia, 1970), pp. 3-7.

32. Jawaharlal Nehru, *The Discovery of India* (New York: John Day, 1946), pp. 347-48, 353-54, 356.

33. *Biographical Vistas* (London: Asia, 1966), pp. 253-58.

34. Quoted in Kulkarni, *The Indian Triumvirate,* pp. 184, 187.

35. *The Discovery of India,* pp. 364, 393-96.

36. *The Indian Struggle, 1920–1942* (Bombay: Asia, 1964, pp. 155-56.

37. Sri Prakasa, *Pakistan: Birth and Early Days,* pp. 4, 46-51, 83-85, 112-17, and passim.

38. Sahni, *Fifty Years of Indian Politics,* 153-54, 199-202, 292.

39. Sharma, *The Pakistan-China Axis,* p. 16.

40. Ibid., p. 17.

41. *The Indian Triumvirate,* pp. 100-103.

42. B. N. Pandey, *The Break-up of British India* (London: Macmillan, 1969), pp. 147-48, 154-56, and passim.

43. Quoted in D. C. Gupta, *Indian National Movement* (Delhi: Vikas, 1970), p. 173.

44. Sahni, *Fifty Years of Indian Politics,* p. 153; T. V. Parvate, *Makers of Modern India* (Delhi: University Publishers, 1964), pp. 91-96; Kulkarni, *The Indian Triumvirate,* p. 100.

45. Kanji Dwarkadas, *India's Fight for Freedom* (Bombay: Popular Prakashan, 1966), pp. 322-26, 350-52, 441; S. K. Majumdar, *Jinnah and Gandhi,* pp. vi, xi, xvii, chaps. 22-23, pp. 27-29; Sasadhar Sinha, *Indian Independence in Perspective* (Bombay: Asia, 1964), pp. 23-24, 27, 50-51, 188. See also Jyoti Prasad Suda, *The Indian National Movement* (Meerut: Jai Prakash Nath and Co., 1969), p. 283.

46. A. K. Majumdar, *Advent of Independence* (Bombay: Bharatiya Vidya Bhavan, 1963), pp. 40-42. See also J. Chinna Durai, *The Choice Before India* (London: Jonathan Cape, 1941), pp. 12, 65, 135-38.

47. *Times of India,* Apr. 10, Nov. 8, 1958; *Dawn,* June 5, 1958.

48. Patel, *For a United India* (New Delhi: Government of India, Ministry of Information, 1949), pp. 6-9, 62, 118-19, and passim. (Next to Jinnah, Liaquat Ali Khan was the most influential leader in the struggle for Pakistan. He was assassinated in 1951 while addressing a public meeting in Rawalpindi.)

49. Sharma, *The Pakistan–China Axis,* pp. 20-27.

50. Sahni, *Fifty Years of Indian Politics,* pp. 461-64; Kulkarni, *The Indian Triumvirate,* pp. 686-87.

51. Sangat Singh, *Pakistan's Foreign Policy,* chaps. 1-2; Saxena, *Relations with India,* pp. 12-13; Sinha, *Indian Independence,* pp. 223-24; Mahajan, *Fifty Years,* p. 419; Kulkarni, *The*

Indian Triumvirate, p. 661; G. S. Bhargawa, *Pakistan in Crisis* (Delhi: Vikas, 1971), pp. 104-13.

52. In addition to the materials cited immediately above, see Jamna Das Akhtar, *Pak Espionage in India* (Delhi: Oriental Publishers, 1971). This writer would have us believe that Pakistan maintains a massive network of spies, saboteurs, and assassins in India and has, from time to time, hired Indian citizens to commit political murders. Happily, none of these designs have succeeded.

53. Patel, *For a United India,* passim.

54. K. M. Panikkar, *Common Sense about India* (New York: Macmillan, 1961), pp. 123-24.

55. Kulkarni, *The Indian Triumvirate,* p. 701; Sangat Singh, *Pakistan's Foreign Policy,* p. 77; A. B. Shah, ed., *India's Defense and Foreign Policies* (Bombay: Manaktalas, 1966), pp. 52-53.

56. See, for instance, Bhutto's piece, "Pakistan Builds Anew," in *Foreign Affairs,* April 1973, pp. 541-54.

57. B. M. Naqvi, "Our Foreign Policy: Assumptions, Motivations, and Frustrations," *Pakistan Observer,* Aug. 14, 1966, quoted approvingly in Sangat Singh, *Pakistan's Foreign Policy,* pp. 76-77. See also Tariq Ali, *Pakistan: Military Rule or People's Power* (New York: William Morrow, 1970), pp. 79, 132, and passim.

58. Cf. Gordon W. Allport, *The Nature of Prejudice* (Cambridge, Mass.: Addison-Wesley, 1954),

chap. 12, and his essay, "The Role of Expectancy," in Hadley Cantril, ed., *Tensions that Cause War* (Urbana, Ill.: University of Illinois Press, 1950), pp. 62-64. See also Walter Lippmann's classic work, *Public Opinion* (New York: Macmillan, 1922), pp. 79-156, for an extended examination of stereotypes. As Allport says, to Lippmann must go the credit for establishing the concept of stereotypes in modern social psychology.

59. Bhatia, *The Ordeal of Nationhood,* pp. 301-2.

60. Lippmann, *The Stakes of Diplomacy* (New York: Henry Holt, 1915), chaps. 3-4.

61. Otto Klineberg, *The Human Dimension in International Relations* (New York: Holt, Rinehart and Winston, 1964), p. 40.

62. Allport, *The Nature of Prejudice,* pp. 202-4. See also Klineberg, *The Human Dimension,* pp. 35, 47.

63. William Buchanan and Hadley Cantril, *How Nations See Each Other* (Urbana, Ill.: University of Illinois Press, 1953), p. 55. See also Gabriel Almond, *The American People and Foreign Policy* (New York: Harcourt, Brace, 1950), pp. 92-99.

64. Noting that Hinduism and Islam have not integrated during the last 750 years and that the idea of their assimilation now is "vain and meaningless," Panikkar suggests that such assimilation is not necessary to India's national unity. Muslims should

not be asked to "merge their identity in a wider Indian community." The Hindus should accept the Muslims "as an integral part of Indian life, organized separately, possessing a culture of their own and constituting an important part of the Indian nation, though a minority". The Muslims, on their part, must adjust themselves to a minority status and to the fact that in independent India the Hindus constitute the dominant society and culture. Muslims should have equal rights and the protection of their religion and culture. *The Foundations of New India* (London: Allen and Unwin, 1963), pp. 222-25.

65. Bhatia, *The Ordeal of Nationhood,* pp. 64-65.

66. Ibid., pp. 282, 302.

67. Apparently the idea of American military assistance to Pakistan had received attention in the U.S. State and Defense Departments as early as 1951. Talks were held with Pakistani officials the following spring and an agreement in principle made in the summer. But the matter did not go forward, probably because the Truman administration was coming to the end of its term and also because influential officials, such as Chester Bowles and George Kennan, opposed it vigorously. See William J. Barnds, *India, Pakistan, and the Great Powers,* (New York: Praeger, 1972), pp. 91-97; Selig Harrison, "India, Pakistan, and the United States — Case History of a Mistake," *New Republic,* August 10,

1959, part 1; and James W. Spain, "Military Assistance for Pakistan," *American Political Science Review,* September 1954.

68. The dimensions of American military aid to India were in fact rather modest. Between 1962 and 1965 arms worth about $85 million were actually supplied. Barnds India, Pakistan, and the Great Powers p. 323.

69. For the most part, U.S. assistance took the form of grants during the 1950s and of loans during the 1960s. By fiscal year 1970 agricultural commodities worth about $1.3 billion had been made available. These were supplied against rupee sales until 1968, after which part of the payment was expected to be made in dollars over a 40-year period at low interest rates. Nearly 75 percent of the rupee proceeds was again granted or loaned to Pakistan for financing development projects. Between 1958 and 1968 Pakistan received a total of $1,335.7 million in development loans ($566.6 million in project loans and $769.1 million in non-project loans). Until fiscal year 1969 technical assistance amounting to $225.2 million had been given. The United States contributed $652 million ($531 million in grants and $121 million in loans) towards the Indus Basin Development Fund. Loans were of two kinds: "hard" loans from the Export-Import Bank at 6 percent for periods of 5 to 20 years; "soft" loans made by U.S. AID at 2

percent for the first 10 years and 3 percent for the subsequent period. I have taken these figures from Samad Hafezi, "Transformation of the United States-Pakistan Alliance 1954-1969" PhD. Diss. University of Massachusetts, Amherst, 1971).

70. See pp. 88–93.

71. Barnds, *India, Pakistan, and the Great Powers,* p.105. Also see my "Foreign Aid: Case Studies in Recipient Independence," *Pakistan Horizon,* 23, No. 1, (1970), pp. 15-36.

72. In *The Continent of Circe* Nirad C. Chaudhuri writes: "India held the pistol at the head of Pakistan, until, in 1954, the American alliance delivered the country from that nightmare." He goes on to say that "at least twice, if not three times, between 1947 and 1954, India intended to invade Pakistan and was deterred only by American and British remonstrances" (p.244).

73. Cf. Wayne Wilcox, "India and Pakistan," in Steven L. Spiegel and Kenneth L. Waltz, eds., *Conflict in World Politics* (Cambridge, Mass: Winthrop, 1971), pp. 251-56.

74. Barnds, *India, Pakistan, and the Great Powers,* pp. 250-51, and Wilcox, *"India and Pakistan,"* p. 259. On Nehru's thinking and intentions regarding Kashmir at this time, see also G. W. Chowdhury, *Pakistan's Relations With India,* (Delhi: Meenakshi Prakashan, 1971), pp. 86-89. Barnds suggests also that apart from security consid-

erations, which undoubtedly carried weight, considerations of personal and organizational influence and power motivated the Pakistani request for American arms. Bogra, he says, would have preferred economic to military assistance. But he was overruled by the civil and military "hierarchs" who wielded real power behind the facade of his prime ministership. Ayub Khan had taken a leading part in discussions with American officials. Convinced that the army alone could keep the country together and defend her from foreign aggression, he wished to consolidate his predominance within the military. The more aid he was able to negotiate the more he could present himself as the man "who could get what the military wanted" (pp. 102, 104). But such calculations of personal interest in making policy choices are not uniquely characteristic of Pakistani leaders. Nor does their presence show that Ayub Khan and others had invented or even unduly exaggerated the national security problem for reasons of personal profit.

75. See *Dawn,* Nov. 7, 1958, *Pakistan Times,* June 13, 1959, and, for trade figures, Barnds, *India, Pakistan, and the Great Powers,* p. 231.

76. *Dawn,* Sept. 27, Nov. 24, 1958.

77. Ibid., Mar. 4, 1959.

78. Mar. 5, 1960.

79. *Dawn,* Mar. 14, 1960.

80. Ibid., Mar. 14, 29, 1960.

81. Ibid., May 8, 9, 11, 1960; *Pakistan Times*, May 14, June 2, 1960.

82. The vehemence of *Dawn's* attacks on Khrushchev, the dictator of a superpower, may have been prompted partly by an unquestioning faith in the assurance that the United States would protect Pakistan if Moscow carried out its threats. But it is to be explained partly by the fact that its editor at the time, the late Altaf Hussain, was widely known for the vigor of his prose when it came to attacking someone.

By way of "rehabilitating" Pakistan, a Soviet writer has recently noted that despite her military alliances with the United States Pakistan did not permit the establishment of American "thermonuclear missile bases" on her soil. Furthermore, Pakistan "unflinchingly refrained from participating in the imperialists' hostile actions with regard to the USSR." Disillusioned by the insufficiency of American support on the Kashmir and Pukhtoonistan issues, Pakistan sought a "rapprochement" with the Soviet Union. The American "ruling circles" timed the U-2 mission so as to disrupt "the formation of normal, good-neighborly relations" between Pakistan and the USSR that was then going forward. I. M. Kompantsev, *Pakistan i Sovetskii Soiuz* [Pakistan and the Soviet Union] (Moscow: Nauka, 1970), pp. 193-97.

83. Others have since made the same observation. See especially Neville Maxwell, *India's China War* (London: Jonathan Cape, 1970). But see also Bhabani Sen Gupta, *The Fulcrum of Asia* (New York: Pegasus, 1970), pp. 157-64, and Barnds, *India, Pakistan, and the Great Powers,* p. 318.

84. See *The Current Digest of the Soviet Press,* Sept. 15, 1965, pp. 15-16.

85. According to U. S. State Department intelligence sources, Soviet arms — tanks, artillery, and armored personnel carriers — worth no more than $10 million were actually supplied to Pakistan before the 1971 Pakistani civil war. See William J. Barnds, "Moscow and South Asia," *Problems of Communism,* May-June 1972, p. 19 n. 17.

86. The Sino-Soviet conflict has received abundant scholarly attention and does not need an extended statement here. Suffice it to say that it is both intense and protracted. It has gone on for more than a decade and shows no signs of ending in the near future. A million Soviet troops stand guard at the Chinese border; the Chinese have built underground shelters for their civilian population in fear of a Soviet strike. Chinese newspapers and radio regularly hurl abuse at Soviet leaders, and according to Leopold Labedz, not a day passes without the Soviet media" discovering some new Chinese abomination, such as . . . the claim that the Soviet Union is not an Asian

power, or the claim to 1.5 million square kilometers of the Soviet territory in the new Chinese atlas." See Labedz, "The Soviet Union in Asia," in *East Asia and the World System,* Adelphi Papers, no. 91 (London: IISS, 1972), pp. 11-12.

87. In the case of the United States, the commerical consideration is now being openly voiced. Justifying the recent decision to sell some two to three billion dollars worth of high performance aircraft and other weapons to Iran over the next several years, State and Defense Department officials argue that, apart from other considerations, the deal would help American arms manufacturers "caught in a post-Vietnam slump" and also help redress the U. S. balance of payments deficit. *New York Times*, Feb. 22, 23, 1973.

88. There are reports that in the summer of 1969 Moscow offered to help Pakistan with a 5-year project for developing Gwadar into a major port that might also be used by her "growing navy." Some Indian sources interpreted these reports to mean that the USSR wished to develop a naval base at Gwadar capable of servicing Soviet submarines. See T. B. Millar, *Soviet Policies in the Indian Ocean Area* (Canberra: Australian National

University Press, 1970), p. 16. But it is possible also that Soviet interest in Gwadar is mainly commercial and only potentially strategic. The USSR is a specialist in overland transit systems. Her railways play the role sea lanes play for other nations. Nearly 80 per cent of her foreign commerce is carried by rail or pipeline (57.5 percent with Eastern Europe and 20 percent with noncommunist countries to which she has rail or pipeline connections), and only about 20 percent by sea. See Geoffrey Jukes, *The Indian Ocean in Soviet Naval Policy* (London: IISS, 1972) Adelphi Papers, no. 87, p. 3.

89. Robert H. Donaldson, "India: The Soviet Stake in Stability," *Asian Survey,* June 1972, pp. 479-83. The Chinese clearly viewed the project as directed against their country and denounced it as something Brezhnev had picked up "from the garbage heap of John Foster Dulles," a "sinister plot" for advancing Soviet "social-imperialist policy of aggression and expansion in Asia." T. B. Millar, "Soviet Policies in the Indian Ocean Area," p. 5.

90. Donaldson, "India: The Soviet Stake in Stability," pp. 482, 487.

91. Donaldson, "India: The Soviet stake in Stability," p. 485.

Chaper 3

1. *Dawn* editorials of Oct. 3 and 17, 1949.

2. New China News Agency (NCNA), June 6, 1955. Chinese materials—NCNA releases, newspaper comments and articles, speeches and statements of Chinese and Pakistani leaders—have been consulted in English translation provided in the *Survey of China Mainland Press*, prepared and issued by the United States Consulate–General in Hong Kong. Materials would normally appear in the *Survey* within a week or so of their date of issue.

3. NCNA, May 22, 1955. The Bandung Declaration is invoked apparently because it had urged that arrangements for collective self-defense should not serve the "particular interests" of any of the big powers and that nations should abstain from exerting pressure upon other nations.

4. NCNA, May 20, 1955.

5. NCNA, Dec. 8, 1955.

6. Hu Chin in *People's Daily*, Feb. 23, 1955. See also Chiang Yuan-chun in *People's Daily*, Jan. 13, 1955.

7. Chiang Yuan-chun, *People's Daily*, Jan. 13, 1955.

8. NCNA, Apr. 29, 1955, excerpting the *People's Daily* of the same date.

9. NCNA, Jan. 12, 1955.

10. "It has become increasingly clear to the people of Asia and Africa that it is of the utmost importance to consolidate and fight for their independence and freedom by overcoming the economic backwardness created by protracted colonial rule. To this end, they must maintain peace in Asia...and adopt a policy of non-participation in any military bloc and coexist in peace with all countries.... Even among some Asian countries in SEATO, there has developed a demand to be free of U. S. control and to pursue an independent policy" (Chiang Yuan-chun in the *People's Daily,* Dec. 8, 1955). In an earlier issue of the same paper (Jan. 13, 1955), Chiang had written: "the American aggressors neglect the fact that the people in large areas of Asia are no longer people who allow themselves to be pushed around by others. They will never permit the war-makers to materialize their intrigues."

11. With reference to adverse Egyptian reactions, a senior Pakistani diplomat recalled, in an interview with the author, that during a visit to Cairo in 1954 Governor General Ghulam Mohammed had assured President Nasser that Pakistan would not join any American-sponsored pact in the Middle East without first consulting him. Yet no such consultations were ever held.

12. NCNA, Mar. 23, 1954.

13. To this effect it quoted, among others, H. B. Jatoi, Chairman of the Sind Hari (peasants) Committee; B. K. Dutta, an MP; Mahmud Ali, an executive of the Azad Pakistan party; Mohammad Shafi, member of the West Paki-

stan Legislative Assembly; Syed Sibte Hasan, a Communist leader; Maulana Abdul Hamid Khan Bhashani, United Front leader; Mian Iftikhar-ud-Din, MP and Azad Pakistan party leader; Sheikh Qamar-ud-Din, Punjab Islam League; Executive Committee of the Jamat-e-Islami; speeches at public meetings and rallies; editorials from *Dawn, Pakistan Times, Times of Karachi, Imroze,* and some other, not so well-known, papers. See NCNA dispatches of Mar. 18, Mar. 30, May 27, and Sept. 27 of 1954 and Mar. 9, 1955.

14. NCNA, Apr. 7, 1954.

15. *People's Daily,* June 4, 1956.

16. NCNA, Mar. 18, May 3, 1954.

17. Vidya Prakash Dutt, *China and the World* (New York: Praeger, 1966), pp. 230-31.

18. Cf. Franklin W. Houn, "The Principles and Operational Code of Communist China's International Conduct," *Journal of Asian Studies,* Nov. 1967, pp. 21-40.

19. George McT. Kahin, *The Asian-African Conference* (Ithaca: Cornell University Press, 1956), pp. 4-5.

20. Ibid.

21. Ambassador Raza recalls that he proposed to have a dinner party at which the two prime ministers might meet. Chou replied that Raza need go to no trouble and that he would be happy to call on Bogra. And this he did.

22. Ibid., p. 28.

23. Ibid., p. 36.

24. Ibid., pp. 24-25.

25. Ibid., pp. 19-20.

26. Ibid., pp. 52-55.

27. Apparently there was a tense moment during one of their meetings when Bogra, with his characteristic frankness, suggested that perhaps, after all, the Chinese were not entirely serious about communism! Author's interview with General Raza.

28. These reports may have made an even larger impact than one might ordinarily expect since they introduced an element of contrast inasmuch as Pakistan's own leaders at that time were not exactly famous for selfless devotion to their nation's social, economic, and political advancement.

29. NCNA, July 25, 1958.

30. NCNA, Sept. 3, 1958.

31. NCNA, June 24, 1957.

32. NCNA, Jan. 31, 1956.

33. At a banquet that he gave for the Pakistani prime minister, Chou En-lai said: "Our two countries do not have any conflicts of interests, but we have many things in common. In the past we both suffered long from the evils of colonialism. Both our peoples eagerly desire to develop their national economies and get rid of the backwardness created by past colonial rule.... Experience shows that as long as the principles of mutual respect for sovereignty and territorial integrity, non-aggression, non-interference in each other's internal affairs and equality and mutual

benefit are adhered to, our two countries can live together in peace very well." NCNA, Oct. 19, 1956.

34. Editorial of Oct. 18, 1956. Similar editorials appeared in *Kuang Ming Jih Pao, Ta Kung Pao,* and the *Daily Worker.*

35. NCNA, Oct. 19, 1956.

36. NCNA, Oct. 18, 19, 1956.

37. NCNA, Oct. 20, 1956.

38. NCNA, Oct. 24, 1956.

39. NCNA, Dec. 26, 1956.

40. NCNA, Dec. 24, 1956.

41. NCNA, Dec. 21, 1956.

42. NCNA, Dec. 24, 1956.

43. NCNA, Dec. 25, 1956.

44. NCNA, Dec. 25, 1956.

45. Full text of the editorial reported by NCNA, Aug. 28, 1953.*

46. *Dawn,* Feb. 7, 1957.

47. Ibid., Sept. 15, 1958.

48. NCNA, Aug. 14, 1955.

49. NCNA, July 7, 1956. It should be noted that while the Pakistani press generally favored China's admission to the UN, the leftist newspapers were naturally the more eloquent. The following editorial of the *Pakistan Times,* on Apr. 3, 1956, would be typical: "China does not seek the seat in the United Nations as a special favor. She does not have to beg for what is her due.... The suggestion that Chiang Kai-shek, hiding in U. S.-sheltered Formosa, is the real representative of the 600 million Chinese would be laughable, if it were not mischievous and dangerous.... The government at Peking, whatever its political complexion, has come to stay and is firmly rooted in the

people. Its voice is the true voice of China."

50. Bhutto, *Foreign Policy of Pakistan,* pp. 29-30.

51. *New York Times,* July 12, 1957.

52. CF. Noon, *From Memory,* p. 260.

53. Talking of Mr. Suhrawardy, an eminent Pakistani commentator writes: "In the matter of foreign policy, Pakistan leaned toward the Western countries right from the time of Liaquat Ali Khan. Subsequently, this tendency became more pronounced, but it was Suhrawardy who performed the task of carrying forward this pro-Western policy to a point of preponderance." Syed Noor Ahmad, *Marshal La Se Marshal La* [From martial law to martial law] (Lahore: Deen Mohammadi Press, 1965), p. 480; my translation of Urdu text. In his *Government and Politics in Pakistan,* (Karachi: Pakistan Publishing House, 1963), Mushtaq Ahmad writes: "he [Suhrawardy] was a staunch champion of the West and lent his country's unqualified backing to its policies in Hungary, the Middle East, particularly the Suez, much against a powerful current of public opinion running in favor of Egypt. Indeed, he went far out of his way to support the West and had to suffer a loss of popularity and prestige at home when the West let him down in the Kashmir and Canal Waters disputes with India" (p. 68).

54. *Pakistan Times,* editorial of

Oct. 1, 1957.

55. July 24, 1957.

56. *New York Times,* July 11, 13, 1957. Suhrawardy did carry a movie camera on his trips abroad and insisted upon operating it personally. This, together with such frivolities as emerging from the airplane at the New York airport carrying a toy tiger and asking reporters what they thought of it, did not exactly make for a statesmanlike image. A friendly assessment of Suhrawardy, including reference to these lighter aspects of his personality, may be seen in Shorish Kashmiri, *Husian Shaheed Suhrawardy* (Urdu) (Lahore: Chatan Publications, 1967).

58. *Dawn,* May 31, 1961.

59. *Pakistan Times,* Oct. 22, 1960.

60. *Dawn,* editorial of July 4, 1959. But, prudently, *Dawn* advised the government not to overreact to the Tibetan situation in view of Nehru's determination not to let Tibet detract from his government's appearance of cordiality toward China.

61. *Pakistan Times,* editorial of Oct. 25, 1959.

62. Ibid., Oct. 15, 1959.

63. NCNA, Mar. 9, 1957.

64. NCNA, July 21, 1959 (NCNA paraphrase of the official Chinese protest lodged with the government of Pakistan).

65. NCNA, July 23, 1959. For some time to come Pakistan kept an open mind regarding the two-China idea. Appearing on a "Meet the Press" program in New York on July 16, 1961, President Ayub, while urging that Communist China should be seated at the United Nations, expressed the hope that negotiations in a spirit of give-and-take might lead to a formula that would enable both China and Formosa to remain in the UN *(Speeches and statements of Field Marshal Mohammad Ayub Khan,* 4:52).

66. NCNA, Feb. 27, 1959.

67. NCNA, Apr. 25, 1959.

68. Cf. Noon, *From Memory,* p. 269.

Chapter 4

1. See Warren Unna, "Pakistan: The Friend of Our Enemies," *Atlantic,* March 1964, pp. 79-80, 83-84. See also *Time,* Sept. 6, 13, 1963, Feb. 28, 1964.

2. *Dawn,* Oct. 1, 1959.

3. *Pakistan Times,* Oct. 15, 1959.

4. Ibid.

5. Mr. Bhutto claims that this was done, somewhat reluctantly, by way of testing the argument for a more cordial relationship with China which he had been pressing for some time. Manzur Qadir, on the other hand, recalled that toward the end of December 1958, two months after entering the government as foreign minister, he prepared a position paper on Pakistan's international environment in which he argued that while Pakistan's relations with

India and the Soviet Union were not likely to improve significantly, those with China could: he recommended a policy of closer relations with China. The paper was presented at a cabinet meeting. Ayub Khan did not reject the idea, but of all the ministers present Bhutto alone spoke in its favor. As Qadir remembers it, Bhutto said, "Get close to China; yes, that's it." Author's interviews with Prime Minister Bhutto and with Manzur Qadir.

6. Mohammad Ayub Khan, *Speeches and Statements,* 4:52.

7. Ibid., pp. 15-16.

8. *Morning News,* Jan. 14, 1962.

9. *Dawn,* Apr. 27, 1962, and *Times of India,* Apr. 28, 1962.

10. *Dawn,* May 4, 1962 and *Pakistan Times,* May 5, 1962, editorials.

11. *Dawn,* May 4, 1962.

12. Ibid., May 26, 1962.

13. *Morning News,* editorial of May 26, 1962.

14. *Dawn,* July 3, 1962.

15. Bhutto, *Foreign Policy of Pakistan,* pp. 79-80.

16. See editorials in *Morning News, Dawn,* and *Pakistan Times,* all of Dec. 28, 1962.

17. *New York Times,* Mar. 4, 1963.

18. *Manchester Guardian,* editorial of Mar. 5, 1963.

19. *New York Times,* May 4, 1962.

20. Ibid., Mar. 4, 1963.

21. *Times* (London), Mar. 4, 1963.

22. *Manchester Guardian,* editorial of Mar. 5, 1963.

23. *Times of India,* Dec. 28, 1962.

24. *New York Times,* Dec. 29, 1962.

25. Ibid., editorial, and Dec. 31, 1962, "The Week in Review."

26. Ibid., Feb. 25, 1963.

27. Ibid., Feb. 26, 1963, Mar. 6, 1963.

28. *Dawn,* Dec. 28, 1962:

29. *New York Times,* Dec. 28, 1962. In one of my conversations with him, Raza confirmed Ayub Khan's explanation and added that it was not his (Raza's) job, at the time, to worry about the impact the announcement might have on Swaran Singh's mission in Rawalpindi!

30. *Peking Review,* Dec. 14, 1962, p. 26. See also *Dawn,* Dec. 12, 1962.

31. *Times,* Dec. 29, 1962. The Chinese themselves seemed to take the same view. At the banquet on Mar. 1, 1963, to greet Bhutto, who was in Peking to sign the border accord, Chen Yi viewed the agreement as showing that "so long as the two parties concerned treasure the fundamental interests of the friendship between their peoples and the common interests of Asian-African solidarity, treating each other with good faith and in a spirit of . . . mutual accommodation, and do not attempt to impose one's own will on the other, all questions, however complicated, can be settled fairly and reasonably." Sino-Pakistan agreement, he hoped, would show the light to others,

including India. *Peking Review,* Mar. 15, 1963, pp. 5-6.

32. *New York Times,* editorial of Dec. 29, 1962.

33. *Daily Telegraph,* Dec. 29, 1962.

34. *New York Times,* Dec. 1, 1962.

35. *Times,* Dec. 24, 1962. Commenting on Nehru's statements on the eve of the Indo-Pakistan talks, the *Guardian* observed that the prospects of a Kashmir settlement were dim. "The blame for that must go predominantly to Mr. Nehru—perhaps to him personally, for although most politically conscious Indians need no encouragement for their 'firm' attitude on the question, such leadership as Mr. Nehru has given has on the whole been in the wrong direction" (editorial, Dec. 27, 1962).

36. *New York Times,* Dec. 29, 1962.

37. Ibid., Jan 25, 1963.

38. Ibid., Dec. 29, 1962.

39. Paul Grimes in ibid., Dec. 20, 1962.

40. Ibid., Feb. 26, 1963.

41. *Manchester Guardian,* editorial of Dec. 28, 1962.

42. *New York Times,* Mar. 13, 1963.

43. *Manchester Guardian,* editorial of Mar. 5, 1963.

44. PIA suspended this service effective Oct. 4, 1963.

45. *Aviation Week and Space Technology,* June 24, 1963.

46. *Ibid.,* Oct. 21, 1963. The Foreign Office preferred a more gradual approach. Officials were apprehensive that the air agreement coming so soon after the border agreement with China might jeopardize Pakistan's relations with the United States. But apparently Nur Khan was able to convince Ayub that the Foreign Office apprehensions were exaggerated. My interview with a senior Pakistani diplomat.

47. *New York Times,* Sept. 1, 1963, and *Aviation Week,* Sept. 2, 1963.

48. *Peking Review,* July 3, 1964, p. 33.

49. *New York Times,* Sept. 1, 5, 1963. As a gesture of self-assertion and independence, Pakistan finalized her air agreement with China and raised her legation in Cuba to embassy status before Ball's arrival in Rawalpindi. According to one report, during Ball's visit five Chinese delegations, including poets and Ping-Pong players, were being welcomed in Pakistan. The Chinese poets were not sitting altogether idle. One of them published the following verses in the Pakistani press: "You [Pakistanis] are on the Western coast of the Sea / and we are on the east. / The tidal waves of the ocean roar, / and, intermingled, / we can hear the sound of our heartbeat." Quoted in *New York Times,* Sept. 4, 1963. See also *Time,* Sept. 13, 1963, p. 42.

50. *New York Times,* Sept. 18, 1963.

51. *Aviation Week,* Jan. 20, 1964.

52. *Peking Review,* May 8,

1964, pp. 6, 36.

53. Stephen Hugh-Jones, "Pakistan Flirts," *New Republic* (Sept. 5, 1964), pp. 15-16.

54. *Times*, editorial of July 18, 1963.

55. Bhutto, *Foreign Policy of Pakistan*, p. 123.

56. Ibid., p. 75.

57. National Assembly of Pakistan, *Debates*, July 23, 1963, pp. 1964–65.

58. *New York Times*, July 18, 19, 1963.

59. Ibid., Sept. 13, 1963.

60. Ibid., Sept. 6, 1963. (Pakistani officials recall that China had indeed proposed a nonagression pact after the border agreement was made, but the Pakistan government, wishing to proceed "one thing at a time," thought the time was not yet propitious for such an accord. Author's interview with a senior Pakistani diplomat.

61. National Assembly of Pakistan, *Debates*, July 23, 1963, p. 1968.

62. Ibid., July 24, 1963, pp. 2006, 2014.

63. Ibid., pp. 2035-36.

64. Ibid., p. 2023.

65. Bhutto, *Foreign Policy of Pakistan*, p. 66.

66. Ibid., p. 97.

67. Ibid., p. 31.

68. *Dawn*, Oct. 20, 1962.

69. *Pakistan Times*, Dec. 16, 1962.

70. "First of the Month Broadcast," Oct. 1, 1963, *Speeches and Statements*, 6: 29-30. The president reiterated this view in several subsequent speeches; see ibid., pp. 56, 117-18, 145.

71. Bhutto, *Foreign Policy of Pakistan*, pp. 40-41.

72. Ibid., pp. 6-9, 40.

73. Sardar Bahadur Khan, leader of the Opposition, called the Sino-Indian conflict a "minor border dispute." So did Begum G. A. Khan and Raja Hasan Akhtar, among others. Abdul Hye Choudhury pointed out that India had not even broken diplomatic relations with China. He saw no danger of a major war. He and Farid Ahmad thought the Anglo-Americans were trying to use India against China for their own purposes. Jahan Khan Busal described the Sino-India conflict as a "hoax." Nehru, he said, was throwing dust in the eyes of the world to get military hardware that he would subsequently use against Pakistan (National Assembly of Pakistan, *Debates*, Nov. 24, 1962, pp. 41-68).

74. See, for instance, Palmer, *South Asia and United States Policy*, pp. 263-64.

75. See the editorial and also David Binder's dispatch from Washington, D. C.

76. *New York Times*, May 3, 1963.

77. American assistance consisted largely of light infantry weapons, artillery, radar equipment, and heavy winter clothing. It did not include tanks or aircraft.

78. *New York Times*, Nov. 23, 1962.

79. *Speeches and Statements*, 6:56.

80. Ibid., p. 12.

Chapter 5

1. A nonpartisan account of this fighting and the following war may be found in Russell Brines, *The Indo-Pakistani Conflict* (London: Pall Mall, 1968).

2. *Dawn*, Sept. 5, 1965. The same argument appeared in the *People's Daily* on Sept. 5, 1965. An editorial declared that Kashmir was a disputed territory whose status, India and Pakistan had agreed, would be settled through a plebiscite. But the Indian government had gone back on its word and now claimed that Kashmir was an integral part of India. It had "barbarously" cracked down on the Kashmiri people, persecuted them, denied their demand for self-determination, deprived them of democratic rights, and otherwise made life "impossible" for them. The Kashmiris, no longer able to tolerate this "brutal" rule, had risen in revolt. This was understandable and justified, for "where there is oppression, there is bound to be revolt." (See text of the editorial in *Peking Review*, Sept. 10, 1965, pp. 7-8). The paragraphs on Kashmir in the official Chinese statement of Sept. 7, noting that the "Indian Government has always been perfidious on the Kashmir question," repeated the reasoning of the *People's Daily* almost verbatim.

3. See text of the statement in *Peking Review*, Sept. 10, 1965, p. 6.

4. Cited in ibid., Sept. 17, 1965, p. 10.

5. Text in ibid., pp. 12-13.

6. U. N.—the Sanctuary for the Indian Aggressor," *People's Daily*, editorial of Sept. 14, 1965, cited in *Peking Review*, Sept. 17, 1965, pp. 15, 18.

7. Observations to this effect also appeared in the American press during the Indo-Pakistan conflict. Commenting on the U. S. decision to suspend military supplies to the subcontinent, Max Frankel wrote in the *New York Times* of Sept. 8, 1965, that the action was aimed especially at Pakistan, which would suffer the more, for since 1954 she had relied largely on U. S. military assistance. This decision was reinforced by "diplomatic moves that stripped away more and more of the veneer of U. S. neutrality." Officials in Washington, said Frankel, had made "short shrift" of Pakistan's efforts to invoke CENTO assistance. They favored a cease-fire on terms that were known to be acceptable to India but not to Pakistan.

Discussing the American "dilemma," the *New York Times* wrote: "Whatever the genesis of the crisis, the war was one in which the United States, if forced to a bitter choice, would side with India. For all the frustrations and dismay . . . over India's piety in international affairs, her recent hopes of coexistence with Peking, her obstinacy over Kashmir, her failures and her weakness at home . . . India was always the centerpiece of the American design for 'Free Asia" (Sept. 12, 1965, in the section, "News of the Week in Review"). According to Drew Middleton, Gromyko, the Soviet foreign minister, told Dean Rusk in New York that his government regarded India as its "chief ally" in Asia, especially in the context of containing China. The Soviet Union, he said, supported India against Pakistan in the Kashmir dispute but wanted to see the Indo-Pakistan conflict ended because it invited Chinese pressures on India (ibid. [international edition], Oct. 1, 1965). Both the United States and the Soviet Union, wrote a commentator in the *Christian Science Monitor*, "tend to be sympathetic toward India but dare not say so lest Pakistan take further steps in the direction of Peking" (Sept. 10, 1965, dispatch of Mario Rossi, *Monitor's* special correspondent at the UN.) See also the *Monitor's* editorial on the same date, and *Time*, Sept. 17, 1965. Another expression of the view that the Soviet Union regards India as her "most important" ally in Asia will be found in Philip Ben, "China's Presence at the UN," *New Republic*, Oct. 2, 1965, p. 9.

8. *People's Daily,* editorial of Sept. 18, 1965, in *Peking Review,* Sept. 24, 1965, pp. 13-16.

9. Ibid., pp. 14-15.

10. Ibid., Sept. 17, 1965, p. 10.

11. Peking Radio carried Anant's report in its "International Service in English," 1544 GMT, Sept. 13, 1965.

12. Text of the note is in *Peking Review,* Sept. 24, 1965, p. 10.

13. Ibid., p. 9.

14. Ibid., Oct. 1, 1965, pp. 19-20 (emphasis added).

15. *Dawn,* Sept. 14, 1965.

16. See Max Frankel's report in the *New York Times,* Sept. 11, 1965, and another correspondent's report in ibid., Sept. 19, 1965, "Supplementary Material" from the New York Times News Service and WQXR, hereafter referred to as "supplementary material." Because of a strike, the *New York Times* published a slim edition during this period; many items not included in the regular printed edition are available as "supplementary material" following each day's issue on microfilm.

17. Saville R. Davis in the *Christian Science Monitor,* Sept. 11, 1965.

18. Editorial, Sept. 10, 1965.

19. *Manchester Guardian,* Sept. 9, 1965.

20. See Max Frankel's dispatch in the *New York Times,* Sept. 11, 1965.

21. Reported by Victor Zorza in the *Manchester Guardian,* Sept. 14, 1965.

22. *Christian Science Monitor,* Sept. 18, 1965. Some observers thought that Indian apprehensions were overstated in order to secure Western help; see Victor Zorza in the *Guardian,* Sept. 22, 1965.

23. Anthony Lukas in the *New York Times,* Sept. 19, 1965 (supplementary material); Clare Hollingworth in the *Guardian,* Sept.

18, 1965.

24. *New York Times* (international edition), Sept. 18-19, 1965.

25. Editorial of Sept. 20, 1965.

26. Tom Wicker in the *New York Times,* Sept. 19, 1965 (supplementary material).

27. Ibid. (international edition), Sept. 21, 1965.

28. "China the Peacemaker," editorial of Oct. 4, 1965 (emphasis added).

29. Thomas F. Brady in *New York Times,* Sept. 20, 1965.

30. Editorials of Sept. 10, 17, 18, 1965.

31. It is not clear how many Indian divisions China was able to keep from the Pakistan front. On one occasion, the *New York Times* wrote that of India's roughly twenty-one divisions half were posted on the northern border. ("News of the Week in Review," Sept. 12, 1965.) *Time* (Sept. 17, 1965) and *Newsweek* (Sept. 20, 1965) put the number at six divisions. In a statement answering Indian criticism that the British government and press had been favorable to Pakistan during the Indo-Pakistan conflict, Prime Minister Harold Wilson observed that India had attacked Pakistan with her entire army minus two divisions, which remained on the Sino–Indian border.

32. "China's interest in humiliating India in the eyes of Asians and the rest of the world is far greater . . . than any desire to help Pakistan, wrote the *Christian*

Science Monitor, Sept. 21, 1965.

33. *Dawn,* Sept. 13, 1965.

34. In a poem broadcast from Radio Pakistan, Habeeb Jaleb, a well-known Urdu poet, wrote: "May you live on, O China and Indonesia, / Because of you is peace sustained in Asia. / With great sincerity you have given us succor, / The truth is you have redoubled our vigor / The call of friendship you have answered well, / May you live on, O China and Indonesia." My free translation of the first three couplets of the poem, "Zindabād ai Cheen ō Indōnesia," in *Nāghmat-e-Jehād,* ed. Abdur Rasheed Arshad [Mian Channun: Maktaba-e-Rasheediya, 1965], p. 160.)

35. The following interesting statements will be found in Amad Siddiqui's voluminous story of the Indo-Pakistan war, entitled *Mujahideen-e-Saf Shikan* (Lahore: Kahkashan Publishers, 1965): "The Chinese warning to India caused disarray in London's official circles. . . . Unnerved by the Chinese warning, Prime Minister Wilson announced the suspension of British military aid to India in an attempt to convince Pakistan that Britain did not support India's expansionist designs" (pp. 112-13). "The very thought of Chinese intervention gave American officials sleepless nights" (p. 158). "The Indians, already weary of fighting Pakistan's valiant army, were stunned by the Chinese ultimatum. The Indian political circles were completely put

out. Men and officers of the Indian army cursed the Indian warlords. They well remembered the crushing defeat they had taken from the Chinese in the NEFA not long ago. ... When China challenged India, all became alert to the threat and started considering plans for getting an Indo-Pakistan cease-fire" (pp. 287-89). (My translation from the Urdu text.)

36. *Dawn,* Sept. 30, 1965 (emphasis added).

37. *New York Times,* Sept. 19, 1965 (supplementary material).

38. John Finney's dispatch in the *New York Times,* Sept. 21, 1965. See also Paul Grimes's delayed report from Rawalpindi in, the same paper, Sept. 22, 1965 (supplementary material), and the *Times* (London), editorial of Sept. 23, 1965.

39. *New York Times,* Sept. 16, 1965.

40. Ibid. But according to the paraphrased version in *Dawn* (Sept. 16), "The President wished India would realize how much she is losing by not having good neighbourly relations with Pakistan." The phrase "working arrangement" appears in the next paragraph but is modified by the phrase "ensuring good relations" between the two countries. If the *New York Times* version, which is a direct quotation, is correct, then it would seem that *Dawn* wanted to avoid attributing to the president a desire for having a "working arrangement" with India.

41. Asked how he would react if Johnson told him he would not stand for this war, Ayub reportedly said: "Well, I think they would have to tell both, cease fire, and then after that, 'Let's have a little arrangement that these unfortunate things don't happen,' Pakistan would understand it" (*New York Times,* Sept. 16, 1965).

42. Jacques Nevard reporting from Pakistan in ibid., Sept. 19, 1965 (supplementary material).

43. Bill Moyers, speaking for President Johnson, told newsmen that the road to peace started from the United Nations and not the White House. He added: "At what time and to what extent the President personally can be helpful is a judgment only the President can make." This was interpreted as a "rebuke to President Ayub" for suggesting "how much pressure the United States ought to exert and when." (Max Frankel in ibid., Sept. 16, 1965).

44. *Pakistan News Digest,* July 1, 1966, p. 1.

Chapter 6

1. My interviews with Pakistani diplomats.

2. Russell Brines, *The Indo-Pakistani Conflict,* pp. 396-98.

3. Prime Minister Bhutto recalled this in an interview with the author.

4. Ibid., pp. 401-9.

5. *Peking Review,* Feb. 4, 1966, p. 11, and Feb. 18, 1966, p. 21.

6. *Peking Review,* Apr. 1, 1966, p. 5; July 8, 1966, p. 23; Aug. 5, 1966, p. 5; Aug. 12, 1966, p. 3.

7. Ibid., Apr. 22, 1966, pp. 3-4.

8. Ibid., June 3, 1966, p. 31.

9. Ibid., Aug. 5, 1966, p. 5.

10. Ibid., Oct. 7, 1966, pp. 34-35. During a recent interview with the author, Pakistan's ambassador to Peking (at that time) recalled that Chou En-lai and Chen Yi had "explained" the Cultural Revolution to him on several occasions.

11. See for instance Ayub Khan's speech at a banquet for Chou En-lai on June 29, 1966, carried by the *Pakistan Times* the following day and in *Peking Review,* July 8, 1966, p. 23.

12. *Dawn,* Oct. 22, 1967.

13. Ibid., Nov. 14, 1968.

14. *Statesman,* May 14, 1968.

15. *Pakistan Times,* Feb. 17, 1971.

16. *Statesman,* June 20, 27, 1969.

17. Ibid., June 27, 1969.

18. *Dawn,* June 6, 1969.

19. *Indo–Pakistani Conflict,* pp. 147-49, 184, 201-6.

20. Dupuy, *Almanac,* p. 299.

21. *Washington Post,* July 12, 1966.

22. Dupuy, *Almanac,* p. 299.

23. International Institute of Strategic Studies, *Military Balance 1971-1972* (London, 1971), p. 50.

24. New York Times, Mar. 5, 1972. Eighty–three Pakistani aircraft and 220 tanks were reported to have been destroyed or otherwise put out of action. See IISS, *Strategic Survey, 1971* (London, 1972), pp. 50-52.

25. *Pakistan Times,* Nov. 30, 1973. (I heard Aziz Ahmad make an announcement to this effect in the National Assembly during a foreign policy debate on Dec. 17, 1973.)

26. Government of Pakistan, Ministry of Finance, *Pakistan: Basic Facts, 1969-70* (Islamabad, 1971), p. 83; and Government of Pakistan, Central Statistical Office, *Pakistan Statistical Yearbook, 1968* (Karachi, 1970), pp. 238–39, 258-59. Figures in these two sources do not match exactly which may be because they are rounded off to the nearest million in *Basic Facts* and to the nearest thousand in the *Yearbook.*

27. *Dawn,* Nov. 20, 1966.

28. Tables 47 and 48 (pp. 104-11) in *Pakistan Economic Survey 1972-1973,* which contain these figures and should be read together, are placed as appendix 3 at the end of this volume. These tables also document assistance Pakistan has received from other sources.

29. News of the project has appeared in the Pakistani and international press from time to time. See, for instance, *Dawn* of Mar. 4, 1967; Jan. 19, Apr. 6, May 1, July 28, 1968; Dec. 7, 1969. See also Government of Pakistan, Ministry of Finance, *Pakistan Economic Survey, 1970-1971* (Islamabad, 1971), p. 46.

30. My interviews with Pakistani diplomats and military officials.

31. My interview with a Chi-

nese-speaking Pakistani diplomat who has recently returned from a tour of duty in Peking.

32. The account which follows is based on my interviews with senior Pakistani diplomats.

33. My interviews with Pakistani diplomats.

34. Tariq Ali, *Pakistan: Military Rule or People's Power*, p. 140.

35. I heard the Maulana say this in a speech he made on arrival at the Lahore airport in March 1969.

36. My interviews with Pakistani diplomats.

37. *New York Times*, Apr. 13, 1971.

38. *Peking Review*, Apr. 16, 1971, p. 3.

39. *New York Times*, Dec. 6, 7, 1971.

40. *Dawn*, Nov. 8, 9, 1971.

41. *Dawn*, Feb. 4, 1972.

Chapter 7

1. The text of the Simla Agreement may be seen in *New York Times*, July 4, 1972.

2. *New York Times*, Apr. 5, 29, May 6, 1972; and Overseas *Hindustan Times*, Apr. 8, May 6, 1972.

3. Overseas *Hindustan Times*, Apr. 8, 1972.

4. Ibid., June 10, 1972.

5. Ibid., Mar. 25, 1972.

6. *The Hindu*, March 1972.

7. *Indian and Foreign Review*, May 1, 1972, p. 24.

8. *New York Times*, Dec. 1, 1972.

9. Malhotra, "After Victory What?" *Illustrated Weekly of India*, Jan. 30, 1972; Shah, "India in 'New' Asia," ibid., Jan. 9, 1972; Malik, "India's Peace Role in Asia," *Indian and Foreign Review*, Apr. 15. 1972. p. 18; Bhargawa, Overseas *Hindustan Times*, Feb. 5, 1972.

10. Overseas *Hindustan Times*, Apr. 1, 1972.

11. President Bhutto made the first of these statements to Loren Jenkins of *Newsweek* and the second to a Pakistani newsman; see *Pakistan Times*, Dec. 12, 18, 1972.

12. This was set forth in the Indian Defense Ministry's annual report to Parliament last May; see overseas *Hindustan Times*, May 13, 1972. India lost 54 aircraft and Pakistan 83 during the 1971 war. On the basis of the International Institute of Strategic Studies' *Strategic Survey, 1971*, pp. 50-52, at least 23 and possibly more of the planes on the Pakistani side were F-86 fighter-bombers. Some of those lost were MIG-19s. A companion IISS publication, *Military Balance, 1971-1972*, credited Pakistan with having one squadron of I1-28 bombers (p. 50). But the 1972–73 edition of this series makes no mention of I1-28 in its listing of Pakistani combat aircraft (p. 53). If this is not an oversight, it may mean that the entire I1-28 squadron was lost. Losses of F-104s and Mirage IIIs were minimal, if any. Pakistan

received a small number of
F-104's and F-5s from Jordan
and Libya during or shortly after
the war. In the spring of 1972 she
received 60 additional MIG-19s
from China.

13. Details of Indian and Pakistani military capabilities (army,
navy, air force) are given in IISS,
Military Balance, 1972-1973
(London, 1972), pp. 49, 53. This
publication puts the number of
Pakistani combat aircraft at 200,
whereas the 1971–72 issue listed
285. The latest figure, 200, is
apparently derived by sub-
tracting the war losses. This
means that it does not include the
60 MIG-19s Pakistan received
last spring. The report about Pakistan getting Mirage Vs appeared
in the *New York Times*, Mar. 29,
1972. My interviews with Pakistani officials in the fall of 1973
indicated that these squadrons
had not yet arrived.

14. The relative capabilities of
these aircraft may be seen in William Green, *The World Guide to
Combat Planes* (London: Mac-
donald, 1966), 1: 76-79, 110-14,
133-40, 143-50.

15. See the register of major
weapons transfers to developing
countries for 1969 in *SIPRI Yearbook of World Armaments and
Disarmament, 1969-1970*
(Stockholm: Almqvist and Wik-
sell, 1970), pp. 342-56, for an
indication of prices at which various types of weapons have
recently been sold.

16. This and the figures for
naval craft will be found in David

Vital, *The Inequality of States*
(Oxford: Clarendon, 1967), pp.
65-66.

17. *Military Balance, 1971-
1972*, p. 75.

18. Ibid., pp. 60-61.

19. My interview with a senior
Pakistani diplomat. Reports of
this project appeared in the Pakistani press in early January
1974.

20. A few years ago George
Liska argued that while the
American imperial role (which he
compared to that of ancient
Rome) might usefully give way to
a balance–of–power strategy in
Europe, the same could not be
done in Asia. The Soviet Union
might become a fit and acceptable candidate for a position of
"primacy or paramountcy" in
Europe; but in Asia there was no
one to take America's place.
China, he thought, was not
respectable or moderate enough
to be trusted with wider responsi-
bilities in the area. He maintained also that a premature
American withdrawal from her
imperial role in Asia would be
symptomatic of the imperial
community's decline and decay
"both as an international actor
and as national body politic"
(*Imperial America: The International Politics of Primacy* [Balti-
more: The Johns Hopkins Press,
1967], pp. 81, 110-13). The
opposing argument, to wit, that
such a withdrawal will have no
adverse effect on American
security or the quality of her
domestic life, is presented in

Robert W. Tucker, *Nation or Empire?* (Baltimore, the Johns Hopkins Press, 1968).

21. There has been some talk of American assistance in China's industrial development. If it were offered, and if China were to accept it, her industrial capacity could rapidly advance to a point where, given her present asceticism at home, she could offer the Soviet Union stiff competition in Asia and elsewhere. This would lighten American burdens and enable the United States to compete with the Soviet Union more selectively.

22. Washington columnist Jack Anderson somehow obtained and published secret memorandums, from the files of the assistant secretary of defense and the joint chiefs of staff, covering the Special Action Group's meetings. The texts of these documents may be seen in *New York Times,* Jan. 6, 1972.

23. The group noted that because of a congressional ban on the supply of weapons to Pakistan none could be sent to her even through third countries. After the war it transpired that she had received, possibly on a loan basis, a few F-104s from Jordan and F-5s from Libya. But it is not known whether these countries acted with the Nixon administration's prior knowledge or consent.

24. The *Enterprise* mission had no impact on the course of events in East Pakistan. By the time the ships were ordered to

sail (around Dec. 12), the Nixon administration already knew that the Pakistani army was about to surrender. As I was told by a senior Pakistani diplomat at the UN, Gen. Farman Ali's request for safe-conduct out of East Pakistan was received in the UN secretary-general's office in the early morning of Dec. 10 and circulated to the members of the Security Council later the same morning.

25. *New York Times,* Jan. 6, 1972.

26. Along with these dispositions is the one against any U. S. military undertaking in Asia after a withdrawal from Vietnam is affected. How America could then be the balancer in Asia is not clear. If in the foreseeable future America's power is to rest at home, her exclusion from the Asian balance of power is the more likely development. In that case, Soviet and Indian pressures against Pakistan, and possibly also China, may become more severe.

27. Precedents of indirect control exist in the experience of both countries. The British system of indirect rule in India's princely states is well known. Until about the end of 1947 the Soviet Union treated Albania as a sub-satellite of Yugoslavia. Stalin professed to be ready even to endorse Albania's and Bulgaria's unification with Yugoslavia. But he changed his mind when he found that Tito and his colleagues would not be unquestioning and obedient tools of Soviet interest

and policy: Tito's example might disrupt Soviet control in eastern Europe. Hence the break with Yugoslavia and the Cominform's public call for the overthrow of Tito and his associates. For further detail, see Adam B. Ulam, *Expansion and Coexistence: The History of Soviet Foreign Policy, 1917-1967* (New York: Praeger, 1968), pp. 422, 461-67; and his *Titoism and the Cominform* (Cambridge: Harvard University Press, 1952), Chaps. 3, 4. See also Milovan Djilas, *Conversations with Stalin* (New York: Harcourt, Brace, 1962), pp. 135-85. Soviet policy and tactics have undoubtedly become more sophisticated than those of Stalin in 1948. India in 1972 is different from Yugoslavia in 1948. But this earlier phase of Soviet policy does suggest the possibility of Soviet-Indian tensions developing over relations with other states of the subcontinent.

28. Texts of these speeches will be found in *Pravda*, Mar. 18, 1972. *Current Digest of the Soviet Press*, Apr. 12, 1972, carries an English translation and also contains the text of the joint Soviet-Pakistan communiqué issued at the end of Bhutto's visit.

29. My conversations with senior Pakistani diplomats. But reports to this effect have appeared in the press also. See Peter Kann's massive account of an interview with Sher Mohammad Marri, a Marxist advocate of Azad (free) Baluchistan *(Wall Street Journal*, Apr. 6, 1970). For

a more recent report, see *Pakistan Times*, Feb. 28, 1973. Also see *Pakistan Times*, Feb. 19, Mar. 1, 2, 1973.

30. Senior Pakistani diplomats provided this assessment in conversations with the author.

31. Bhutto's interview with C. L. Sulzberger in *New York Times*, Feb. 13, 1972.

32. IISS, *Strategic Survey, 1971*, p. 56.

33. Ibid.; and IISS, *Military Balance, 1971-1972*, p. 6.

34. A Doak Barnett, *A New U. S. Policy toward China* (New York: Brookings, 1971), pp. 104-5. See also IISS, *Strategic Survey, 1971*, p. 57.

Chapter 8

1. Vital, *The Inequality of States*, and *The Survival of Small States* (London: Oxford, 1971).

2. *Small Nation Survival: Political Defense in Unequal Conflicts* (New York: Exposition Press, 1969).

3. Alfred Cobban, *National Self-Determination* (London: Oxford, 1945); and Annette Baker Fox, *The Power of Small States* (Chicago: University of Chicago Press, 1959).

4. The next three paragraphs are based mainly on Robert L. Rothstein, *Alliances and Small Powers* (New York: Columbia, 1968).

5. Ibid, p. 29.

6. Bhutto, *The Myth of Inde-*

pendence, pp. 13, 139-40.

7. Ibid, p. 15.

8. Ibid., p. 16.

9. Physical remoteness or a rival global power's support for the smaller state will raise the costs of applying coercion.

10. Ibid., pp. 179-181.

11. Ibid., pp. 178-80.

12. Ibid., p. 187.

13. Meaning that the Muslims of the Indian subcontinent were a separate nation from the Hindus and were therefore entitled to a separate homeland, that is, Pakistan.

14. A full-scale discussion of Pakistan's nation-making problems cannot be undertaken here. A brief discussion of some related issues may be seen in my "Reflections on the Ayubian Decade in Pakistan," *Pakistan Administrative Staff College Journal,* December 1971, pp. 26-35.

Index